THE CRISIS OF THE REVOLUTION

FROM THE ORIGINAL PAINTING BY ANDRE, IN THE POSSESSION OF J. W. BOUTON ESQ., NEW YORK.

THE CRISIS OF THE REVOLUTION

BEING THE STORY OF

ARNOLD AND ANDRÉ

NOW FOR THE FIRST TIME COLLECTED FROM ALL SOURCES, AND ILLUSTRATED
WITH VIEWS OF ALL PLACES IDENTIFIED WITH IT

BY

WILLIAM ABBATT

ILLUSTRATIONS FROM ORIGINAL PHOTOGRAPHS BY

EDWIN S. BENNETT

With a new preface:
WILLIAM ABBATT AND HIS HISTORICAL WORK
by Jeff Canning

NEW YORK
WILLIAM ABBATT
1899
Reprinted by
HARBOR HILL BOOKS
Harrison, New York
1976

Library of Congress Cataloging in Publication Data

Abbatt, William, 1851-1935.
    The crisis of the Revolution.

    Reprint in re-arranged form of the 1899 ed. published
by W. Abbatt, New York, with supplements of 1909 and 1915.
    Bibliography of Major André, by C. A. Campbell (from
Magazine of American history, Jan. 1882): p.
    1. Arnold, Benedict, 1741-1801. 2. André, John,
1751-1780. I. Title.
E236.A12 1976   973.3'092'2 [B]   76-2604
ISBN 0-916346-20-X

Preface by Jeff Canning copyright 1976 by Harbor Hill Books

Reprinted from a copy in the
Library of the United States Military Academy,
West Point, New York

The 1909 supplement reprinted from a copy in the
New York Public Library.

The present edition is a complete reprint of the 1899 edition
in somewhat rearranged form. Illustrations, which appeared
in the original edition interspersed with the text, have been
placed at the end of the volume, in the order in which the pas-
sages referring to the pictures occur in the text. The plates
have been numbered and references to the numbers placed at
the bottom of the proper text pages.

Most corrections and additions listed on the errata sheet pp.
99-100 have been repeated at the foot of the respective text
pages. Further errata appear in the 1909 supplement, placed
in this edition after the index (page 120) and before the 1915
supplement.

Harbor Hill Books, P.O. Box 407, Harrison, New York, 10528

I conceive that every circumstance connected with it cannot fail of being interesting to Americans —

CAPTAIN ALDEN PARTRIDGE, U. S. A.,
SUPERINTENDENT OF THE UNITED STATES MILITARY ACADEMY,
WEST POINT, N. Y.,
1818.

TO THE DESCENDANTS OF THE MEN OF "SEVENTY-SIX," AS REPRESENTED IN
OUR PATRIOTIC-HEREDITARY SOCIETIES, THIS RECORD OF THE
MOMENTOUS EVENTS ALONG THE HUDSON FROM
SEPTEMBER 21 TO OCTOBER 2, 1780,
IS DEDICATED.

WILLIAM ABBATT AND HIS HISTORICAL WORK

William Abbatt's intensive study of the André-Arnold affair is typical of his thorough-going approach to historical research. Although he directed his writing primarily to the general public, he held himself to the highest standards of exhaustive research, and his works abound with references to his sources. His intense dedication to his labors left him little time for the social graces, and most of his Tarrytown neighbors considered him something of a brooder.

Abbatt was born Nov. 16, 1851, the son of William D. and Agnes Alice Dean Abbatt, in a house that stood at Broadway and 13th Street in Manhattan. Details of the first 40 years of his life are obscure; it is known that he attended private schools in New York City and Westchester County, the northern neighbor of the metropolis, but whether he went on to higher education is uncertain. One thing is definite -- somewhere along the line he became skilled in the techniques of historical research.

Abbatt's earliest printed work appears to be a transcript of a poem, "The Hunters of Kentucky; a famous old song; contributed by William Abbatt," which was published in 1891 in 'The Magazine of American History' vol. 25, p. 244. A footnote states that the lines were first sung in a New Orleans theater just after the Battle of New Orleans in 1815 and that they were reprinted in Democratic newspapers before the election of President Andrew Jackson in 1828. Meanwhile, he was sharpening his literary skills as editor of 'Interstate' and assistant editor of 'The New York News Letter' in the early 1890s.

Abbatt is frequently but erroneously identified as the editor and publisher of 'The Magazine of American History,' beginning in 1898. Actually, he was the editor and publisher of 'The Magazine of History' from 1905 to 1922, which he advertised as "the virtual successor" of the older magazine. 'The Magazine of American History' was founded in 1877 by John Austin Stevens, general secretary of the New York Historical Society. Stevens was succeeded a few years later by Martha J. Lamb, author of the comprehensive two-volume 'History of the City of New York,' which was completed in 1880. Mrs. Lamb edited the magazine until her death 1893, by which time 30 volumes of it had been published. It was revived under the identical title by the Westchester historian Alvah P. French in 1901 and published variously in Mount Vernon and Port Chester until 1917. French continued the numbering system of Mrs. Lamb, labeling his issues volumes 31 to 46.

Abbatt's writings indicate that he considered his magazine, launched in 1905, as the true heir of Mrs. Lamb's magazine, even though the word "American" was missing from the title. A notice in Abbatt's magazine's first issue June 1905, reads in part: "'The Magazine of American History,' which was founded in 1877, ceased to appear in 1893, not long

after the death of Mrs. Martha J. Lamb, who had been its editor for nearly ten years; and has never since been equalled, until the present time.
A legal obstacle preventing the use of the word 'American' in connection
with the title, the present Magazine will bear the name of 'The Magazine
of History, with Notes and Queries' (the latter phrase formed a part of
the title of 'The Magazine of American History' in 1880 and is adopted
as peculiarly descriptive of an important part of the new publication)...
It will be as near an exact duplicate of the original 'Magazine of American History' in form, size - even in type - as possible...''

Just what constituted the "legal obstacle" is a matter of conjecture,
but one may assume that the enterprising Alvah P. French had seized
the evidently unprotected name and copyrighted it when he started his
periodical in 1901. Thus, when Abbatt began his magazine four years
later, obviously long since planned as a continuation of Mrs. Lamb's
publication, he had no choice but to adopt a different name, which he did
by dropping the word 'American'. The "notes and queries" that Abbatt
considered so important contained requests from readers for specific
points of information about topics of history, genealogy, etc. and were,
of course, fashioned after the popular English magazine 'Notes and Queries.'

'The Magazine of History' was published regularly from 1905 to 1922,
comprising a total of 26 volumes. Publication was suspended for unknown
reasons from July to December 1912 and from January 1918 to June 1921.
Abbatt gave up publication of the magazine proper in 1922, perhaps in
order to devote more time to the books he was writing and editing, but
continued to publish the popular "Extra Numbers", which he launched in
1907 and continued until his death in 1935, issuing a total of 200. This
series of Americana contained reprints of rare historical works, best
described by Abbatt's printer, W. F. Humphrey of Geneva, New York
(who claimed to be "Central New York's Finest Printer") in the preface
to his catalogue of the "Extra Numbers", issued in 1936:

"...the work of the Magazine of History has been a labor of love to
carry on the unbroken file of the Magazine, which is a veritable store-
house of original material on American history and which has been,
through the years, a rich vein of source material for the research student
...Each number (of the 'Extra Numbers') was a reprint of a scarce and
much sought after item of American history. At first, these 'Extras'
were printed biennially, but the large libraries of the country soon recognized the value of such a work and made so many suggestions that the
'Extras' have totalled 200 volumes during the past 30 years (they are
really new editions since notes are added to each and illustrations to
many). As the library subscription list was small and the price per issue
only $5.00, there was always a struggle during the three decades to meet
the printing costs. But through the indefatigable efforts of Mr. Abbatt,
the work was carried out.''

In addition to the extensive work with his magazine, Abbatt also was
getting involved with books. His major works include Ladies on Life In-
surance; notable Opinions (1896); The Crisis of the Revolution; being the

Story of Arnold and André (1899); The Battle of Pell's Point (or Pelham) October 18, 1776 (1901); The Colloquial Who's Who; an Attempt to Identify the Many Authors, Writers and Contributors Who Have Used Pennames, Initials, etc., 1600-1924 (1924-1925); and The Attack on Youngs' House (or Four Corners), February 3, 1780 (1926). He also edited a number of books about colonial days and the Revolution, including General Heath's Memoirs, Sargent's Life of Major John André, Winfield's Block House by Bull's Ferry, Codman's Arnold's Expedition to Quebec and Hopkins' Memoir of the Housatunnuk Indians.

Abbatt had most of his works printed privately in limited editions. "The Crisis of the Revolution" and "The Attack on Youngs' House" were limited to 250 copies each, while 500 copies were printed of "The Battle of Pell's Point." The "Extra Numbers" - or 'Abbatt's Reprints' as they were often referred to - were each printed in 55 copies only.

No pains were spared by Abbatt in preparing his book on the André-Arnold affair. In addition to standard research efforts with old books and records, he packed up his notebook and camera and personally retraced the routes of the participants, visiting and photographing the buildings and locations that played a part in the incident. The result was an exhaustive study of Benedict Arnold's aborted effort to betray the American stronghold at West Point, New York, to the British; his secret liaison with Major John André, adjutant general of the British army; the capture of André at Tarrytown September 23, 1780 by three American militiamen (John Paulding, Isaac Van Wart and David Williams); and the major's trial and execution across the Hudson River at Tappan, New York. The value of Abbatt's work is enhanced by the fact that many of the old inns and houses associated with the incident have been demolished since Abbatt, with his associate Bennett, photographed them shortly before the turn of the century.

Abbatt settled in Tarrytown before World War I and for many years lived on the first floor of a two-family house at 28 West Elizabeth Street near the center of town, less than a mile from the site of André's capture. One of his neighbors at the time, Tarrytown village historian William C. Gross, remembers him well and has furnished the following personal recollections. He presented a somber, even sullen, appearance to his fellow townsmen -- he invariably wore a black suit, black top hat and dark gray spats, carried a gold-headed cane and never smiled through his bushy full beard. He was always well dressed, and his clothes reflected his conservative outlook on life. In winter, he wore a black topcoat that nearly brushed the ground and covered the tops of his high black shoes. In warm weather, when the neighborhood youngsters were outside playing ball, he invariably slammed shut the window next to the desk where he did much of his work. Those who knew him said he rarely spoke to anyone he passed on the street. In contrast, his sister Caroline, with whom he lived, was a friendly, outgoing woman. His upstairs neighbor was Chester Lyon, a druggist and partner in the Tarrytown drug store Russell & Lawrie, Inc.

The only Tarrytowner ever known to make Abbatt crack a smile was William Dwyer, who worked in the post office and also ran an undertaking establishment. According to Tarrytown oral tradition, Abbatt went to the post office one morning and was greeted by a cheery "Good morning, Mr. Abbatt!" from Dwyer. "What's good about this morning?" grumbled the historian. "Mr. Abbatt, any morning you can get up is a good morning. I know. I am an undertaker." Upon hearing that, Abbatt's face broke into a grin and he chuckled in agreement.

William Abbatt left Tarrytown to return to New York City in 1932, where he lived at 189 Madison Avenue until his death September 7, 1935. He never married, and was survived only by his two sisters, Caroline Abbatt and Cornelia Abbatt. But in a larger sense, he had thousands of survivors--his books and magazines. As his printer, Humphrey, put it in his catalogue of the "Extra Numbers":

"...one man has suffered and labored, that scarce and fastly disappearing works on American history might be readily available to the research student. As a delver into the vast dust bin of oblivion, the writer cannot begin to express how happy he was to know that this man William Abbatt was always walking before him, was carrying the torch, so to speak, blazing the trail through the dark and bloody ground, with his excellent reprints of rare Americana which this humble laborer had neither the time nor the means to discover for himself... You will find there a treasure house of source material, the great preserving ground of American history in which an unsung, patriotic American has labored long and well to preserve for you and me the personal histories of our great and honored past..."

JEFF CANNING

Tarrytown, January 1976.

PREFACE

I N putting forth a new book on so familiar a subject as the conspiracy of Benedict Arnold
with Major André, I am not unmindful of the opening words of Lossing's *Field-Book*,
"The story of the Revolution has been well and often told." My excuse for again
telling this part of it must be, first, to again quote Lossing: "A large proportion of our
people are but little instructed in many of the essential details of that event, so important for
every intelligent citizen to learn," and secondly, that while so much has been printed that I
cannot add much new material, it has not been published in any complete form. Hence the
student who seeks for all its details has been obliged to consult a wearisome succession of
books, periodicals, newspapers, and some *MSS.*, many accessible only to the favored few
living within reach of our great libraries.

Finally, no complete itinerary of André's journey has been published,[1] nor has any
authority given more than a few illustrations of the various places identified with him. In
this last respect I flatter myself I have left no scene of any interest unrepresented; and to
this feature I trust in part for popular endorsement of my work. To obtain the photographs
Mr. Bennett and myself visited almost every site, and traveled over the greater part of
André's path.

The map showing his route has been carefully drawn from authentic surveys, and
shows every detail. I am greatly indebted for their aid in preparing it, and for valuable
topographical information, to Mr. Lavalette Wilson, of Haverstraw; Rev. Amos C. Requa,
of Peekskill; Judge J. O. Dykman, of White Plains; Mr. William H. Bleakley, of Verplanck's
Point; Rev. David Cole, of Yonkers, and Mr. Edward Hagaman Hall, of New York; and
for access to their libraries, to Dr. Thomas Addis Emmet and Mr. William L. Stone.

If my book shall increase interest in Revolutionary history and lead to further investi-
gation of the many events for which general histories cannot afford adequate space, it will
not have been written in vain. In that hope it is now confided to the individual whose
qualifying adjective, in view of the numerous membership of ladies in our patriotic societies,
assumes a new and pleasing significance — the "Gentle Reader."

W. A.

West Chester, N. Y., 1899.

---

[1] Save Judge Dykman's *Last Twelve Days of Major André*, in 1889.

DRAMATIS PERSONÆ

ANDRÉ -
ARNOLD - - - - - - - - - - - - - - - - - -
ARNOLD, Mrs. - - - - - - - - - - - - - - - -
ABBOT, Benjamin - - - - - - - - - - - - Drummer, — Regiment.
ABERCROMBY, Lieut. Col. Robert - - - - - - - - 37th Regiment.
ACKER, Benjamin - - - - - - - - - - Fourth N. Y. Continentals.
ALLEN, Capt. William - - - - - - - - - - Second Rhode Island.
ALLEN, Lieut. Solomon - - - - - - - - - Col. Seth Murray's Mass. Militia.
"BALDWIN" - - - - Unknown Private of Col. Jeduthun Baldwin's Regiment, — Massachusetts.
BARLOW, Joel - - - - - - - - - - - - Chaplain Gen. Poor's Brigade.
BEEKMAN, Gerard G. - - - - - - - - - - - - - -
BEEKMAN, Mrs. Gerard G. (Cornelia) - - - - - - - - - -
BOWMAN, Ensign Samuel - - - - - - - - - Third Massachusetts.
BOYD, Captain Ebenezer - - - - - - - - - Third Westchester Militia.
BRONSON, Isaac, M. D. - - - - - - - Assistant Surgeon Second Dragoons.
BRUNDAGE, Sylvanus - - - - - - - - - Second Westchester Militia.
BURNET, Major Robert - - - - - - - - - Aid to Gen'l Greene.
BURR, Aaron - - - - - - - - - - - - - - -
BURROWES, Major John - - - - - - - Col. Spencer's New Jersey Regiment.
CILLEY, Col. Joseph - - - - - - - - - - First New Hampshire.
CLINTON, Gov. George - - - - - - - - - - - -
CLINTON, Sir Henry - - - - - - - - - - - -
CLINTON, Gen'l James - - - - - - - - - - -
COLQUHOUN, Joseph - - - - - - - - - - - -
COLQUHOUN, Samuel - - - - - - - - - - - -
COOLEY, Capt. John - - - - - - - - - Fourth Westchester Militia.
COX, Major James - - - - - - - - - - Ordnance Department.
CROSBIE, Lieut. Col. William - - - - - - - - 22d Regiment.
DEAN, Sergeant John - - - - - - - - - First Westchester Militia.
DEARBORN, Lieut. Col. Henry - - - - - - - First New Hampshire.
DEWEES, Samuel - - - - - - - - - - Fifer Tenth Pennsylvania.
DWIGHT, Rev. Timothy - - - - - - - Chaplain First Conn. Brigade.
EUSTIS, William, M. D. - - - - - - - Surgeon Knox's Artillery.
FOOTE, Captain Ebenezer - - - - - - - Commissary Department.
FRANKS, Major David S. - - - - - - - - - Aid to Arnold.
GARDINER, Nathaniel, M. D. - - - - - - Surgeon First New Hampshire.
GILBERT, John - - - - - - - - - - - - -
GLOVER, Gen'l John - - - - - - - - - - - -
GOUVION, Col. J. B. - - - - - - - - - Chief of Rochambeau's Artillery.
GREENE, Gen'l Nathanael - - - - - - - - - - -
HALL, Timothy, M. D. - - - - - - - - Surgeon Fifth Massachusetts.
HAMILTON, Alexander - - - - - - - - - - - -
HAMMOND, David - - - - - - - - - - - - -
HAMMOND, Sally - - - - - - - - - - - - - -

HAMMOND, Staats - - - - - - - - - - Sergeant First Westchester Militia.
HAND, General Edward - - - - - - - - - - - - -
HARWOOD, Major Peter - - - - - - - - - - Sixth Massachusetts.
HAY, Col. Ann Hawkes - - - - - Haverstraw Regiment, Orange County Militia.
HEATH, Gen'l William - - - - - - - - - - - - -
HERON, William - - - - - - - - - - - - - -
HOOGLAND, Captain Jeronemus - - - - - - - - - Second Dragoons.
HOWE, General Robert - - - - - - - - - - - -
HUGHES, Capt. John - - - - - - - - - Second Canadian Regiment.
HUNTINGTON, General Jedediah - - - - - - - - - - -
JACKSON, Col. Henry - - - - - - - - - - Sixteenth Massachusetts.
JAMESON, Lieut. Col. John - - - - - - - - - Second Dragoons.
JAMESON, William - - - - - - - - - - - - — Regiment.
KIERS, Major (E.) William - - - - - Haverstraw Regiment, Orange County Militia.
KING, Lieut. Joshua - - - - - - - - - - - Second Dragoons.
KNOX, Gen'l Henry - - - - - - - - - - - - -
LAFAYETTE - - - - - - - - - - - - - - -
LAMB, Col. John - - - - - - - - - - - Second Artillery.
LAMBERT, Cornelius - - - - - - - - - Fourth N. Y. Continentals.
LAMBERT, Henry - - - - - - - - - - First Westchester Militia.
LAMBERT, Lambert - - - - - - - - - First Westchester Militia.
LARVEY, James - - - - - - - - - - - Fifth Massachusetts.
LAUNE, Peter - - - - - - - - - - - - André's Servant.
LAURANCE, Col. John - - - - - - - - - Judge Advocate General.
LIVINGSTON, Col. James - - - - - - - - Second Canadian Regiment.
MASON, Rev. John - - - - - - - - Chaplain to Hudson River Posts.
McHENRY, James, M. D. - - - - - - - - - - Aid to Lafayette.
McKINLEY, Alexander, Drum-Major - - - - - - - - — Regiment.
McKNIGHT, Charles, M. D. - - - - - Surgeon Gen'l of Hospital, Middle Dep't.
MEADE, Lieut. Col. R. K. - - - - - - - - - Aid to Washington.
MEIGS, Col. Return J. - - - - - - - - - - Sixth Connecticut.
MEKEEL, Lieut. John - - - - - - - - - Second Westchester Militia.
MILLER, Andreas - - - - - - - - - - - - -
ODELL, Rev. John - - - - - - - - - - - - -
OGDEN, Captain Aaron - - - - - - - - - Lafayette's Light Infantry.
PARSONS, Gen'l Samuel H. - - - - - - - - - - - -
PATERSON, Gen'l John - - - - - - - - - - - - -
PAULDING, John - - - - - - - - - - First Westchester Militia.
PETTINGILL, Major Thomas - - - - - - - - - Ninth Massachusetts.
ROBERTSON, Lieut. Gen'l James - - - - - - - - - - -
ROBINSON, Col. Beverly - - - - - - - - - "Loyal Americans."
ROGERS, Lieut. Jedediah - - - - - - - - - - Second Dragoons.
ROMER, James - - - - - - - - - - First Westchester Militia.
ROMER, Mrs. Jacob - - - - - - - - - - - - -
ROMER, John - - - - - - - - - - - - - -
RUSSELL, Benjamin - - - - - Worcester County Regiment, Massachusetts Militia.
SCAMMELL, Col. Alexander - - - - - - - - - Adjutant General U. S. A.
SCOTT, Gen'l John Morin - - - - - - - - - - - -
SEE, Isaac - - - - - - - - - - - First Westchester Militia.
SHAW, Major Samuel - - - - - - - - - - - Aid to Knox.
SHELDON, Col. Elisha - - - - - - - - - - Second Dragoons.
SHIPPARD, Lieut. Samuel - - - - - - - - - - First New Jersey.
SHREVE, Col. Israel - - - - - - - - - - Second New Jersey.
SIMCOE, Colonel John G. - - - - - - - - - - Queen's Rangers.
SMITH, Captain Ebenezer - - - - - - - - - Thirteenth Massachusetts.
SMITH, Joshua Hett - - - - - - - - - - - - -
SMITH, Richard - - - - - - - - - - - - - -

SMITH, Thomas - - - - - - - - - - - - - - - -
SMITH, Lieut Col. Wm. S. - - - - - - - - - Aid to Washington.
STARK, Gen'l John - - - - - - - - - - - - -
ST. CLAIR, Gen'l Arthur - - - - - - - - - - -
STEUBEN, Gen'l Baron - - - - - - - - - - - -
STIRLING, Gen'l Lord - - - - - - - - - - - -
SUTHERLAND, Lieut. Andrew - - - - - - - - - Royal Navy.
TALLMADGE, Major Benjamin - - - - - - - - Second Dragoons.
THACHER, James, M. D. - - - - - - - Surgeon Sixteenth Massachusetts.
THORNE, Jesse - - - - - - - - - - - - - -
THORNE, Stevenson - - - - - - - - - - - -
TOMLINSON, Ensign Jabez H. - - - - - - - - Ninth Connecticut.
UNDERHILL, Mrs. Isaac - - - - - - - - - - -
VAN DYK, Captain John - - - - - - - - - Second Artillery.
VAN WART, Isaac - - - - - - - - - First Westchester Militia.
VAN WART, William - - - - - - - - - - - -
VARICK, Col. Richard - - - - - - - - - - Aid to Arnold.
WADE, Col. Nathaniel - - - - - - Essex County Regiment Massachusetts Militia.
WASHINGTON - - - - - - - - - - - - - -
WAYNE, General Anthony - - - - - - - - - - -
WEBB, Captain John - - - - - - - - - - Second Dragoons.
WEBB, Col. Samuel B. - - - - - - - - - Ninth Connecticut.
WELLS, Lieut. Col. Jonathan - - - - - - - Nineteenth Connecticut.
WILLIAMS, Abraham - - - - - - - - - First Westchester Militia.
WILLIAMS, David - - - - - - - - - - First Westchester Militia.
YERKS, John - - - - - - - - - - - First Westchester Militia.
YOUNGS, Lieut. Samuel - - - - - - - - - - Second Dragoons.

From the original engraving, after MAJOR ANDRÉ's drawing, made the day before his execution.

By permission of the LENOX LIBRARY, New York. The extent of scene is a little over four miles.

THE CRISIS OF THE REVOLUTION.

CHAPTER I.

New York to King's Ferry—Safety.

The aspiring youth that fired the Ephesian dome
Outlives in fame the pious fool that reared it.
COLLEY CIBBER—*Richard III*.

KIP HOUSE.

SOMETHING like Cibber's cynical words might be applied to the men of the Revolution. Many a brave patriot is less remembered than Arnold, and distinguished British officers than André. Of the latter's prototype in misfortune, the heroic Nathan Hale, Thacher, the Revolutionary surgeon, quoting Hannah Adams' *History of New England*, says: "Whilst almost every historian has celebrated the virtues and lamented the fate of André, Hale has remained unnoticed,[1] and it is scarcely known that such a character ever existed;" and Fenimore Cooper says, "Arnold has acquired a notoriety that promises to be as lasting as that of Erostratus."

The reason for this is not far to seek. Hale's story is exceedingly brief, and almost entirely lacking in details, while André's is just the reverse. Hence it has always been invested with a peculiar degree of interest, heightened by the personal and social attractions which he possessed to such an extent as won friendship and admiration from enemies no less than friends.

It is no part of my plan to repeat the familiar story of how Arnold, the hero of Quebec and Saratoga, came to plan the surrender of West Point and the betrayal of his country, to which in 1778, only two years before, he had solemnly sworn allegiance. Nor shall I give any detailed account of André's life. Both are to be had in general histories and other works easily accessible to the reader.

---

[1] I am glad to know that a gentleman in New York has long been gathering materials for a new life of Hale, which may be published in two or three years.

On the night of Monday, the 18th of September, 1780, there was a brilliant military assemblage in New York City, then occupied by the British army under General Sir Henry Clinton. The place was the ancient stone house of the Kip family, built in 1696 (and standing as lately as 1850), where is now the corner of Second Avenue and Thirty-fourth Street. At the time it was the quarters of Colonel Williams,[1] of the 80th regiment. The occasion was a dinner given by him to Clinton and his staff. André, as Adjutant General and Clinton's favorite, was prominent among the guests.[2] At the close of the festivities he sang the song attributed to General Wolfe, and then very popular,[3] the second and best-known verse beginning:

> Why, soldiers, why,
> Should we be melancholy boys?

Though officers of the Highland regiments were present, no soothsayer like he of Clan Ivor was there, to see the winding sheet almost as high on André's breast as the *Taishatr* had seen it on Colonel Gardiner's the day before Prestonpans. Little thought any of the party that just two weeks later he would be a corpse, buried at the foot of an improvised gibbet in a little hamlet of Orange County (the present Rockland County was formed out of Orange).

From New York he went the next day, Tuesday, by way of King's Bridge to Dobbs' Ferry, and thence to the sloop-of-war *Vulture*,[4] then probably at anchor off North Point, Teller's Point.[5] Reaching her about 7 P. M., he waited all the next day (Wednesday) without message or news from Arnold.[6] The next point of interest in the drama — its opening scene, in fact, regarding the Williams dinner as the prologue, — is the spot where the interview with him occurred. At the period we are noticing, the correspondence with Arnold had continued for eighteen months,[7] or from about the spring of 1779, under the guise of proposed mercantile transactions. His letters, in a disguised hand, were

---

1 It is significant that so early in the story I have to note that while I insert this name on the strength of Lossing, I can find in Mr. Worthington C. Ford's valuable *List of British Officers, 1774–80*, no Williams who was a Colonel, nor any Williams among the 80th officers. From whom did Lossing quote?
For the view of the Kip House I am indebted to Mr. S. Victor Constant, of New York.

2 Lossing (*The Two Spies*) says Clinton had intimated that he was about starting on a mission of importance, and openly declared he would become Sir John André if he successfully accomplished it.

3 See Appendix.

4 She was a third-rate, carrying fourteen guns, and commanded by Lieutenant Andrew Sutherland, R. N. "If any omen might be derived from her name and history, she was a fortunate ship for the enterprise, having been very successful in avoiding our privateers. Thirty-five years before (1745) a band of prisoners, some of them detained as spies (comprising not only Home, in whose tragedy of *Douglas* André had delighted to bear a character, but Witherspoon, now active for the Congress, and Barrow, in arms for the King,) had escaped from Charles Edward's hands, and flying from Doune Castle by Tullyallan, were received on board her."—*Sargent.*

5 See map, *post.*

6 The meeting planned by Arnold for September 11 at Dobbs' Ferry had failed, owing to his never-explained neglect to provide his boat with a flag of truce, and its consequent hostile reception by the British. He then wrote again, September 15 : "I will send a person to meet you at Dobbs' Ferry, at the landing on the east side, on Wednesday, the 20th, who will conduct you to a place of safety, where I will meet you. It will be necessary for you to be disguised * * * * *. Smith (see *post.*) failed to get one of the Colquhoun brothers as boatman, hence the delay until Thursday.   7 It became necessary, page 3.

signed "Gustavus," and addressed "Mr. John Anderson, merchant, to the care of Mr. James Osborne, to be left at Rev. Mr. Odell's."[1]

Aboard the *Vulture* André found Beverly Robinson, and after fruitlessly waiting over Wednesday wrote thus to Clinton:

> On board the *Vulture*,
>
> 21 September.
>
> SIR : As the tide was favorable on my arrival at the sloop yesterday, I determined to be myself the bearer of your Excellency's letters as far as the *Vulture*. I have suffered for it, having caught a very bad cold, and had so violent a return of a disorder in my stomach which had attacked me a few days ago, that Captain Sutherland and Colonel Robinson insist on my remaining on board till I am better. I hope to-morrow to get down again.

In this letter he enclosed one meant for Clinton only:

> SIR : I got on board the *Vulture* at about seven o'clock last evening; and after considering upon the letters and the answer given by Col. Robinson,[2] "that he would remain on board, and hoped I should be up," we thought it most natural to expect the Man I sent into the Country here,[3] and therefore did not think of going to the Ferry. Nobody has appeared. This is the second expedition I have made without an ostensible reason, and Col. Robinson both times of the party. A third would infallibly fire suspicions. I have therefore thought it best to remain here on plea of sickness, as my enclosed letter will feign, and try further expedients.

From the vessel, a letter dated "Morning of 21st September," and written by André though signed by Sutherland, was sent to Colonel James

Ja.ˢ Livingston

---

[7] It became necessary at this instant that the secret correspondence under feigned names, which had so long been carried on, should be rendered into certainty; both as to the person being General Arnold, commanding at West Point, and that in the manner in which he was to surrender himself, the forts and troops, to me, it should be so conducted under a concerted plan between us, as that the King's troops sent upon this expedition should be under no risk of surprise or counterplot; and I was determined not to undertake the attempt but under such particular security. I knew the ground on which the forts were placed, and the contiguous country, tolerably well, having been there in 1777; and I had received many hints touching both, from General Arnold. But it was certainly necessary that a meeting should be held with that officer, for settling the whole plan. * * * General Arnold had also his reasons, which must be so very obvious as to make it unnecessary for me to explain them. Many projects for a meeting were formed, and consequently several attempts made, in all of which General Arnold seemed extremely desirous that some person who had my particular confidence might be sent him; some man, as he described it in writing, *of his own mensuration.* I had thought of a person under this important description who would gladly have undertaken it, but his peculiar situation at the time, from which I could not release him, prevented. * * * General Arnold finally insisted that the person should be Major André, who had been the person who managed and carried on the secret correspondence.—CLINTON, in *Sparks.*

The "Hon. and Rev." (as he is generally styled) Jonathan Odell was born in Newark, N. J., September 25, 1737, and died in Fredericton, N. B., November 25, 1818. He studied medicine, and became a surgeon in the British army, but by 1767 had studied theology, and eventually became rector of the Episcopal church at Burlington, N. J. His Toryism obliged him to leave the state, and he settled in New York, where he became chaplain of one of the Loyalist regiments. He was possessed of considerable musical ability, and one of his songs is said to have suggested the tune of *Hail Columbia.* He left the United States with the British army, and settled in New Brunswick, where, and in Nova Scotia, his descendants still live.

[2] To Arnold.

[3] That Arnold or his messenger would come aboard.

See plate 1: Portrait of Jonathan Odell

Livingston, of the Additional Continentals,[1] who commanded at both Verplanck's and Stony Points. It complained of a violation of a flag of truce the day before.[2] When the letter was shown Arnold, the handwriting of course showed him that his correspondent "Anderson" was aboard the vessel. Having previously had his own barge go up Canopus Creek, above Peekskill, and bring thence to Crom Island, in Haverstraw Creek, a rowboat, he was now ready to have André and Robinson[3] brought ashore. To do this required a third person, as confidant. Such an one he had found not long before, in Joshua Hett Smith, of Haverstraw. This man's character is of great interest. He was very well connected, rich, if not wealthy, intimate with prominent patriots, and was a lawyer by profession, as were also two of his brothers.[4] He was born May 27, 1749, being a brother of William Smith, the Chief Justice of New York, and in 1770 married Elizabeth Gordon, of Belvedere, South Carolina.[5]

When General Robert Howe turned over the command of West Point to Arnold, the previous third of August, he recommended Smith to him as a man who could be very useful in securing important news of the enemy's plans. Having secured his consent to aid in the desired interview, Arnold gave him an order on Major Kierse[6] for the rowboat, furnished him with the necessary passes, and left him to get the two rowers for the boat. Two tenants of his own, the Colquhoun brothers, Samuel[7] and Joseph, were asked to serve. Refusing at first, Arnold threatened them with arrest as persons disaffected to the American cause, and they reluctantly yielded.

[1] **James Livingston,** not Henry B., as Lossing says. (See Washington's letter to Lamb, Chap. II.) He is also found as Colonel of the First Canadian regiment, and was with Montgomery at Chambly and Quebec. He was born in Canada, March 27, 1747, and died in Saratoga County, N. Y., November 29, 1832. Washington, after these events, wrote him: "I am gratified that the post was in the hands of an officer so devoted as you were to the cause of your country." Mrs. Elizabeth Cady Stanton is his granddaughter.

[2] To this occurrence a good deal of invention attaches, with the necessary result of confusing history. A careful examination of all authorities leads me to summarize it thus: On the 20th, Moses Sherwood and Jack Peterson (a mulatto soldier of Van Cortland's—the 3d—regiment of Westchester militia, who had been a prisoner in the *Jersey* ship, and who died at 103, in Tarrytown), concealed in the underbrush at North Point, fired on a boat—presumably a flag—from the *Vulture*.

On this one fact a mass of traditionary and legendary romance has been built. As a specimen: So practical a man of business as Freeman Hunt (*Letters about the Hudson*) states that the event was on the 22d; that the boat was filled with men, but that they had only one musket among them (!); that it was to take aboard André, who, soon after its repulse, came down near the shore, but had to go back to Crompond (!!) where he spent the night at the house of Mr. Smith (!!!)

Such is history "as she was wrote," even forty years nearer André than are we to-day.

The firing of Livingston's cannon, on the 22d, was an entirely separate affair.

[3] There is no doubt he expected and wished to see Robinson.

[4] While previously living in New York, he is said to have been one of the "Sons of Liberty," with Marinus Willett and other Whigs. Jones (*N. Y. in the Revolution*) says Smith was one of the mob which, in 1775, tried to seize Rev. Dr. Myles Cooper, President of King's (now Columbia) College, and maltreat him for his Tory sympathies. In 1776 he and his brother-in-law, Colonel Hay (of whom more hereafter), were members of the New York Convention, which drafted the State Constitution. He always asserted his ignorance of Arnold's designs, but Dr. Thacher (*Military Journal*) says he "had long been suspected of a predilection for the British interest." Compare Lamb's opinion of him, *post*.

[5] They had three children—Joshua Gordon, Sarah and Laura Sophia (the latter by his second wife, see Chapter V.). Sarah married Thomas Hay, probably son of Colonel A. H. Hay. Laura married — West, and a daughter of Thomas Smith (Joshua's brother) married John C. Spencer, Secretary of the Navy in 1842, and became the mother of the unfortunate Midshipman Philip Spencer, of the brig *Somers*.

Dr. Thacher, who had met her at West Point, at the house of Major Bauman, says: "Mrs. Smith was an accomplished and interesting woman."

[6] Major and Quartermaster, ⎱
[7] Samuel had previously, ⎰ page 5.

The Orderly-Book of Captain E. Stearns' company, Colonel John Rand's Massachusetts regiment, now in the possession of the Massachusetts Historical Society, records: "August 6, 1780: The Honorable General Arnold takes command in this department."

The passes read:

Headquarters,
Robinson House,
Sept. 20, 1780.

Permission is given to Joshua Smith, Esquire, a gentleman, Mr. John Anderson, who is with him, and his two servants, to pass and repass the guards near King's Ferry at all times.

B. ARNOLD, M. Gen'l.

Headquarters,
Robinson House,
Sept. 21, 1780

Permission is granted to Joshua Smith, Esq., to go to Dobbs' Ferry with three men and a Boy with a Flag to carry some Letters of a private Nature for Gentlemen in New York, and to return immediately.

B. ARNOLD, M. Gen'l.

N. B. He has permission to go at such hours and times as the tide and his business suits.

B. A.

To protect him still further he was given a letter to Beverly Robinson, who had previously written Arnold for an interview on the subject of his confiscated property:[1]

"This will be delivered to you by Mr. Smith, who will conduct you to a place of safety. Neither Mr. Smith nor any other person shall be made acquainted with your proposals. If they (which I doubt not) are of such a nature that I can officially take notice of them, I shall do it with pleasure. I take it for granted that Colonel Robinson will not propose anything that is not for the interest of the United States as well as himself."

The start was made at about midnight of Thursday, the 21st. By Arnold's orders the oars were muffled with pieces of sheepskin. As the moon did not rise until six o'clock Friday morning, the flag of truce could not have been seen, had it been used that night—a fact which had an important bearing on the results of the trip. The countersign, to pass the American guard-boats, that night, was "Congress."[2] The boat was allowed to come alongside, or seems to have done so almost unperceived by the sentinel, and Smith got aboard by a convenient rope, only to be received—as he says—with threats from the watch-

---

6 Major and Quartermaster William Kiers (Kierse or Kierce), seems to have been in charge at Stony Point. It is to be presumed he was of Livingston's regiment, though the only record of him in the State's archives is as a captain of the Haverstraw militia, in 1778. This regiment was commanded by Colonel Hay. I have found it impossible to find his descendants, or to obtain any definite information about him.

7 Samuel had previously refused to row Smith to the *Vulture* on the twentieth, and Smith sent him on horseback to Arnold, with a letter to that effect, which brought the traitor at once to Haverstraw.

1 On the seventeenth, when Washington and Arnold were together at Smith's house, Arnold showed the Chief a letter from Robinson about his confiscated estates, addressed to General Putnam, or the officer commanding at West Point. The writer requested an interview, which Washington discouraged, adding that Arnold might send a trusty representative if he chose. In telling the story to Luzerne he added: "I had no more suspicion of Arnold at the time than of myself." 2 The question of, page 6.

Major Kiers is also referred to in the *American Archives:* His store (Haverstraw) is mentioned, July 19, 1776 (Vol. X., p. 452). On October 10, 1776, he is mentioned as paid £27 11s. 2d. for apprehending deserters (page 236), and the sum of £400 is acknowledged due to him for provisions for the public use (page 338).

See plate 2: Portrait of Joshua H. Smith

officer, who evidently had not been taken into his superiors' confidence. He was allowed to enter the cabin, where he found Sutherland and "old Colonel Robinson."[1] The third person, who was to play so important a part in the events of the week—André himself—was in his berth at the moment, but soon came out and joined the party. After Smith had given Robinson the letter from Arnold and announced his errand, André offered to go ashore with him, as Robinson refused. Several authorities agree that both Robinson and Sutherland expected Arnold, though it is difficult to understand why, in view of his letter. In fact each party to the transaction seems to have expected the other to take the risk of coming to him. Robinson and Arnold were each too cautious to run into danger, but not so André. Though both Robinson and Sutherland opposed him, he was tired of inaction aboard ship, and was not to be dissuaded from trying to close the long correspondence by a personal interview. Entering Smith's boat, both were soon on shore, at a spot at the foot of Long Clove Mountain, about two miles below Haverstraw. It is now identifiable only by the remains—visible at low tide—of "André's dock," on the beach at the terminus of a road extending from the Clove to the river. The slope is steep, and the road itself, many years disused, is overgrown with trees and underbrush, yet its course, northeast from the old highway,[2] is still fairly plain. In the view of the landing-place[3] the large boulder on the left stands almost on a line with the north side of the dock, and is the most prominent object on the shore. Suitably inscribed, this would constitute an admirable monument for the spot identified with an event of so much historic importance.

---

[2] The question of the tide on this occasion is one which apparently does not admit of solution. Sargent says the boat was started on the last of the ebb, and by the time the *Vulture* was reached it was young flood. But Gaine's *Register* for 1780 says high tide was at three A. M. of Thursday, or about four A. M. of Friday. "Thus the tide would have been against the rowers all the way down—nearly twelve miles. The Coast and Geodetic Survey authorities at Washington give me the time of high water as 3.12 A. M. Friday, which makes no material difference." (E. H. HALL, *Spirit of '76*, March, 1898.)
Smith's historic statement is that it was strong ebb at about that time.
In this connection the table from Gaine's *Register* will be found interesting :

MOON, September, 1780.

First Quarter, Tuesday   5th, 5 P. M.
Full Moon,   Wednesday, 13th, 8   "
Last Quarter, Thursday,   21st, 6 A. M.
New Moon,   "   28th, 2   "

TIDES.	High Water.	Sun rises.
Sept. 20, Wed.	2 hr. 2	5.57
21, Th.	3 " 0	5.58
22, Fri.	3 " 54	5.59
23, Sat.	4 " 50	6. 0
24, Sun.	5 " 48	6. 1
25, Mon.	6 " 40	6. 3
26, Tues. *May rain*	7 " 38	6. 4
27, Wed.	8 " 30	
28, Thurs.	9 " 27	6. 5
29, Fri.	10 " 12	6. 7
30, Sat.	11 " 6	6. 8
Oct. 1, Sun.	11 " 56	6.10
2, Mon.	12 " 50	6.13

[1] His son, Beverly, Jr., was lieutenant-colonel of his regiment.
[2] See map, opposite page.   [3] In the view, page 7.

See plates 3-4: Andre's Landing Place
See plate 68: Map of Andre's Landing Place

We may now return to our traveller for a brief retrospect of his career. Having been captured at St. John's in 1775,[1] and imprisoned successively at Lancaster and Carlisle, Pennsylvania, André was not unfamiliar with the American character—in fact, by 1780 he had probably been longer in the country than most of his companions in arms. It was to Clinton's esteem he owed the personal request to the War Office, in the previous August, which had secured his promotion to the rank of Major (in the 54th Regiment), and the appointment as Adjutant-General. That same esteem had won his Chief's consent when Arnold asked that he be sent as the British representative; but, in spite of his personal attractions and professional attainments, his course in the important business now entrusted to him clearly shows him to have lacked the prudence and readiness vital to success under such conditions. It was a fortunate choice, for the patriot cause, for, as I shall have occasion to show, Arnold's treason was several times almost successful, failing only because of trifles which a cooler head than André's might have easily foreseen and as easily overcome. This leads me to call these three weeks the crisis of the Revolution. Clinton remembered that the capture of Fort Washington, the first great success of the British arms—if we except the battle of Long Island—was achieved by the liberal use of gold, securing the defection of the "first American traitor,"[2] Demont (or Dement), and he naturally looked for much greater success in Arnold's case, for the stake was greater, and he was as ready to buy at any cost as Arnold to sell. The time was opportune, for the colonies had had five years' ceaseless fighting, Continental money was practically worthless, and the future was very dark. Even Washington wrote that he had "almost ceased to hope." The plan was simple enough, and, so far as Arnold was concerned, was carried out—the fatal weakness lay with André.[3] West Point once in British hands, what might not have been the change in our national history? Could independence have been achieved—and at how much greater cost of time, blood and money?[4]

[3] In the view from the south showing Haverstraw in the distance. The other view shows Teller's Point, nearly opposite.

[1] He was quartermaster of the post. His first commission was as Second Lieutenant in the Royal Fusiliers (7th Foot), March 4, 1771. The regiment was sent to Canada by way of Philadelphia, in 1773, so that he was in the future capital of the Colonies while the first Congress was in session. Lossing (*Two Spies*) says he did not arrive until September, 1774, and that he wore citizen's dress, visited New York and Boston, and reached Quebec in November. He thinks Sir Guy Carleton directed him to do this, to gain information of the patriots' plans, etc.
After the battle of Long Island he was exchanged, and soon made Captain in the 26th Regiment—the "Cameronians." While in Philadelphia during its occupation by the British, his fondness for social and theatrical affairs brought him into the circle of acquaintance with Miss Shippen, who became Arnold's second wife.

[2] See W. R. Benjamin's chapter in the S. A. R.'s pamphlet, *Fort Washington* (N. Y., 1897). Strictly speaking, he was not the first, for Dr. Church and Major Zedwitz preceded him and General De Fermoy followed them. Church was head of the army hospital at Boston, 1775, Zedwitz was Major of McDougall's—First—New York Regiment, and was cashiered for a treasonable correspondence with Tryon after the battle of White Plains. De Fermoy set fire to his house on Mount Independence, at Ticonderoga, in 1777, thereby revealing to the enemy the evacuation in progress.

[3] Had André exhibited a presence of mind worthy of his reputation for sagacity, the die had been cast which sealed the fate of the Highland passes.—*Leake*.   [4] In the first place, page 8.

8

André later acknowledged that Clinton had explicitly ordered him not to enter the American lines, change his uniform or receive papers. A caution against putting it out of his power to return to the *Vulture* would have seemed superfluous—but it was just here he made his first mistake. True, part of the responsibility rests on Robinson[1] and Sutherland, but that he would go ashore in a stranger's boat, without providing independent means of return, in the shape of an armed boat from the *Vulture*, either to accompany or follow Smith's, could never have suggested itself to anyone.[2] We may now return to the midnight conference. Arnold awaited his visitor probably very near the centre of the spot shown in the view of "The Firs." Smith says he was "hid in a clump of firs." Though but few such trees are there now, there are enough to retain for the place something of its original aspect. It was dim, even on a bright August morning, when I visited it. At the historic hour we are concerned with, there was no moon, and the stars could have given little or no light through the dense wood.

The steep ascent—nearly fifty feet—from the beach was easy for an active young man like André, and he and his unknown correspondent were soon met. Expressing surprise and regret at Robinson's non-appearance, the traitor asked Smith to return to the boat. To be thus dismissed to the society of his two boatmen-tenants must have been galling to the man whose aid in bringing about the meeting had been sought by Arnold but a few days before. Of course he could not refuse, and the two conspirators were left alone. The place was well suited for a meeting which would not bear daylight—literally or figuratively. It was easily accessible by either road or river, yet remote from any dwelling. Just what passed during the long interview, none but the two principals ever knew. Below, the tired boatmen probably slept, but Smith, suffering alike from wounded pride and the ague to which he was subject, must have had a weary time of waiting in the boat or on the beach. The exact length of the interview is

[4] In the first place, the mere acquisition of a fortress so important, with all its dependencies, garrison, stores, magazine, vessels, etc., was (would be) an achievement of no secondary magnitude. The supplies gathered here were very great, and, once lost, could not have been readily, if at all, restored. The works were esteemed our tower of salvation, an American Gibraltar, impregnable to an army twenty thousand strong. Though yet unfinished, they had cost three million dollars and three years' labor of the army. But the ulterior consequences of its possession were of even greater importance. It would have enabled Sir Henry Clinton to have checked all trade between New England and the Central and Southern States. It was, in Washington's eyes, the bolt that locked this communication. The Eastern States chiefly depended for their breadstuffs on their sisters in the Union, were commercial rather than agricultural communities, and the power that at once commanded the seaboard and the Hudson might easily bring upon them all the horrors of famine. From Canada to Long Island Sound a virtual barrier would have shut out New England from its supplies, as the wall of Antonine barred the free and rugged Caledonians from the Roman colonies and the south of Britain.—*Sparks.*

[1] Colonel Robinson observed that as they had but two men in a large boat, they would find some difficulty in getting on shore, and proposed that one of ours should tow them some part of the way, to which he (Smith) objected, as it might, in case of falling in with any of their guard-boats, be deemed an infringement of the flag.—*Sutherland to Clinton, Oct. 5.*

[2] André's testimony upsets the flag theory (see Chapter V). Smith says he asked for two rowers, to aid the Colquhouns, but was refused. This was very natural on Sutherland's part. Leake pertinently remarks, "This portion of the plot seems to have been most clumsily contrived, and unless it was changed in part of its details, failed from its own stupidity. Why the *Vulture* should not have been ordered to anchor nearer the place of meeting is very difficult to imagine." She was now twelve miles further up-stream than when at Dobbs' Ferry.

See plate 5: "The Firs", below Haverstraw

uncertain, but as Smith says he went up to warn Arnold of the approach of day-light, it could not have been less than three hours, if we allow two hours from midnight to reach the dock from Haverstraw, and the sun to rise at six. Arnold had foreseen a prolonged discussion, and had caused a negro servant[1] to ride a horse to some spot convenient to the meeting place, so that André might have a mount if necessary. The warning of Smith ending the conference, André mounted, the negro going to the boat, which the Colquhouns rowed back up stream to Hay's dock in Haverstraw Creek.[2] The mounted pair took their way over the old highway (now disused and closed by a locked gate). At some distance from the " Firs," it joins the present highway, called the Clove road.

Haverstraw in 1780 was a mere hamlet, the original buildings of which have long since disappeared before the advance of the cavernous brick yards, some of which have in their turn been abandoned. Its southern limit was probably about the spot now called Kierse's dock (formerly owned by descendants of the Stony Point quartermaster.) Near this must have been the sentry[3] whose unexpected challenge must have sent a thrill through André, showing as it did that he had—unwittingly—violated Clinton's first injunction, by entering the American lines. It was too late to draw back—Arnold gave the countersign, and they passed on. The way to Smith's house, whither they were bound, led through a thinly popu-lated tract until Colonel Hay's[4] house was seen, in the gray of morning. Near this was the dock, all traces of which have been obliterated by one of the all-devouring brick yards. Hay's house has also gone, its site alone being identified by an old frame building on an eminence left by cutting down the rest of the plateau for brick-clay.

---

1 Probably Smith's own, whom we shall meet again.
On September 19th Arnold wrote to one Jefferson :

Headquarters,
Robinson House, Sept. 19, 1780.

To Mr. Jefferson,
Fredericksburg, N. Y.
Sir—You will please to pick out of the horses you have now in your custody, or which you may hereafter receive, a pair of the best wagon-horses, as also two of the very best saddle horses you can find, for my use. You 'll send them to me as soon as possible.

I am, Sir, your most obedient servant,
B. ARNOLD, M. G.

The saddle horses may have been those used on this occasion.

2 The vexed question why they did not take André back to the *Vulture*, may be compared with his own state-ment in Ch. V. He evidently expected to return to the vessel next day. My own idea is that the Colquhouns, both tired by their work and angry at being compelled to it by Arnold, were also suspicious of the whole business, and anxious to be rid of it ; so they used the adverse tide as a convenient excuse for refusing Smith's request to return to the *Vulture*. Very probably they were not sorry for the chance of thus " getting even " with Arnold.

3 Of Spencer's New Jersey Regiment (see page 15). 4 Ann Hawkes Hay, page 10.

See plate 69: Map of Haverstraw
See plate 70: Map of Haverstraw Bay

Smith's is about a mile and a half distant, in what is now West Haver-straw, nearly a mile north by west of the West Shore railroad station, and half a mile from the station of the New Jersey and New York road. Here the Stony Point highway comes in from the north at a right angle to that which extends to Garnersville. It is quite straight for some distance, at the foot of a bluff forming the western boundary of the alluvial plain on which stands the greater part of the two Haverstraws. An old road which extended to it from Hay's dock, and which our two riders probably followed, has long disappeared. The tourist is apt to be misled as to which of the residences on the ridge is the landmark he seeks. Two are white, and very similar, but the northernmost is our goal. It is but a short distance from the other, and reached by a very steep road, directly up the face of the ridge. Up this Arnold and André must have ridden. Smith's name for the property was "Belmont." It is just four and one-tenth miles[1] from the scene of the interview at "The Firs." The Smiths—there were fourteen sons and daughters—were extensive landowners in this region, and Joshua seems to have built his house on land belonging to his brother Thomas. This was about 1770, probably just before his marriage. It remains practically as in 1780, save in two minor particulars: the eastern piazza is modern,[2] and the roof balustrade. The east side originally had only the narrow Dutch "stoep" (stoop) with a seat on either side. The hallway is broad and the stairs make a square turn half-way up. The east half of the ground floor comprises a single room, the parlor. Its windows command a magnificent view south and east, only excelled by the same prospect from the second story. Everything about the building (which is locally known as "Treason House" and its site as "Treason Hill) shows its connection with the eighteenth century. Its form is nearly square—55 by 45 feet—its material stone, stuccoed white. The wings are wooden and probably—certainly as to the exterior—of the second generation since 1770, but the same as the

---

[4] **Ann Hawkes Hay** (whose singular Christian name recalls that of De Montmorency, the historic Constable of France) was the son of a Scotch planter in the island of Jamaica, where he was born about 1754. He was sent to New York to be educated, and in 1772 married Martha Smith, sister of Joshua Hett Smith. (A coincidence is that his distinguished contemporary, Alexander Hamilton, was, like him, born the son of a Scotch planter, in the island of Nevis, 1757, and sent to New York for his education. The two may have met at King's College.)

The Tory influence of some of his wife's relatives was exerted to the utmost, to win him to the British cause at the outbreak of the Revolution. Twice a commission in the royal army was offered him, but refused. He was appointed (1776) Colonel of the Haverstraw militia regiment, which did duty on the west bank of the Hudson from Haverstraw to Fort Lee. He attracted the notice of Washington, who was a frequent visitor at his house. Soon after the execution of André a British force was sent, at the instigation of Tryon, to Haverstraw, to burn the dwelling. A negro slave betrayed the place in the garden where the family silver and other valuables had been buried, and they were carried off.

Colonel Hay died suddenly in New York, about 1786, leaving a large family. The present members of it now reside in South Carolina and in Clinton County, New York. I am indebted to his great-grandson, Mr. L. D. Hay, of West Chazy, N. Y., for most of these facts.

In the last letter written by Washington to Arnold (September 14) he says: "I hope Colonel Hay's plan for obtaining a supply of flour from the State of New York, and his application to the people of the [New Hampshire] Grants will both meet with success. He is a faithful and indefatigable officer."

[1] Measured by E. H. Hall, 1897.

[2] Possibly the western, also, but I am not sure of this. An odd feature is, that while there is no approach by road from the west, the house really faces that way, as is shown by the brass knocker still in place on the hall door.

Ann Hawkes Hay. A letter from him to General George Clinton, dated July 14, 1776, records, that "on Friday, the 12th, a barge and cutter from the British fleet of one forty and one twenty-gun ship (the *Rose*, Captain Wallace, and *Phœnix*, Captain Parker) with four cutters, anchored opposite Nyack." Hay's regiment was called out, the barge was fired on and driven off.—*American Archives*, Vol. I., 5th Series, pp. 338, 580.

On August 10, 1776, Hay was appointed Commissary of Militia.

On November 30, 1776, General John Morin Scott, writing to Washington, refers to Colonel Hay as "a gentleman uncommonly spirited in the publick cause." (Page 929.)

originals in size and form. The whole design is that of the best residences of its day, and when new and in good condition it must have been a handsome and dignified abode for a man of means and good social position, which Smith certainly was. A complete list of its visitors of note would be interesting. In its dining-room Arnold, his host and Mrs. Smith dined when the former made his frequent visits from West Point. Mrs. Arnold, with her child, was there overnight, Tuesday, the twelfth[1] of September, and there were to be other and more distinguished guests soon after. Wayne was there on the twenty-seventh, and wrote to Washington, dating from "Smith's white house." William Irvine followed, then Lafayette, and finally Washington, again,[2] nearly a year later, on his way to Cornwallis and Yorktown.

Though contemporary opinions as to Smith's politics varied widely, he was in excellent repute with many good Whigs. Though Colonel Lamb, commanding the artillery at West Point, would not visit him (although their wives were relatives) as he deemed him a Tory, Knox and Robert Howe testified in his favor at his trial, and Major Kierse, of Stony Point, testified that Smith had lent him a thousand dollars that very summer, to aid in shipping quartermaster's stores, and that his predecessor, Quartermaster Henry, had had a similar loan. Colonel Hay testified that in July, 1776, Smith was one of thirteen men who, in the absence of the militia, successfully resisted the landing of a force from some British vessels, to carry off some stores from Haverstraw.

In the parlor, the floor boards attest the building's age. They are spruce, unusually wide and thick, and but little worn, considering their century and a quarter of use. The grate, fender, and iron-work of the fireplace are said to be the originals, but the marble mantel and jambs have been transferred to the dining-room and replaced by others. They are of white marble and were brought from England. On the mantel, some Vandal has roughly scratched the name BURR.[3] In the second story the visitor is shown a curious secret closet under the garret stairs, and then the most interesting apartment of the house, the southeast bedroom, where Arnold and André breakfasted.[4] Smith himself brought the meal upstairs, and Arnold returned to the Robinson House as soon as it was over. Every detail of the conspiracy had been settled between André and himself, and

---

[1] There has been some variance of opinion about this date, some writers claiming it was the nineteenth. I have followed Leake, who says Arnold "brought Mrs. Arnold to the Robinson House, the next day," which was the thirteenth.

[2] King (see Ch. III) says he heard Washington tell Luzerne in October, that he dined with Arnold at Belmont the day he started for his conference with Rochambeau at Hartford.

As Washington was crossing from King's Ferry, in Arnold's boat, two incidents occurred, which although almost unnoticed at the time, assumed some importance when the treachery became known. The *Vulture* was in full view, and while Washington was regarding her through his spyglass, and speaking in a low tone to one of his officers, Arnold was observed to appear uneasy. A second was Lafayette's remark to Arnold, *àpropos* of the expected arrival of the French fleet under Count de Guichen. Alluding to the frequent communications by water between New York and the Hudson river posts, he said: "General, since you have a correspondence with the enemy, you must ascertain what has become of Guichen." Arnold was disconcerted, probably for a moment thinking his plot was discovered; but nothing more was said, as the shore was reached at that moment.—SPARKS, *quoted by Lossing.*

[3] After Aaron Burr. [4] According to Thacher, page 12.

See plates 6-9: Joshua Hett Smith's House

See plate 10: Portrait of John Lamb

the return of Washington from Hartford on the twenty-seventh was to be signalized by the capture of the Chief as well as that of West Point. During breakfast, or, as some accounts have it, as soon as they had reached the house,[1] the two heard the sound of distant cannon, and from the southeast window, which commands an uninterrupted view for miles up and down the Hudson, saw the *Vulture* lying close to Teller's Point—too close for safety. Colonel Livingston had noticed her position a day or two before, and asked Arnold for two cannon to use against her. Arnold evaded compliance, and he was obliged to content himself with a four-pounder, which seems to have been the only gun at Verplanck's. Securing from Lamb a small supply of powder,[2] which the veteran artillerist grudgingly furnished,[3] he went on Wednesday to Croton Landing and thence to the farmhouse of William Teller on the Point, to get a horse[4] to draw the cannon down. By Thursday night—the twenty-first—this was accomplished, and the gun in place on or very near Northwest Point, as shown on the map. This was not over a thousand yards, or two-thirds of a mile, from the sloop. The river here, between Squaw Point and André's dock, is quite two miles wide. The success of the cannonade is historic. Smith says the vessel seemed to be afire. Had she not got away downstream with the tide she must have been sunk or captured.[5] Thus the historic four-pounder was the first link in the chain of events which were to array themselves against him who, as Smith says, was so vehemently wishing himself again aboard the vessel. The return to her, on which he—and perhaps Arnold also—had counted, was henceforth impossible. With her went the safe and easy return to New York, where promotion and honors awaited him. Now, alone within an enemy's country, without means of escape except such as Smith was willing to furnish, he must have passed a day of

---

3 After Aaron Burr resigned from the army, in 1779, with the rank of lieutenant-colonel and an honorable record of four years' service, he began to study law, and in the spring of 1781 went to Haverstraw. Thomas Smith was then occupying "Belmont," Joshua being in jail at Goshen (see Chapter III). Thomas seems to have been forced out of New York City, whether by want of practice during the British occupancy, or because suspected of Whig sympathies is uncertain. The first seems more likely, as a third brother, William, was Chief Justice of New York and in Clinton's confidence (see Chapter IV). As Joshua says he himself had met Burr before, this was apparently not his first visit to Haverstraw. He read law with Thomas at "Belmont" for six months. In the *New York Packet* of November 15, 1783, Thomas advertises "Belmont" for sale or to let, as containing "150 acres or more of good land, situate three miles from King's Ferry, good house, with six fireplaces." (The property was his, not Joshua's).

4 According to Thacher, this was not until ten o'clock. Smith had sent his wife and children away to Fishkill (see Chapter II).

1 Smith says he saw the firing begin while he was returning in his boat. This, however, may mean just as he was landing. He says, "firing from Gallows Point," and several who quote him have evidently not looked at his *errata*, where he says it should be Teller's. On some old maps the name is printed *Tallus*. That printed opposite is from the latest survey (1898) made by Mr. E. H. Hall, of the Sons of the American Revolution.

2 This must have been without Arnold's knowledge.

3 "Firing at a ship with a four-pounder," he wrote, "is in my opinion a waste of powder." Yet, as Leake very truly says, in commenting on this remark of Lamb, "Had Colonel Lamb been aware of the blessed effects to be produced by this cannonade," etc. (see Leake, page 258) "he would not have dispensed his munitions so grudgingly ; for never were balls so well expended as those which were fired upon that occasion."

4 In 1863 the late Mrs. Williams, one of Teller's twin daughters, told Miss Cornelia Van Cortland that she remembered the event, and that she and her sister followed the party all the way over "Cortland's Neck" to Teller's, weeping for fear the horse would never be returned to the farm.   5 Just here I, page 13.

exquisite discomfort. Smith served him dinner[1] in the same upper room, and he accepted—as he had to—his offer to escort him to the British lines, near White Plains. (It was really Arnold's plan. See André's statement later.) In changing his uniform coat and hat for such as Smith lent him, he made another mistake, as he had previously made one in accepting from Arnold the various papers—now preserved at Albany—containing details of the post and garrison at West Point.[2] Thus, in less than one day, Clinton's three specific cautions had all been disregarded. The transaction of the papers is incomprehensible, as they were in no way necessary to his mission. As Sargent suggests, their salient points could easily have been memorized, or embodied in a brief form, intelligible only to himself. To receive and carry them was surprising rashness.[3] Sargent may be right in thinking he exacted them of Arnold as a proof of sincerity, or that the latter offered them as such. The latter seems more likely, as he had them ready. During the day Smith must have crossed the river on the errand which was so nearly successful, and would have changed the whole subsequent history if it had been. The incident has never received the historical prominence it deserves. In 1844 Mrs. Gerard G. Beekman (Cornelia Van Cortland, daughter of General Pierre) was living at Tarrytown, and, although nearly ninety years old, in full mental

THE ANDRÉ TABLE.

---

[5] Just here I may remark on what seems to me a singular omission on the part of all authorities—viz., the action of the *Vulture* herself during the cannonade. Does anyone suppose the commander of a vessel mounting fourteen guns would remain quiescent while a four-pounder was firing on her? Yet no one seems to have thought the "fire" which Smith saw was what it must undoubtedly have been—the flashes of fire and the dense cloud of smoke through which they spurted in rapid succession, giving the vessel the appearance of being actually in flames as her seven guns—the battery on one side—were rapidly replying to Livingston's one small cannon. No doubt part of the crew were making every effort to get her under sail and out of range, but the finding at different places on the Point of cannon balls larger than Livingston's piece could use shows conclusively, I think, that at least part of her battery was actively engaged with the daring foe. It is much to be regretted that no report from Lieutenant Sutherland of the action is accessible.

An unpublished diary of General Henry Dearborn (then Major of the First New Hampshire) records: "Orangetown (the present Tappan), 22 September, 1780. At daybreak two cannon and a howitzer began to play briskly on a ship of war that lay in the river. The wind and tide being unfavorable for the ship, she was not able to get out of reach for more than an hour." Could this have been the *Vulture*? Tappan is about nine miles below Teller's Point. A tradition in the family of Lieutenant-Colonel Ebenezer Stevens, of Lamb's regiment, is that he had himself taken out cannon and fired on the vessel, following her down the river—on the west bank.—*Magazine Am'n History, August, 1880.*

Possibly the two items refer to the same case. Stevens may have taken his guns some distance up-stream, and thus for a while the vessel would be under fire from both banks.

[1] The table on which breakfast and dinner were served is now owned by Mr. C. W. Gordon, Haverhill, Mass. It is circular, of mahogany, claw-footed and with a tilting top.

[3] See André's statement, Chapter V, on this point.　　　　　　[2] The following are, pages 16—18.

vigor. She told Lossing then (and in 1845 repeated the story to J. Watson Webb, with trifling variations) that Colonel Samuel B. Webb's younger brother John, usually called Lieutenant Jack,[1] came to the Van Cortland house,[2] at North Peekskill, where she was living, about the seventh of September. He brought a valise containing considerable specie and his new uniform, and left it with her, cautioning her not to give it to any one without a written order from himself or his brother. Riding on, he dined at Peekskill, presumably at a tavern, for Joshua Hett Smith was present. In the latter's hearing he mentioned the call he had just made, and the fact was not lost upon his auditor, for on the twenty-second Smith rode to Van Cortland's, where he asked for the valise, saying Jack Webb had sent him. Mr. Beekman was about to send a servant for it, when his wife, overhearing the conversation, appeared on the scene and demanded the stipulated written order. Smith readily answered that Webb had not had time to write it; whereupon she refused to give up the valise, and despite Smith's angry remonstrance, he was forced to leave without it. Had his effort succeeded, André's escape in the uniform would have been certain. Fortunately for Smith, Mrs. Beekman does not seem to have told the story at the time, for she was not summoned as a witness at his trial. Her story seems to establish Colonel Lamb's opinion that Smith was a Tory.

Thus Cornelia Beekman is justly entitled to the credit of indirectly, at least, causing André's capture.[3]

To return to the latter—Leaving his hat and scarlet uniform coat in the room we have illustrated, he reluctantly put on a coat belonging to Smith,[4] apparently of a shade between crimson and claret, and a civilian's round beaver hat, also Smith's. Over all he put the long, light-blue cloth cloak, with a cape, which he had worn when leaving the *Vulture*. Thus attired, he started with Smith and the negro[5] for King's Ferry, just before sunset on Friday. His mount was a Government horse, brown, branded U. S. A. on the near shoulder (Smith claims to have furnished the saddle and bridle). From Smith's to King's Ferry is three miles, by a winding, hilly and picturesque road, which crosses two small creeks (Miner's Falls and Florus Falls), passes behind Stony Point and ends at a little cove just north of it. West of the cove, the cut made in constructing the West Shore Railroad destroyed its last hundred yards, and few traces of it remain. Its course, however, was pointed out to me by the venerable John Ten Eyck, son of him who was the ferryman from 1784 to 1844. The dock of 1780,

[1] I do not know why, for his actual rank was Captain, in Sheldon's dragoons.
[2] Called the Mansion house, to distinguish it from the Manor house at Croton.
[3] In *Harper's Monthly* for April, 1876, it is stated that Washington afterwards thanked her. If so, he could not have known of the event at the time of Smith's trial, as it would infallibly have hanged Smith.
[4] This advice—to change his dress—perplexing to unravel as it is, André, with all his sagacity and good sense, was prevailed upon to pursue, for what reason nobody ever knew.—*Jones*, I, page 372.
[5] As Sargent remarks, it is very possible this humble retainer, had he been given a "half-joe" (about $8 specie), and warned to keep silent, might readily have contrived a way to put André safe aboard the *Vulture* again. But nobody gave his possible aid a thought.

of which a timber or two can be seen at low tide, was between the two rows of huge old willows seen in the view. This was taken from the Ten Eyck property on the north, and the boulder seen on a line with the post in the nearer stone wall shows the exact spot. Lonely and deserted as it now is, it is hard to realize that during the Revolution it was the ferry-place of the patriot army and the public, and a link of communication[1] between New England and the South. As a natural sequence, it was constantly occupied by the ferrymen and a detail of soldiers, and near it our party met some of Livingston's officers. One was Captain Cooley, probably Adjutant John, late of the Third Westchester militia, but then of the Fourth (Colonel Crane's). A second was William Jameson.[2] Smith asked Cooley if they could get a boat, and was told they might catch the Government boat if they were quick about it. They had previously met Major John Burrowes, of Spencer's New Jersey Regiment (often called the Fifth Battalion of the Jersey Line),[3] to whom Smith dexterously gave the slip after a brief colloquy, and near a tent—of either Livingston or these officers, probably the latter[4]—Smith stopped, chatted, and without dismounting drank grog or punch from a bowl handed him. André and the negro meanwhile rode on. It may easily be supposed the former was in no mood for unnecessary conversation with the officers, to whom Smith was well known. The ferryboat, which was probably a *bateau* (flatboat or scow) was just starting as they boarded her. Among the rowers were Cornelius, Lambert and Henry Lambert and Benjamin Acker. Henry Lambert[5] was steersman, William Van Wert—or Van Wart—was the ferrymaster, and on reaching the eastern shore Smith paid him eight dollars Continental money for the ferriage. Smith's presence doubtless saved André from unwelcome questions, and once the boat reached her dock, in the deep bay called Green's Cove, nearly a mile southeast of the extremity of Verplanck's Point, he was free to continue his journey—henceforward to be full of danger.

---

1 It was called the lower route, to distinguish it from the upper, terminating at Fishkill. At this time there were 166 "bateau-men" at Verplanck's and Stony Points.

2 He was apparently an officer, as, witnessing at Smith's trial, he spoke of "my tent." Possibly the company tent was meant. The New York records do not contain any officer of the name. Another account says they also met Major Kierse.

3 **John Burrowes** first appears as Captain in Forman's New Jersey Regiment, 1776, then in 1779 as Major in Spencer's. After the war he became Sheriff of Monmouth County, N. J.
He seems to have been commanding officer at Haverstraw, as Smith, on his trial, asked him whether his guards at the lower end had reported to him "meeting (being passed by) two strange gentlemen the night before" (Thursday). These two must have been Arnold and André.

4 On his trial Smith stated that he met Livingston at Verplanck's Point. Livingston corroborated him, adding that he gave Smith two letters to deliver, one each for Arnold and Governor Clinton. Smith adds that Livingston was related to Mrs. Smith, and that he asked André and him to remain to supper, but André declined. While Smith, as a rule, is a discredited authority, I think he may be trusted on minor points.

5 Names which show the craft must have been the Government boat, for all were soldiers. Cornelius was a veteran who had served in the Third New York Levies (Colonel Morris Graham). In the previous May he had enlisted in the Fourth New York Continentals (Colonel James Hughes) in which Acker was also a private. Lambert was a private (Combs' company) and Henry a lieutenant (Orser's company) of the First Westchester militia.

The following are true copies of the several papers :

"West Point, September 5th, 1780.

"*Artillery Orders.* — The following disposition of the corps is to take place in Case of an alarm :

"Capt. Dannills with his Comp'y at Fort Putnam, and to detach an Officer with 12 men to Wyllys's Redoubt, a Non Commissioned Officer with 3 men to Webb's Redoubt, and the like number to Redoubt No. 4.

"Captain Thomas and Company to repair to Fort Arnold.

"Captain Simmons and Company to remain at the North and South Redoubts, at the East side of the River, until further Orders.

"Lieutenant Barber, with 20 men of Capt. Jackson's Company, will repair to Constitution Island ; the remainder of the Company, with Lieut. Mason's, will repair to Arnold.

"Capt. Lieut. George and Lieut. Blake, with 20 men of Captain Treadwell's Company, will Repair to Redoubt No. 1 and 2 ; the remainder of the Company will be sent to Fort Arnold.

"Late Jones's Company, with Lieut. Fisk, to repair to the South Battery.

"The Chain Battery, Sherburn's Redoubt, and the Brass Field pieces, will be manned from Fort Arnold as Occation may require.

"The Commissary and Conductor of Military stores will in turn wait upon the Commanding Officer of Artillery for Orders.

"The artificers in the garrison (agreeable to former Orders) will repair to Fort Arnold, and there receive further Orders from the Command'g Officer of Artillery.

"S. BAUMAN, *Major Comm't Artillery.*"

This and the following document are in Arnold's handwriting :

"*Estimate of Forces at W'st Point and its Dependencies, September* 13, 1780.

"A brigade of Massachusetts Militia, and two regiments of Rank and File New Hampshire, Inclusive of
166 Batteaux Men at Verplanck's and Stony Points 992
"On command and Extra Service at Fishkills, New Windsor, &c., &c., who may be called in occationally 852
"3 regiments of Connecticut Militia, under the com'd of Colonel Wells, on the lines near N. Castle . . . 488
"A detachment of New York levies on the lines 115

Militia, 2447

"Colonel Lamb's Regiment 167
"Colonel Livingston's, at Verplank and Stoney Pts. 80

Continent : 247

"Colonel Sheldon's Dragoons, on the lines, about one half mounted 142
"Batteaux Men and Artificers 250

Total, 3086."

The following document is in the handwriting of Villefranche, a French engineer :

"*Estimate of the Number of Men necessary to Man the Works at West Point and in the Vicinity.*

Fort Arnold	620	Redoubt No. 2	150	Redoubt No. 7	78
—— Putnam	450	ditto 3	120	North Redoubt	120
—— Wyllys	140	ditto 4	100	South Redoubt	130
—— Webb	140	ditto 5	139		
Redoubt No. 1	150	ditto 6	110	Total,	2438

"N.B. — The Artillery Men are not Included in the above Estimate."

The following table is in the handwriting of Bauman, Major Commandant of Artillery :

"RETURN OF THE ORDNANCE IN THE DIFFERENT FORTS, BATTERIES, &C., AT WEST POINT AND ITS DEPENDENCIES, SEPT. 5, 1780."

	Metal	Garrison Carriages	Garrison Carriages	Traveling Carriages	Garrison Carriages	Stocked Carriages	Garrison Carriages	Garrison Carriages	Stocked Carriages	Traveling Carriages	Garrison Carriages	Traveling Carriages	Traveling Carriages	Mortars (Inches)	Mortars (Inches)	Mortars (Inches)	Howitzers (Inches)	Total
Calibers		24	18	12	9		6		..	4		3	0	5½	4⅖		8	
Fort Arnold {	Brass	..	..	..	..	..	..	..	..	..	1	..	..	5	5	1	..	} 23
	Iron	1	6	..	..	1	..	..	..	..	..	..	3	..	..	..	..	
Fort Putnam {	Brass	..	..	..	..	..	..	..	..	2	..	1	..	..	4	..	..	} 14
	Iron	..	5	..	2	..	..	..	..	..	..	..	..	..	..	..	..	
Constitution Island	Iron	..	..	..	4	..	1	5	..	..	..	..	..	..	..	..	..	10
South Battery	Iron	..	4	..	1	..	..	..	..	..	..	..	..	..	..	..	..	5
Chain Battery	Iron	..	..	..	1	2	..	..	..	..	..	..	..	..	..	..	..	3
Lanthorn Battery	Iron	..	..	..	..	..	2	..	..	..	..	..	..	..	..	..	..	2
Webb's Redoubt	Iron	..	..	..	1	..	..	2	..	..	..	1	..	..	..	..	..	4
Sherman's Redoubt	Iron	..	..	..	..	..	..	2	3	..	..	..	..	..	..	..	..	5
Megg's Redoubt	Iron	..	..	..	..	..	..	1	..	..	..	1	..	..	..	..	..	2
South Redoubt	Iron	..	..	..	1	..	..	4	..	..	..	..	..	..	..	..	..	5
North Redoubt	Iron	..	3	..	3	..	..	..	..	..	..	..	..	..	..	..	..	6
Wyllys's Redoubt	Iron	..	..	2	..	..	..	..	..	..	..	..	3	..	..	..	..	5
Rocky Hill, No. 4	Iron	..	..	..	..	..	..	..	2	..	..	..	..	..	..	..	..	2
" No. 1	Iron	..	..	..	1	..	4	..	..	..	..	..	..	..	..	..	..	5
" No. 2	Iron	..	..	..	..	..	2	..	..	..	..	..	..	..	..	..	..	2
Verplanck's Point	Brass	..	..	..	..	..	..	..	..	..	..	..	..	..	2	1	..	3
Stony Point	Iron	..	..	1	..	2	..	..	..	..	..	..	..	..	..	..	1	4
Total		1	18	3	14	5	9	14	5	2	1	3	6	5	11	2	1	100

N.B.—The following ordnance not distributed :

No. 6 iron 12 pounder.	3 brass 24 pounders.
4 " 9 "	7 " 12 "
1 " 6 "	1 " 8-inch howitzer.
1 " 4 "	___
2 " 3 "	11
___	
14	

The following description of the works at West Point and its dependencies is in the handwriting of Arnold, endorsed "Remarks on Works at West Point, a copy to be transmitted to his Excellency General Washington. Sep'r, 1780."

"Fort Arnold is built of Dry Fascines and Wood, is in a ruinous condition, incompleat, and subject to take Fire from Shells or Carcasses.

"Fort Putnam, Stone, Wanting great repairs, the wall on the East side broke down, and rebuilding From the Foundation ; at the West and South side have been a Chevaux-de-Frise, on the West side broke in many Places. The East side open ; two Bomb Proofs and Provision Magazine in the Fort, and Slight Wooden Barrack.—A commanding piece of ground 500 yards West, between the Fort and No. 4 — or Rocky Hill.

"Fort Webb, built of Fascines and Wood, a slight Work, very dry, and liable to be set on fire, as the approaches are very easy, without defences, save a slight Abattis.

"Fort Wyllys, built of stone 5 feet high, the Work above plank filled with Earth, the stone work 15 feet, the Earth 9 feet thick.—No Bomb Proofs, the Batteries without the Fort.

"Redoubt No. 1. On the South side wood 9 feet thick, the Wt. North and East sides 4 feet thick, no cannon in the works, a slight and single Abattis, no ditch or Pickett. Cannon on two Batteries. No Bomb Proofs.

"Redoubt No. 2. The same as No. 1. No Bomb Proofs.

"Redoubt No. 3, a slight Wood Work 3 Feet thick, very Dry, no Bomb Proofs, a single Abattis, the work easily set on fire—no cannon.

"Redoubt No. 4, a Wooden work about 10 feet high and fore or five feet thick, the West side faced with a stone wall 8 feet high and four thick. No Bomb Proof, two six pounders, a slight Abattis, a commanding piece of ground 500 yards Wt.

"The North Redoubt, on the East side, built of stone 4 feet high; above the Stone, wood filled in with Earth, Very Dry, no Ditch, a Bomb Proof, three Batteries without the Fort, a poor Abattis, a Rising piece of ground 500 yards So., the approaches Under Cover to within 20 yards.—The Work easily fired with Faggots diptd in Pitch, &c.

"South Redoubt, much the same as the North, a Commanding piece of ground 500 yards due East—3 Batteries without the Fort."

This was in Arnold's handwriting:

Endorsed:

At a Council of War held in Camp, Bergen County, Sept. 6, 1780.

"Present—the Commander in Chief. The Commander in Chief states to the Council that since he had the honor of laying before the General Officers, at Morristown, the 6th of June last, a general view of our circumstances, several important events have occurred which have materially changed the prospects of the Campaign. That the success expected from France, instead of coming in one body and producing a Naval Superiority in these Seas, has been divided into two Divisions, the first of which only consisting of seven ships of the line, one forty-four and three smaller Frigates, with five thousand land Forces, had arrived at Rhode Island. That a reinforcement of six ships of the line from England having reinforced the Enemy, had made their Naval Force in these seas amount to Nine Sail of the Line, Two Fifties, two forty-fours and a number of smaller Frigates, a Force completely superior to that of our Allies, and which has in consequence held them blocked up in the harbor of Rhode Island till the 29th ult., at which period the British Fleet disappeared, and no advice of them has since been received.

"That accounts received by the *Alliance* Frigate, which left France in July, announce the Second Division to be confined in Brest with several other ships, by a British Fleet of thirty-two sail of the Line, and a Fleet of the Allies, of Thirty-six or Thirty-eight Ships of the line ready to put to sea from Cadiz to relieve the Port of Brest.

"That most of the States in their answers to the requisitions made of them, give the strongest assurances of doing everything in their power to furnish the men and supplies for the expected Co-operation. The effect of which, however, has been far short of our expectations, for not much above one third of the Levies demanded for the Continental Batallions nor above the same proportion of Militia have been assembled, and the supplies have been so inadequate that there was a necessity for dismissing all the Militia whose immediate services could be dispensed with, to lessen our consumption, notwithstanding which the Troops now in the Field are severely suffering for want of Provision. That the army at this Post and in the vicinity, in operating Force, consists of 10,400 Continental Troops and about 400 Militia, besides which is a Regiment of Continental Troops of about 500 at Rhode Island, left there for the assistance of our Allies against any attack of the Enemy, that way, and two Connecticut State Regiments amounting to 800 at North Castle.

"That the Times for Service for which the Levies are engaged will expire the first of January, which if not replaced, allowing for the usual Casualties, will reduce the Continental Army to less than 6000 men.

"That since the State of the Council above referred to, the Enemy have brought a detachment of about 3000 men from Charles Town to New York, which makes the present operating Force in this Quarter between Ten and Eleven Thousand men.

"That the Enemies Force now in the Southern States has not been lately ascertained by any distinct accounts, but the General supposes it cannot be less than 7000 (of which about 2000 are at Savannah). In this estimate the Diminution by the Casualties of the Climate is supposed to be equal to the increase of Force derived from the Disaffected.

"That added to the loss of Charles Town and its Garrison, accounts of a recent misfortune are just arrived from Major General Gates, giving advice of a general action which happened on the 16th of August near Campden, in which the army under his command met with a total defeat, and in all probability the whole of the Continental Troops and a considerable body of the Militia would be cut off. The State of Virginia has been some time exerting itself to raise a Body of 3000 Troops to serve till the end of December, 1781, but how far it has succeeded is not known.

"That Maryland has resolved to raise 2000 men, of which a sufficient number to compose one Battalion was to have come to this army. The remainder to recruit the Maryland line—but in consequence of the late advices, an order has been sent to march the whole southward.

"That the Enemies force in Canada, Halifax, St. Augustine and at Penobscot remains much the same as stated in the preceding Council.

"That there is still reason to believe the Court of France will prosecute its Original intention of giving effectual Succor to this Country, as soon as circumstances will permit; and it is hoped the Second Division will certainly arrive in the course of the fall.

"That a Fleet greatly superior to that of the Enemy in the West Indies, and a formidable land Force had sailed some time since from Martinique to make a combined attack upon the Island of Jamaica—that there is a possibility of a re-inforcement from this quarter also, to the Fleet of our Ally at Rhode Island.

"The Commander in Chief having thus given the Council a full view of our present situation and future prospects, requests the Opinion of each member, in writing, what plan it will be advisable to pursue, to what object Our Attention ought to be directed in the course of this fall and winter, taking into consideration the alternative of having a Naval superiority, whether any offensive operations can be immediately undertaken and against what Point. What ought to be our immediate preparations and dispositions, particularly whether we can afford or ought to send any reinforcement from this army to the Southern States, and to what amount.

"The General requests to be favored with these opinions by the 10th instant at the furthest."

CHAPTER II.

King's Ferry to Tarrytown—Danger.

I have not quailed to danger's brow
When high and happy—need I now?
BYRON—*Giaour*, line 1035.

OFFICER'S BUTTON,
26TH BRITISH REGIMENT.

AS with the western, so the eastern end of King's Ferry —nothing but a few logs, submerged at high water, identify it.

The "King's Ferry Road[1] extends for a mile and a half almost due east. There, on top of a ridge extending north to Peekskill, it joins the old Albany Post Road a little north of where another road leads east, down the ridge to the Montrose station of the New York Central. Our travellers turned north at the junction and in about two miles and a half reached the present Peekskill, and turned east on the Crompond Road. This is a winding, hilly road, now bordered after settled Peekskill is past, by modern residence property and well-kept farms. Diversified by hill and dale, open fields, trim dwellings and spreading trees, it affords a most delightful drive to the lover of Nature. In 1780 the region must have been rather a lonely one, with here and there a farmhouse whence, in most cases, had gone a son or brother to the army or militia. At about four miles from Peekskill, and eight from Verplanck's, occurred Smith's first check, and the one which ultimately caused his companion's capture. Here, at about half-past eight,[2] the party met a sentry, who halted them until his officer, Captain Ebenezer Boyd,[3] of the Third Westchester militia, appeared. Smith dismounted, and talked some time with him, producing Arnold's pass. He took this into his quarters[4] to read by lamplight, and was satisfied with it, but proved uncomfortably inquisitive as to the travellers' business and their wish to proceed that night. Smith tried to meet and parry his questions, but

---

For this button and succeeding similar ones, I an indebted to Mr. W. L. Calver, of New York. All three regiments—the 26th, 7th and 54th were André's.

[1] The view shows it at about midway of its length.

[2] Sunset was at seven that day, so it must have been deep gloom by this time.

[3] **Ebenezer Boyd** was born either in Scotland or near Bedford, Westchester County, about 1735, and died at Boyd's Corners, in the town of Kent, Putnam County, June 29, 1792. He was Captain of what would now be called the second or "B" company. Colonel Van Cortland had been promoted to Brigadier, and was succeeded in command of the regiment by Lieut. Colonel Drake.

[4] The house long since disappeared, and was replaced by a barn, which is just west of Stony Street. On the map it is marked by the figure 3.   *This autograph should have appeared on page 19.*

See plate 11: King's Ferry
See plate 12: King's Ferry Road
See plate 13: Crompond Road

made a false step by saying they would stop overnight further on, with either Colonel Gilbert Drake[1] or Major Joseph Strang, both of Boyd's regiment. At this Boyd must have suspected him, for he told him Strang was absent, and Drake removed to another town. He represented the danger of travelling White Plains-ward by night as so great, because of a band of "Cowboys" known to be within the lines, that Smith's fears were aroused[2] (probably also by Boyd's evident suspicions of him), and he agreed to stop at a house nearby. André, to whom the marauders were far more likely to be friends than foes, and who was depressed by his anomalous and dangerous position, disguised and in the enemy's country, was naturally anxious to push ahead. But Smith carried his point, and they went back to Andreas Miller's house,[3] on the south side of the road, about one-third of a mile east of Hog Lane (an existing road now bearing the more euphonious but absurd name of "Lexington Avenue") and just over the boundary line in the town of Yorktown (Peekskill is in the town of Cortland). Miller's accommodations for travellers were decidedly limited—apparently to one bed, which Smith shared with André, who went to bed in his boots, not even removing his spurs, and spent the time in restless weariness, disturbing Smith's slumbers. The dwelling[4] has disappeared, save the foundation and a few timbers. A growth of young locust trees and flowering shrubs surrounds the spot, and some search is required to find it.

Before dawn—Saturday, the twenty-third—the trio were again in the saddle, and rode to a point half a mile east of the Presbyterian church,[5] at Crompond Corner. By this time André had recovered his spirits, as though feeling entirely safe, and displayed to the full those accomplishments of mind and manner which had invariably charmed all who met him, and which had their effect on Smith. At the Corner, in the angle made by the junction, from the north, of the Somerstown road, stood a tavern known as Strang's[6] (or Mead's). Near it, the three riders were suddenly halted by a picket-guard, and detained

---

1 One account has Lieutenant Colonel Delavan instead of Drake.

2 If Smith suspected André's real character, he knew there could not be much danger from these marauders; but, on the other hand, his Whig reputation would be endangered by the very fact, if they were met, and yet suffered nothing by the meeting. He was, in short, trying to "run with the hare and hunt with the hounds." It was more prudent to allay Boyd's suspicions by staying over night—but the delay was fatal to André the next day.

3 Marked 2 on the map. Smith's *Narrative* is clearly misleading here, when he speaks of going "back some miles, to a tavern kept by one McKoy." At his trial, Captain Boyd testified that Miller's house was "close by."

4 In the case of this house tradition has especial value, as there is but one life between 1780 and 1898. In 1784 the dwelling was sold to John Strang, son of Major Joseph, and a new one took its place. In 1795 this was bought by Abraham Requa, a soldier of the Westchester militia, of much active service. His son Edmund inherited it, and his grandson Amos C. was born in it. The son of Edmund, and grandson of Abraham, Rev. Amos C. Requa, lives in Peekskill, and is my authority for identifying the house.

5 Marked 4 on the map. The edifice itself was not then standing, for on June 24, 1779, Tarleton's and Simcoe's cavalry came up from White Plains by way of Pine's Bridge, and burnt it. The parsonage, ten days earlier, had met the same fate, at the hands of a detachment from Verplanck's Point, under Lieutenant Colonel Robert Abercromby, of the 37th Regiment.
The two incidents well illustrate the harassed condition of the Neutral Ground at the time.

6 Marked 5 on the map. On a map made by Erskine, the patriot geographer, it is called Mead's Tavern.

See plate 14: Ruins of Andreas Miller's House, Yorktown.
See plate 15: Site of Strang's Tavern, Crompond Corner

while the officer in command, Captain Ebenezer Foote,[1] of the Commissary Department, was notified. Arnold's pass was again produced, but the morning was yet too dark[2] for open-air reading, and the Captain went into Strang's — his headquarters — and read it by lamp-light. The scene outside at the moment is readily imaginable to one who has visited the spot, and is worthy the brush of a historical painter. The atmosphere was foggy, threatening rain. Nearby objects were indistinct and distant ones invisible through the gloom. In the foreground the watchful guard, the sentry in front of the tavern, the two white men, one muffled in a light-blue cloak covered with moisture, sitting his horse like a soldier, the other in civilian's dress, and intently awaiting the opening of the tavern door and the re-appearance of the officer. In the middle foreground, a small frame building, and inside, seen through the small-paned window, a grave-faced young officer intently scanning the paper — since grown historic and carefully preserved at Albany — which allows "Mr. John Anderson" to "pass the guards to the White Plains and below if he Chuses."

Nothing wrong about it, thinks the Connecticut Captain, less suspicious than Boyd, so he returns it, and, like Boyd, misses his chance of historic distinction.[3] André's spirits must have risen again with this second escape, and the

[1] **Ebenezer Foote**, son of Daniel and descendant of Nathaniel, who settled in Watertown, Mass., in 1633, was born in Colchester, Conn., April 12, 1756, and died December 28, 1829, in Delhi, N. Y. At nineteen we find him in the ranks of the Minute Men at Bunker Hill, and afterwards as a sergeant of the Second Connecticut. He was taken prisoner at the surrender of Fort Washington. With several companions he escaped from the Bridewell in New York, at night, in the month of December following, gained what were then the open fields, and reached the Hudson at the village of Greenwich, eluding all the British sentinels. On the bank they found no means of escape but an unseaworthy boat, and here the party divided, and his companions, going further, were most or all recaptured. He determined to trust himself to a single plank, rather than run risk of capture. Accordingly he proceeded to swim the Hudson by means of the plank, and after being several hours in the icy water, and safely passing an anchored British man-of-war, he was floated ashore below Hoboken. At first unable to stand after his terrible experience, he eventually reached a house where he was succored. Reaching the American lines we find him in the army at the capture of Trenton, and during the terrible winter at Valley Forge. This, however, added to his previous experience, broke down his constitution, and soon afterwards he secured a transfer to the Commissary Department, where he remained until the end of the war, rising to the rank of Major. After 1783 he began mercantile life in Newburgh, and then went into politics, eventually becoming member of the Legislature, and holding many minor offices until appointed First (Presiding) Judge of Delaware County, an office he held for many years, and to universal satisfaction.

His military ability was inherited by his son, General Frederick Foote, who died prematurely as a result of hardships endured on the frontier during the war of 1812, and by his grandson, Captain and Brevet-Major (really acting Colonel) William Rensselaer Foote, of the Sixth U. S. Infantry, who was killed at the battle of Gaines' Mills, in 1862.

[2] Sunrise was at six. This shows how early the party must have left Miller's — apparently without breakfast.

[3] Foote told Smith — who did all the talking — that the only American forces below were Sheldon's dragoons, who were chiefly at Robbins' Mills (now Kensico) and would give him an escort to White Plains if he wanted it. A few days later this note was written:

"Continental Village,
"28 of Sept. 1780.

"Captain Foote,
"Sir.—Your letter to the General was delivered me on the road. You will on receipt of this permit the officer with the flag to return, delivering him the enclosed letter. This I know to be his Excellenc intention, and he yesterday sent orders which seem not to have reached you.
I am, Sir, your most obedient servant,
A. HAMILTON,
Aid De Camp.

Captain Foote has endorsed this:
"Ordering the return of the flag sent out from New York on account of Arnold's desertion."
I am unable to decide what flag of truce this refers to.

See plate 16: Interior of Strang's Tavern
See plate 17: Portrait of Ebenezer Foote

proof of the value of Arnold's pass. Strang's tavern was demolished about 1825, but the hewn frame of a part of it was moved from the original site, just across the road, to the rear of the house now occupied by Mr. Anson Lee. With modern siding, its exterior is completely changed, but inside the bare, hewn posts, braces and cross-beams attest its age. It is now used as a kitchen, but the chairs, brass warming-pan and polished powder-horn,[1] all older than the Revolution itself, are quite in keeping with its history, and it is not impossible that it is the very room in which Foote read the pass.

Up a long hill and down into a little valley, where now is the track of the New York and Putnam Railroad, rode our party, and, at a point not identifiable, André had a meeting which he afterwards said "made his hair rise." Colonel Samuel B. Webb, of the Third Connecticut,[2] then and since December 29, 1777, a prisoner to the British in New York, and at this time out on parole, met him. Coming on him in this sequestered place at such an hour, Webb — who had often met him in New York, and probably not long before — stared hard at him. André knew him at once, and gave himself up for lost. But Webb's star was not in the ascendant that morning, any more than had been Boyd's or Foote's, and he failed to recognize his acquaintance,[3] and once more fate spared him. As the riders went past the house of Major Strang (where Smith, the night before, had proposed to stop) they were observed by the inmates, who thought them Continental officers.[4] Daylight appeared as they followed the road south and east about three miles and a half, to where, just before it forks on Cat Hill, a small two-story frame house[5] stands, close to the road, on the west side.

Modernized by a narrow "lean-to" in the rear, an addition on the western end and ordinary siding all round, it does not seem old; but it actually dates from

---

[1] The horn is inscribed: "Belong'd to Daniel See — Seth Allen his Horn, 1775." See is still a well-known family in upper Westchester County.

[2] **Samuel Blachley Webb** was born in Wethersfield, Conn., December 13, 1753, and died at Claverack, N. Y., December 3, 1801.
  He was wounded at Bunker Hill, was aid to General Putnam, and in 1776 was appointed aid to Washington, with the rank of Lieutenant-colonel. He was again wounded at White Plains, and at Trenton; was at the battles of Long Island and Princeton, and raised and organized the Third Connecticut almost at his own expense. It was first styled the Additional Continentals, then the 9th and finally the 3d. Webb was not exchanged until January, 1781.
  He and Colonel Joseph Reed it was who refused to receive Howe's letter to Washington, because of its address to "George Washington, Esquire." His regiment acquired the sobriquet of the Decoy Regiment, owing to its being uniformed in red — the uniforms, in fact, captured aboard a British vessel, and slightly changed to adapt them to patriot use. To this circumstance was due the capture (October 10, 1777,) of the British spy, Daniel Taylor, who mistook them for the royal forces, found himself in the presence of General James Clinton instead of Sir Henry, and was hanged at Hurley, Ulster County, N. Y., October 14th. On his expedition to Long Island, in December, 1777, Webb was captured.
  Soon after his return to active service he was brevetted Brigadier-General.
  When Washington took the oath of office as President, in 1789, Webb held the Bible on which it was administered. His son, Henry L., was Colonel of the 18th U. S. Infantry, during the Mexican War, and General Alexander S. Webb, president of the College of the City of New York, is his grandson.

[3] It is a coincidence that on February 12, 1778, Webb's brother Joseph wrote him from New Haven: "Should you meet Captain André, acknowledge from me his politeness to Major Huntington, and I think you will find him much the gentleman."

[4] Dykman. The house is marked 6 on the map.

[5] Marked 7 on the map.

See plate 18: Portrait of Samuel Webb

See plates 19-20: The Underhill House, Yorktown

See plate 21: Portrait of Richard Varick

about 1700. For more than a century, and up to 1895, it was owned and occupied by those by whose name it is still known—the Underhills. In 1780 its owner was Isaac, whose widow, Sarah, survived until 1812. Tradition—practically history, as in the case of the Miller-Requa house—says that a band of Cowboys—(probably those Captain Boyd had referred to)—had driven off all but one of her cows the previous night. The present highway wall did not then exist, so our travellers rode up to the back door—now hidden by the "lean-to"—where both alighted and asked for breakfast. All Mrs. Underhill could give them, under the circumstance of her loss, was the humble dish of "suppawn"[1] (mush and milk). Seated on the step of the back door,[2] the talented young Adjutant ate his last meal as a free man. At this stage of the journey, Smith and he parted—to his speedy ruin. Nothing has ever been disclosed as to why this was done. White Plains was still fifteen miles distant; André knew nothing of the region between, while Smith knew it well. He had agreed to take his companion there, but made no further effort to that end.[3] The other could not force him to do it,[4] and possibly did not greatly desire his further company, feeling tolerably confident, as Smith told him he was now beyond the American outposts.[5] So, paying Mrs. Underhill, dividing with André his Continental money, and giving him a message[6] to his brother William, the Tory Chief-Justice at New York, whom André knew, he and his servant returned to Crompond and thence northwest to Arnold's quarters at the Robinson House, just below West Point on the east shore, and told his story to the expectant traitor, with whom he says he dined.[7] Unless Arnold was concerned about André's being abandoned short of White Plains, he must have felt assured of the success of his plot. Smith went on to Fishkill to rejoin his family. His Whig connections have a fresh proof here. Colonel Ann Hawkes Hay, of the Haverstraw militia, was married to Smith's sister, Martha, and lived at Fishkill at this time. It was to his house that Mrs. Smith and the

[1] A curious coincidence is that of André's contemptuous reference to this homely dish, in the *Cow Chace*. See Appendix.

[2] The view of this was made under difficulties, it being necessary to place the camera outside the back window. The house is in good condition, and may last another century. If the owner, Mr. George Gregory, carries out his expressed intention of removing the "lean-to," the back will appear in its original condition, showing the "André door." In the side view Miss Gregory is shown standing just where the "lean-to" joins the original building.

[3] The horse and equipments André promised should be returned or paid for.

[4] A singular fact is that André, although knowing he was entering the enemy's country when leaving the *Vulture*, was unarmed.

[5] Had Smith forgotten Foote's statement that Sheldon's force was at Robbins' Mills?

[6] One of his captors subsequently stated that when first seen by them he was intently studying a piece of paper containing a rough map of the region south of Pine's Bridge. An obvious inference would be that Arnold or Smith made it for him. No trace of it exists. It may have been lost when his boots were taken off at Tarrytown.

[7] He was no stranger to the house, but Colonel Richard Varick, Arnold's senior Aid, thoroughly disliked and distrusted him, and not long before had tried to pick a quarrel with him at dinner, until Mrs. Arnold became annoyed and asked him to desist. Varick was so unsuspicious of the real relations existing between Smith and his chief that he warned Arnold against him. Leake says Smith and Lamb were invited guests at dinner on the eighteenth of September. This may have been the date of the quarrel between Varick and Smith, but Leake does not mention it.

Richard Varick was born in Hackensack, N. J., March 25, 1753, and died in Jersey City, July 30, 1831. Commissioned a Captain in McDougall's New York Regiment in 1775, he rose to the rank of Lieutenant Colonel in 1777 as Deputy Muster-master General. He was an ardent admirer of Arnold's military genius and became his Aid. The discovery of the treason nearly upset his reason (as it did that of Major Franks). He became Recording Secretary to Washington soon afterwards, and after the war was Recorder of New York City (1783-89), and from 1791 to 1801 he was Mayor (the first) of the city. He was many years President of the Merchants' Bank and of the American Bible Society. In all the relations of life he was most exemplary, a model man in both public and private life.

children had been sent, to have them out of the way while Arnold's mysterious visitor should be at "Belmont," and Smith now proposed to take them back with him. On Monday,[1] the twenty-fifth, he rode to Poughkeepsie on business, and returned in time to be present at the dinner given by General John Morin Scott in honor of Washington. He is said to have had a seat at the same table with the Chief.[2]

We will now return to Yorktown. André continued on the road which passes Underhill's to Pine's Bridge, which then spanned the Croton river about half a mile further up stream than the present structure.[3] Crossing it, he turned to the right and followed the highway down the south bank about a mile, to Hog Hill. Then turning to the left he ascended the hill to Underhill's Corners, where Henry C. Allen now lives, about three miles from the bridge.[4] Here the road extends nearly north and south, and at its intersection with the Chappaqua road, becomes Kipp Street. In the angle between the two on the east side of Kipp Street, is the dwelling of Mr. Allen. In 1780 the house[5] then existing was occupied by Stevenson Thorne, a member of the Society of Friends. The fugitive reached the spot about ten o'clock,[6] when the fog had changed to a fine, drizzling rain. In doubt as to whether he ought to keep on the road, or take that to Chappaqua, southeast, he checked his horse, and seeing Jesse Thorne, a twelve-year old boy who was standing on the wood-pile near the front of the house, asked his way to Tarrytown.[7] Jesse jumped from the wood-pile and went to the house-door to call his father, who came out. A brief colloquy ensued between them, the way to Tarrytown was pointed out, the stranger touched his horse with the spur[8] and galloped away southwards on Kipp Street.[9]

Jesse, with the curiosity of a country boy, watched him whilst he spoke with his father, and many years afterwards described him accurately, as "very genteel in his manners and intelligent, wearing a wide-brimmed hat, military cape overcoat, high boots with spurs, and riding a brown horse branded U.S.A. on the shoulder, and having one white forefoot and a white star on his forehead."

André pursued his journey down Kipp Street to the Hardscrabble road. So far, no obstacle had arisen, and the way to safety seemed open, if he could but follow Smith's directions for reaching either White Plains or Dobbs' Ferry.

---

[1] Smith's *Narrative*.

[2] Another authority says he called on Washington that day, at the house of Dr. McKnight, where the Chief was quartered, and where the dinner was probably given. If Smith is to be believed, he and Colonel Hay dined with General Knox that day at "Dr. McKnight's, where General Scott also lived." After supper, he says, Washington came out and stayed a few moments with them.

[3] The old abutments were visible until the recent raising of Croton Dam increased the depth of water.

[4] Dykman.

[5] Marked 8 on the map.

[6] Jesse Thorne to his grandson, Rev. C. C. Thorne, of Windham, N. Y., who is my informant.

[7] That inquiry was fatal. Had he taken the Chappaqua road he would almost certainly have reached the British lines.

[8] This spur, of silver, was in 1882 preserved in Washington's Headquarters at Newburgh.

[9] The road shown in the centre, ascending the hill.

See plate 22: The Thorne House, near Chappaqua
See plate 23: Sgt. Sylvanus Brundage's House, Pleasantville
See plate 24: The Roadside Spring, Pleasantville

At the house[1] in Pleasantville then occupied by Sylvanus Brundage, and now by his grandson, William H. Brundage, on this road, he stopped to water his horse at the spring opposite the house. Brundage, himself a soldier, of the Second — or Middle — regiment of Westchester militia (Colonel Thomas) was then at home.[2] Some words were exchanged between them, and the traveller went on. Continuing on he reached the old Bedford road, and passed down it to Rossell's — now Mekeel's — Corners.[3] Here he turned to the left. At a point about a mile further, the road descends to the little valley where the Nepperhan[4] river, here a mere brook, is crossed, and feeds the pond for the sawmill still existing and known as Hammond's. To his left, on a slight eminence, stood the dwelling of Staats Hammond,[5] the miller. Here, for the second time that morning, the fugitive unwittingly met a patriot soldier. Hammond was a sergeant in the First Westchester, and had been wounded through the left leg in an encounter near Sing Sing, June 17, 1779.[6] The unhealed wound still disabled him and he was lying on the floor in his house.[7]

It was a beautiful September day when I visited the scene. Hammond's house disappeared long ago, but that lately occupied by Floyd Powell stands on the same site.

Riding quite close to the well, where stood David and Sally Hammond, fourteen and twelve years old, the stranger asked for a drink. Sally filled a cup or bowl and handed it to him, while David held the horse and noticed the handsome double-snaffle bridle, and the mane full of burrs. André remarked on the excellence of the water,[8] gave Sally a sixpence, which was treasured for many years afterwards, and then asked David[9] about the distance to Tarrytown and the likelihood of meeting a Whig force at Young's tavern, about a mile further on. The boy told him there was a party of scouts there. Alarmed at this, he turned his horse and retraced his journey as far as Mekeel's Corners. Here he continued over the old Bedford road, on to Tarrytown Heights to the old Albany Post road, which he followed to Tarrytown.

Here Fate awaited him, and the consequences of the night's delay at Miller's house, and his fear of the party at Young's tavern were to deliver him into the hands of his enemies. Had he gone on, towards Dobbs' Ferry, past

---

[1] Marked 9 on the map.

[2] The term of service of many of the militia had expired the previous June.

[3] Marked 10 on the map. John Mekeel was a first lieutenant in the Third Westchester militia.

[4] Spelled also Nepperan, but generally known by the barbaric name of Sawmill.

[5] Marked 11 on the map.

[6] Howe was there in July — possibly "June" should be July.

[7] Through the window he had a glimpse of the rider, and afterwards expressed distrust of him on account of his being muffled to the chin in his cloak.—*David Hammond in 1847.*

[8] The "André well" still furnishes excellent water. In the illustration it is not shown, but is directly on a line with the left end of the house.

[9] Mrs. Hammond, according to Campbell.
    David lived until 1853, and to the end clearly recalled the scene.

See plate 25: Staats Hammond's House
See plate 26: Mekeel's Corners, Pleasantville

Young's tavern, which was doubtless the route Arnold laid out for him, or had he been but an hour and a half earlier, all would have been well with him, for the road was then free. At this point I would digress a moment, to consider the state of that part of Westchester County—its greater part—then known as the Neutral Ground, from not being permanently occupied by either army. Strictly speaking, the Neutral Ground was all below the Croton river, but the frequent British forays beyond that line rendered its actual extent indefinite. Dr. James Thacher,[1] surgeon of the Sixteenth Massachusetts, whose *Military Journal* is so full of valuable details of the period, was present with his regiment during November, 1780, when a large detachment of Washington's army, under Stark, crossed the Hudson and moved down through the county as far as West Farms, only eight miles from King's Bridge, and endeavored to draw the British into a general engagement.[2] He thus graphically describes the region and inhabitants:

"The miserable inhabitants are not much favored with the privileges which their neutrality ought to secure to them. They are continually exposed to the ravages and insults of infamous banditti, composed of royal refugees and Tories. The country is rich and fertile, but now has the marks of a country in ruins. The few farmers who remain find it impossible to harvest the produce. The meadows and pastures are covered with grass of a summer's growth, and thousands of bushels of apples and other fruit are rotting in the orchards. Some on either side have taken up arms, and become the most cruel and deadly foes. There are within the British lines, banditti of lawless villains who devote themselves to the most cruel pillage and robbery among the defenceless inhabitants between the lines; many of whom they carry off to New York after plundering their houses and farms. These shameful marauders have received the names of Cowboys and Skinners. By their atrocious deeds they have become a scourge and terror to the people."

Rev. Timothy Dwight, of New Haven, who was Chaplain to General Silliman's Connecticut Brigade—the First—in 1778-9, and afterwards President of Yale College, has left a still more distressing description of the same region:

"These unhappy people were exposed to the depredations of both armies. Often they were actually plundered, and always were liable to this calamity. They feared everybody whom they saw, and loved nobody. Fear was apparently the only passion by which they were animated. The power of volition seemed to have deserted them. They yielded, with a kind of apathy, what you asked and what they supposed it impossible for them to retain. Their houses were in a great measure scenes of desolation, and their furniture was extensively plundered or broken to pieces. The walls, floors and windows were injured both by violence and decay, and were not repaired, because they had not the means and because they were exposed to the repetition of the same injuries. Their cattle were gone, their enclosures were burnt where they were capable of becoming fuel, and thrown down where they were not. Their fields were covered with a rank growth of

---

[1] **James Thacher** was born in Barnstable, Mass., February 4, 1754, and died in Plymouth, May 24, 1844. He entered the army in 1775, and served throughout the war, successively as surgeon of the First Virginia and the Sixteenth Massachusetts. He was prominent professionally and socially throughout his life after the end of the war, and exerted a marked influence for good on the community in which he dwelt.

[2] Under pretext of a foraging expedition, this force was intended by the Commander in Chief to co-operate with the main army in an attack against the Enemy's post on (New) York Island. By some cause, known only to the Chief, this enterprise was unfortunately defeated.—*Thacher*.

weeds and wild grass. Their world was motionless and silent, except when one of these unhappy people went upon a rare and lonely excursion to the house of a neighbor no less unhappy, or a scouting party alarmed the inhabitants with expectations of new injuries and sufferings. The very tracks of the carriage roads were obliterated by disuse, and when discernable resembled the faint impressions of chariot wheels said to be left on the pavements of Herculaneum. The grass was of full height for the scythe, and strongly realized to my own mind, for the first time, the proper import of that picturesque allusion in the Song of Deborah : ' In the days of Shamgar, the son of Anath, in the days of Jael, the highways were unoccupied, and the travellers walked through by-ways. The inhabitants of the villages ceased, they ceased in Israel.' '' (*Judges V.*, 6, 7.)

It was through this very region, and among a people thus harried and ruined that Clinton's Adjutant-General was now making his way—and it was to the recent brutalities of a party of Cowboys that he was indirectly to owe his capture, within an hour of the time he left Hammond's house.

At about one o'clock in the afternoon of the previous day—Friday, the twenty-second—John Dean, John Paulding, James Romer, Isaac See, Isaac Van Wart, Abraham Williams and John Yerks,[1] all young men,[2] left Salem on a "scout" or errand of more or less independent and irregular warfare, having for its object the capture of any Cowboys or others who might drive cattle towards New York. As they passed the house of Joseph Benedict, where David Williams was at work, he recognized them, asked their errand and volunteered to join them. His personal aim was to revenge the death of a neighbor named Pelham, killed by Cowboys the day before, and his property stolen. All of Yerks' party were militiamen,[3] and had secured, through Paulding, leave of absence from their officers to take part in the scout. Sleeping that night in John Andrews' hay barn at Pleasantville,[4] they reached Tarrytown Saturday morning, at about half-past seven, and went to the house of Jacob Romer, father of James, which has now disappeared. It stood close to the present reservoir, near the Tarrytown station of the New York and Putnam road. Here they had breakfast, and Mrs. Romer put up dinner for them in a basket.[5] They went next to Isaac Reed's house, borrowed a pack of playing

---

[1] Yerks originated the scout, having proposed it to Paulding.

[2] David Williams, the oldest, was not quite twenty-three. Van Wart and Paulding were cousins ; also, apparently, Romer and Paulding. Yerks was a cousin of Dean's on his mother's side.

To Williams, more than anyone else, history is indebted for many minute details about the capture and the events immediately preceding it. He only it is that has given the particulars about the party of Cowboys of which Boyd, Foote and—later—Jameson and Washington himself, were apprehensive. He says the band had raided Poundridge (the easternmost town in the county, lying next to Connecticut) the night before his party started (Thursday the twenty-first) and that they were led by a noted Tory named Smith. Tory Smiths were numerous, and three were noted bandits—Claudius, of Orange County, the greatest villain of the three, had been hanged in 1778, and a second's head was cut off, in Schoharie County, by infuriated Whigs in 1779, so the son of Claudius, Richard, is the one probably meant. While they were on Pelham's farm, driving off his live-stock, the unfortunate owner had run out in his nightshirt to save his horse, when the ruffians killed him.

What a graphic picture of a midnight foray on a defenceless homestead in the Neutral Ground this brief statement gives !

[3] The First Westchester.

[4] Paulding says Pleasantville ; Williams, Salem. It was a few yards from the present Methodist church at Pleasantville.

[5] The pewter basin accompanying it is now in the possession of Colonel J. C. L. Hamilton, of Elmsford, N. Y.

cards, and then proceeded to the spot where the business of the day might be looked for—the two roads leading to New York. Here they separated into two squads. Paulding, David Williams and Van Wart were posted on what was known as the old Post Road, near where stood an enormous white-wood or tulip tree,[1] just south of the little stream then known as Clark's Kill, but ever since as André Brook, Just opposite was afterwards built St. Mark's Episcopal Church. (The old Bedford road at that time came into the Post road at that point.) The other five were to watch the old Bedford road on Davis' Hill.[2] The two were not far apart, and it was agreed that either party needing aid should fire a gun, and that any plunder taken should be shared equally by all. While they are waiting, we may consider the epithets of "marauders," "banditti," etc., afterwards applied to them, and the irregularity which some have insisted attended their action and nullified their patriotism. Certainly they were not an organized body, detached by superior authority for a definite military expedition. But all were militia accustomed to active service—Dean, David Williams and Paulding particularly so. Paulding had been twice a prisoner in British hands[3] in New York. The party was actually under the direction of one of their number who was a veteran, not only of militia service, but of the Canada expedition of 1775. There he had endured great hardships, and left behind him an elder soldier-brother, entombed in the tremendous snowdrifts of the Plains of Abraham. He alone of the party was not a private, being at the time a sergeant in the First Westchester, and was later promoted and commissioned as ensign. I refer to John Dean,[4] to whose methodical disposition of the party its success was probably largely due, yet whose modesty prevented his receiving a just share of the praise bestowed on the three known to history.[5] To return to our story—they, whom Fortune was to favor that day, had the pack of cards, and drew lots to see who should watch while the others played. Van Wart lost, and took his place by the roadside,[6] at about eight o'clock. None but persons whom he knew passed until about half-past nine, when the sound of horse hoofs was heard on the bridge

---

[1] *Liriodendron.* It was 112 feet high, and stood, a noted landmark, until July 31, 1801, when destroyed by lightning. A coincidence was that on the same day the news reached Tarrytown of Arnold's death in London. The spot is marked 12 on the map.

[2] It is a curious fact that on Tarrytown Heights André rode past those who were watching the Bedford road from Davis' Hill, without being seen by them.—*Judge J. O. Dykman,* in a note to the author.

[3] He says the first time he was confined in the Sugar House, and the second in the North Dutch Church.

[4] That he was recognized as the leader appears from Jameson's question. See *post.*

[5] **John Dean** was born September 15, 1755, and died in Tarrytown April 4, 1817. After his service in Canada, as noticed, he was in the militia almost constantly until the end of the Revolution. In most of the encounters between the patriots and their enemies, whether British regulars, their Tory allies, or the Cowboys, he bore a prominent part, and his death was directly due to an injury received in a skirmish at King's Bridge in 1781.
His entire life after the close of hostilities was spent in Tarrytown, where his descendants still reside, and where his name appears amongst those of his companions in arms of the Neutral Ground, on the monument erected in 1894 to the memory of the soldiers of the Revolution.

[6] Williams says all sat down.

spanning the "kill."[1] The rider was intently scanning a small map, though his animal was galloping.[2] On this, either Van Wart or Williams said, "Here comes a gentleman-like looking man, who appears well-dressed, and whom you had better step out and stop, if you don't know him."[3] Paulding did so, presenting his musket at the rider's breast.[4] "I asked him which way he was going." "My lads," he replied, "I hope you belong to our party."[5] "What party?" "The lower."[6] "We do—my dress shows that," artfully said Paulding, who wore the uniform coat, green, faced with red, of a German *Jäger*. This dress naturally helped to deceive André.[7] As a matter of fact, Paulding had but a few days before escaped from a British prison—the North Dutch church, Fulton Street—in New York, and by the friendly keeper of a livery stable had been furnished with the coat, to help him pass the King's Bridge outposts.[8] The horseman, now addressing the group collectively, said: "I am a British officer, have been up the country on particular business, and would not wish to be detained a minute"—and to prove his claim to be an officer, took out his gold watch.[9] "Upon this, I told him to dismount,[10] and we told him we were Americans."[11] At this the stranger started, changed color, and "fetched a deep sigh."[11] "God bless my soul," he exclaimed, "a body must do anything to get along now-a-days,"[11] and produced Arnold's pass. Paulding, who alone of the three could read or write, read it. "You had best let me go, or you will bring yourselves into trouble, for your stopping me will detain General Arnold's business: I am going to Dobbs' Ferry, to meet a person there and get information for him," said the rider, whom Van Wart afterwards accurately described as "a light, trim-built man of a bold military countenance, and with dark eyes." The party hesitated—Arnold's pass was undoubtedly genuine, and his authority

---

[1] Van Wart.

[2] Williams. Van Wart says he was riding slowly, which seems more likely. Both may be right, for he may have checked the animal just as he crossed the bridge. As he was halted he thrust the map (which Arnold or Smith had given him) into his off boot-leg.

[3] Paulding.

[4] Van Wart says all three presented their guns.

[5] Williams.

[6] André's fatal question has been the wonder of all historians. With the pass in his pocket which had brought him safely through so many dangers, he made his crowning blunder.
The suddenness of the surprise seemed to deprive him of his wonted presence of mind.—*Jones.*
Instead of producing Arnold's pass, which would have extricated him from our parties, and could have done him no harm with his own, he asked the men if they were of the "upper" or "lower" party.—*Hamilton.*
With a want of self-possession so difficult to be accounted for in a mind equally brave and intelligent that it would almost seem Providential, instead of producing the pass from Arnold, he asked the man (Williams) where he belonged.—*Marshall.*

[7] General Van Cortland says André exclaimed: "Thank God! I am once more among friends." The buttons of this coat were long preserved at the Van Cortland manor house at Croton.

[8] The "fierce spirit of liberty" which the British acknowledged actuated the people of New England, was found also in the devastated Neutral Ground. Twice a prisoner, yet in arms again as soon as he escaped, is a typical record of a young militiaman.

[9] He carried two, one of silver.

[10] Paulding.

[11] Van Wart.

extended to Tarrytown.[1] Once more André's fate hung in the balance,[2] but he had just avowed himself a British officer,[3] displaying as a proof a gold watch, an article possessed by but very few Americans at the time—and Paulding, the master spirit of the three, whose acquaintance with British officers was recent and probably painful, was not satisfied, and said, doubtfully, "I hope you will not be offended, we do not mean to take anything from you, but there are many bad people on the road, and I don't know but you may be one. What is your name?" "John Anderson," was the reply.[4] Still unsatisfied, Paulding told him he must dismount and accompany them into the thicket, where they would be out of sight of passers-by.[5] This was done, Williams bringing up the rear and replacing the fence rails behind them.[6] Paulding told Williams to search him, which was done, and even his outer clothing removed, but to no purpose. Then he was told to sit down and take off his boots, "which," naïvely adds Williams, "he seemed to be indifferent about, but we got one off and found nothing in it." Van Wart says: "We found his stocking sagged a little, and, taking it off, found three unsealed letters within. Paulding hastily read them, and exclaimed, 'He's a spy!'"

Williams continues: "We found three more papers in the other stocking, then made him dress himself, and I asked him what he would give us to let him go."[7] "Any sum you want," was the prompt reply—if money could save him, the fugitive had no fear of the result. "A hundred guineas, with the horse, saddle, bridle and your watch?" queried Williams. "Yes, and the money shall be sent here if you want." "Will you not give more?" pursued the relentless

---

1 As Sheldon's regiment, on duty as low as White Plains, was under Arnold, I infer that his authority extended to Tarrytown. Yet on August 3, Washington, in appointing him commander at West Point, made out his notice: "West Point and its dependencies, in which all are included, from Fishkill to King's Ferry." Possibly this refers only to the fortifications.

2 We were about allowing him to pass, and he was reining his horse into the road, when Paulding exclaimed, in an undertone, "D——n him! I don't like his looks."—*Williams.*

3 "I would have let him go, had he shown his pass before he said he was a British officer," Paulding afterwards admitted.

A curious story may be found in the "Life and Observations of Rev. E. F. Newell" (C. W. Ainsworth, Worcester, Mass., 1849,) to this effect: In 1799 he was told by Rev. Duncan McColl, a well-known Methodist clergyman, in Connecticut, and an associate of Rev. Jesse Lee, the founder of New England Methodism, that during the Revolution he was employed as a clerk by the British "field-officers" (Headquarters?) and in such capacity was aboard the *Vulture* when she lay in the Hudson awaiting the return of André, "who had gone ashore to ascertain whether Burgoyne had reached Albany, and to secure information about the American troops." That he (being then recently converted) desired to prevent further hostilities and, with another man on the *Vulture* (whose name he did not give), prayed to that effect—and that the two believed André's capture was an answer to their prayers.
The story comes so directly that it may receive more consideration than it would otherwise, considering the variance in time between Burgoyne's campaign (1777) and Arnold's treason.

5 A singular circumstance is that on July 4, 1807, at the "Old South" Theatre, Philadelphia, a play concerning André was produced, in the course of which was used a drop scene which he had painted for the theatre used by the officers of Howe's army during the occupation of Philadelphia. It was introduced as representing the scene of his capture.

6 Williams' account, as printed, says they went about seventy rods into the thicket—an almost manifestly impossible distance. It is probably a typographical error for seven, or twenty—most likely the latter.
Williams says André's underclothing was of fine quality—"thread." His faculty for noticing details would have made him a good newspaper reporter.　　　　7 This admission, page 31.

See plate 27: The Capture of Major Andre

captor.[1] "Yes, any quantity of drygoods,"[2] was the reply, André finally rising to ten thousand guineas — an amount which surpassed the bribe paid to Arnold,[3] and must have seemed simply fabulous to his hearers.[4] "Where did you get these papers?" he was asked. "Of a man at Pine's Bridge, a stranger to me," was the reply — too transparent to deceive for a moment.[5] His watch — the gold one — was now taken from him, and the eighty dollars Continental bills which Smith had given him.[6] The fence was replaced, the order given him to mount

[7] This admission certainly tends to make one believe André's subsequent declaration to Tallmadge that they ripped open his saddle for money, and finding none, said : " He may have it in his boots," and so those were taken off.

The truth is, to the imprudence of the man (André himself) and not to the patriotism of anyone, is to be attributed the capture. Had money been at command after the imprudent confession, or any security given that the "patriots" could put confidence in, he might have passed on to Clinton.— *King*, in 1823.

Sargent prints this interesting affidavit :

Crom Pond, July 9, 1780.
    Miss Hannah Sniffen says that * * * and Isaac Van Wart did, on the night of the 27th ult. take from Mr. James Sniffen, an inhabitant of White Plains, without civil or military authority, three milch cows, which they converted to their own private use.

HANNAH SNIFFEN,
in behalf of her father.

Sargent says this is among the Rufus Putnam papers in Ohio.
Sargent further says that Williams and others, twice in the Summer of 1780, made seizures of people and cattle, but the civil authorities interfered and compelled restitution in both cases.
The disbelief of Tallmadge, King, and others, in the purity of the captors' motives, is an old story, and need not be repeated here. I am, however, enabled to give a valuable statement bearing on the characters of Van Wart and Williams, which has never before been printed, and which proves beyond question that they had been marauders (as Colonel A. G. Hammond wrote to Tallmadge). My informant is Rev. Chester C. Thorne, of Windham, New York, grandson of Jesse Thorne, whom I have quoted on page 24.
" My grandfather came to visit my father at the time we were living near West Oneonta, N. Y., and I remember his calling me to him, saying, 'I have something to tell thee'—and he told me this story so vividly that I never forgot it: In speaking of the captors, he said repeatedly (referring to Williams and Van Wart) 'They were Cowboys.' (While my great-grandfather, Stevenson Thorne, suffered terribly at the hands of the 'Cowboys' he never complained particularly of the 'Skinners.' He was repeatedly plundered by the former—of live stock and household goods.) It become known that he had money secreted, and one day (the exact date cannot be positively given, but was probably in 1777 or '78) an armed gang came to his house, and demanded it. Failing to force him to surrender it or reveal its hiding place, they endeavored to break open a wardrobe where it was really hidden, but failed. They then proceeded to hang him to one of the trees in his orchard, and strung him up twice, each time letting him down just in time to save his life, and then demanding the surrender of the gold.
A third time they drew him up to the limb, and on letting him down life was almost extinct. Convinced that death would be his portion if he persisted in further resistance, the unfortunate man, after being revived, surrendered the hidden treasure, which amounted to $1,300 in gold. One of the gang engaged in the robbery was Isaac Van Wart and David Williams was not far off. (So naïvely adds Jesse Thorne, in the written narrative.) This incident in his life is known to all of Stevenson Thorne's posterity, and being given in such detail by his son, an eye-witness to the cruel treatment of his father, the *status* of Van Wart and Williams not long before 1780 may be regarded as definitely settled, as that of Cowboys.

[1] Though neither knew it, captive and captor had met before, for when André was captured at St. John's, in 1775, Williams was a soldier of Montgomery's command.

[2] "Any amount you may name, in cash or drygoods."—Dr. Eustis to Dr. Thacher, on Van Wart's testimony.

[3] As Grant Thorburn remarked in 1840 (when Williams, the last survivor, had been dead only ten years) this sum would have made the three so rich that they could have owned more live stock than Job in the height of his prosperity. The very magnitude of the sum may have over-reached its object. It is highly probable no one of the three had ever possessed a hundred guineas at any one time.

He offered also to let them keep him concealed while their messenger should go to the British lines with the letter he would write. They held a long consultation (as he told Tallmadge subsequently) but finally decided the risk was too great, "a detachment would probably be sent out against them, they be captured and imprisoned in the Sugar House" (probably that in Liberty Street, near Nassau). The fear was realized in part, in Paulding's case, soon afterwards. He was wounded, a third time captured and was in a British hospital until the end of the war.

[5] "We refused to accept his bribes, unless he would say from whom he got the papers. He refused to say."— *Williams, in 1817.*   [6] The law allowed, page 32.

and go in advance.[1] The other five now joined them — perhaps summoned by the agreed-on musket shot. Paulding said: "We have taken a prisoner,[2] searched him, and found papers in his boots, and don't know what to do with him."[3] "Take him to General Washington," advised Yerks.[3] Possibly as a compromise, it was agreed that he be taken to the nearest outpost, which was one of Sheldon's Dragoons. The whole party accordingly started, but not before André had vainly repeated his offer of ten thousand guineas. At this point he surrendered his silver watch, saying "it was their prize,"[4] and the party began their march for the Romer house, which they had left that morning.

---

[6] The law allowed captors in such cases, all the prisoner's property found on him. It was restored to him at Tappan, by Washington's order. The sixpence he had given to Sally Hammond seems to have been the only small change he had with him. At Tappan he told Bowman that they robbed him of the few guineas he had. Of course he did not know that the law permitted it.

[1] Yerks says Paulding led the horse up the hill.

[2] The news was soon spread, for that afternoon "a runner passed our house, stopping a moment to say to my father, 'They have taken a spy at Tarrytown.'"—*Jesse Thorne*, see p. 24.

[3] Yerks must have thought the Chief was at Arnold's quarters, instead of at Hartford.

[4] Williams. (Abraham Williams, See and Romer appear to have been minor figures.) Yerks says Paulding demanded it.

CHAPTER III

Tarrytown to the Robinson House — Detection.

Now a' is done that men can do,
And a' is done in vain.
BURNS.— *It was a' for our rightfu' king.*

OFFICER'S BUTTON,
7TH BRITISH REGIMENT.

THE distance to Romer's was fully a mile and a half or two miles. During the march, Sergeant Dean was in command, as is shown by the fact that when Williams annoyed the prisoner by persistent questioning, he appealed to the Sergeant for protection, and the latter ordered his tormentor to desist. Van Wart has left this graphic picture of the march: "You never saw such an alteration in any man's face. Only a few moments before he was uncommonly gay in his looks, but after we had made him prisoner, you could read in his face that he thought it was all over with him. After travelling one or two miles, he said: 'I would to God you had blown my brains out when you stopped me.'"

Paulding preceded the others to the Romer house,[1] and cautioned Mrs. Romer, saying: "Take care what you say, Aunt Fanny; I believe we have a British officer with us." On arrival it was found the basket containing dinner had been forgotten in the excitement of the morning, and John Romer, James' younger brother, a boy of sixteen who was destined to live to be ninety-one, was sent back to the tulip-tree for it. It is not clear whether the party waited at Romer's for his return,[2] or went at once to Reed's,[3] where they had borrowed the cards that morning. This — now known as the Landrine house — still stands on the north side of the old White Plains road, about one and a half miles from the New York Central's Tarrytown station, and half a mile from the East View or Tarrytown stations on the New York and Putnam road. The small addition to it, shown in the illustration, is modern. André was taken into the right-hand room. Here, at the right of the fireplace, is a box stairway,[4] and on its first step he sat while eating bread and milk. The stairs remain unchanged, but the door

---

[1] The party probably also visited the Dean house, though this is not certain.

[2] Yerks says all had some food while there, but André refused to eat. It may be that this house was the scene of the dinner referred to by Irving. See page 34.

[3] Marked 13 on the map.

[4] A stairway closed in and hidden by a partition, but without balusters — usually without handrails. It is common in old houses. At this house one authority — J. S. Lee, of Beekmantown — says the party dined on eggs and bacon.

See plate 28: The Reed Tavern, East Tarrytown
See plate 29: The Captor's Monument, Tarrytown

seems modern. When young Romer came back with the basket, the time must have been past noon, and its contents were probably eaten before the journey was resumed. Sheldon's nearest post was, as Foote had said, at Robbins' Mills, the present Kensico. I quote from Judge Dykman, illustrating the minutely careful record he has made of the route, enabling the tourist to easily identify sites:

They passed along the road East, turned to the north on the hill west of the county almshouse, up that road, under Buttermilk Hill, across the Sawmill river at the bridge just below the mill. Passing up the road near Raven Rock, they went to the corner at the late residence of Carlton Clark. Turning to the right they ascended the hill to the Upper Cross Roads, down another hill, past Ebenezer Newman's, across the hollow now traversed by the Harlem Railroad, and up Reynolds Hill on the White Plains road to the old Foshay house.

This building[1] was unfortunately destroyed before I could visit and photograph it. Here they stopped awhile, and drank water or milk. Their objective point was John Robbins' house, where the officer in command of Sheldon's detachment was supposed to be. It is a small frame building, on land recently — 1896 — acquired by New York City as part of the Kensico reservoir watershed, and is soon to be removed or destroyed on that account. Of all I visited, it is about the only one in bad condition. Its siding, though probably not the original, is nearly black from age and exposure, and the front porch, where André probably entered, has disappeared, though the old Dutch half-door remains.[2]

It was, probably, at this house that occurred the episode told only by Irving.[3] The party arrived as the family were at dinner. André was asked to

[1] Site marked 14 on the map.
[2] This side the building was in such bad condition that Mr. Bennett preferred to photograph the other, where the obliging housewife went to the trouble of taking down her Monday wash to allow the camera a clear field. It is marked 15 on the map.
[3] *Life of Washington*, Vol. iv., p. 124.

See plate 30: The Robbins-Wright House, Kensico
See plate 31: Sands' Mills, Armonk
See plate 32: Portrait of John Jameson

share the repast, and its humble nature apologized for. He replied: "Oh, madam, it is all very good, but indeed I cannot eat." A young girl of the company was Irving's informant in her old age, and said she could never restrain her tears when recalling the scene. The house had been the quarters of Lieutenant-Colonel John Jameson,[1] of Sheldon's regiment.[2] As the Colonel himself was under arrest[3] at the time, for some unknown military offense, Jameson was in temporary command, and possibly for that reason had transferred his headquarters to Sands' Mills, in the town of North Castle. Hence the squad resumed their march, over the North Castle road.[4] One-half the distance from Tarrytown had been covered, and six miles remained. It could not have been earlier than three o'clock, and was probably somewhat later. André was still riding his brown horse, which one captor after another led by the rein, the others marching on either side and behind. Sands' Mills would be reached by five or half-past.[5] The "Mills" is merely a sawmill and two or three houses in the northern part of the small town of Armonk, formerly called Mile Square. None of the present dwellings are of Revolutionary age, the Sands house being dated 1809. Probably Sands' original dwelling and that we are interested in, the outbuilding or annex to the barn,[6] were the only ones there in 1780, besides the mill. The second and third are not a hundred feet apart. The mill was closed on the day of our visit, but is modern, at least outside. It is run by the power of Wampus Pond, a pretty little lake on the higher ground westward. To the north and west are the "Heights of North Castle," where Washington's forces encamped after the battle of White Plains (1776).

The farm's outbuilding,[7] like most others of its time, has lost its appearance of age with its ancient shingle siding. Smooth modern boards effectually

---

1 **John Jameson,** of a distinguished Virginia family, was born in either Culpeper or Fairfax, Va., in 1751. At the time we are considering he had been for three years an officer of Sheldon's regiment, to which he had been promoted from Major of Bland's First Dragoons, a Virginia regiment, as Sheldon's was of Connecticut. He had been wounded near Valley Forge in 1778, and served creditably throughout the Revolution. He was for many years Clerk of Culpeper County, dying in Culpeper, November 20, 1810. He was a member of the same Masonic Lodge in Alexandria as Washington. The portrait shown has never before been published. I am indebted for it to his grandson, Mr. Philip R. Jameson, of Culpeper.

2 Sheldon's was a "crack" regiment, the arms and accoutrements of which had been bought in France. That part of it on duty in Arnold's district comprised only 142 men, "about one-half mounted" (see page 16). The paper with this detailed information was at that moment in possession of Paulding (or Dean).

3 Sheldon was tried by court martial at West Point, October 23, 1780, Colonel Hazen, of the "Congress," or Second Canadian Regiment, being president, and acquitted.

4 Williams' account says: "We kept to the by-ways, and went as quickly and silently as we could. He suffered much in mind, as was apparent from his great dejection, but he acted like a gentleman, candidly and politely, and never once attempted to escape."

5 History has generally stated that only the three captors went to Sands' Mills. But in 1832 Samuel Youngs, who had been a private in the First Westchester when commanded by Colonel Hammond, and became a lieutenant in Sheldon's in 1782, endorsed the pension application of Ensign John Dean's widow, to this effect: In 1780 he himself was employed as a guide for Sheldon's regiment, and as such was at Mile Square on the twenty-third of September, and there witnessed the arrival of the eight, whom he mentions by name. When Dean was asked by Jameson for their names, he gave only those of Paulding, Williams and Van Wart.

6 The 1780 barn has given place to another.

7 Marked 16 on the map.

Samuel Youngs was born in 1760, and died in 1837. He was a well-known figure in Westchester County, and held the office of Surrogate for several terms.
It has been claimed that from him Irving drew the character of *Ichabod Crane.*—M. D. Raymond, *Souvenir,* etc., Tarrytown, 1880.

36

disguise the oldest structure, making it resemble a "modern antique." The frame, and probably most of the floor, is as when Jameson there received the prisoner whose real importance he so misunderstood. As the owner was absent, with the key, we were unable to make a photograph of the interior, which is now a carpentry workshop. As this building, like Robbins' house, is on "reservoir land" it must soon be removed or destroyed, and by the time these lines reach the reader both will probably be things of the past. My visit to the scenes just described was during the same week in September as that in which André was there in 1780. I passed over almost every foot of the road he traversed, and realized that the landscape could not differ greatly from that which he saw. The fence-corners were ablaze with purple asters, golden rod, tansy, and Virginia creeper; cardinal flowers were blooming here and there, and the occasional call of "Bob White" from an unseen bevy of quail, or the caw of a crow as he winged his way across the valley of the Bronx—here a little brook—were almost the only sounds which broke the rural quiet. Just such André must have seen and heard, as he rode at the slow pace of his guard those six miles from Robbins' Mills[1] to Mile Square.

Jameson at length found, and "Anderson" turned over to him, all but Paulding, Van Wart and Williams returned to their several homes. If their names were asked, neither Jameson nor anyone else mentioned them. Jameson's decision to send "Anderson" at once to Arnold with a letter[2] is familiar history,[3] and has been severely criticised. But of the honesty of his purpose—and possibly also of the military propriety of his action—there has never been any question. In a subsequent letter[4] to Washington, he acknowledged his unfortunate mistake. Now once again André's star seemed emerging from the clouds of danger surrounding him. Could he but reach Arnold once more, he was safe—and he must have been eager to start. The guard sent with him oddly enough did not include any of his captors. It was composed of four Connecticut militia, undoubtedly of one of the three regiments of such, on the North Castle lines, commanded by Lieutenant Colonel Jonathan Wells, Nineteenth Connecticut. The squad was commanded by Lieutenant Solomon Allen of Northampton, Mass., of Colonel Seth Murray's three months' regiment of Hampshire County militia.[5] (He was Adjutant at this time.)

[1] Van Wart afterwards referred to his distress of mind, as shown by the great drops of sweat which kept falling from his forehead.

[2] Whether or no André asked him to do this is a disputed point (Lossing says he did). The letter is as follows:
North Castle, 23 Septr.
Sir,—I have sent Lieutenant Allen, with a certain John Anderson, taken going into New York. He had a passport signed in your name. He had a parcel of papers taken from under his stockings, which I think of a very dangerous tendency. The papers I have sent to General Washington. They contained (see description, pages 16-18).

[3] Van Wart afterwards testified that Jameson cautioned the captors to keep the matter secret, as there were probably others concerned in the plot, who must not be frightened off before they could be seized. I doubt this. An officer of his rank would not have been likely to thus take an unknown militiaman into his confidence.

[4] See Chapter IV.　　　　　　　　　　　[5] Solomon Allen was born, page 37.

See plate 33: Portrait of Solomon Allen
See plate 34: Portrait of Col. Benjamin Tallmadge

These events took place on Saturday, the twenty-third, probably at about six in the evening. André, who had now been in the saddle almost continuously since five in the morning, was at once hurried off for Arnold's headquarters,[1] to his own secret satisfaction. Nothing but the arrival a little later of one whose reminiscences of the period are among the most readable of such, prevented him from safely arriving there.

This person was Benjamin Tallmadge, of Wethersfield, Connecticut, an active and intelligent young officer, the Major of Sheldon's regiment. Being on duty below White Plains, he did not return to headquarters until some time after the Allen party had left.

His suspicions of Arnold, remonstrances against Jameson's action, and the consequent sending of a messenger to overtake Allen,[2] are all familiar incidents of history, as is also Jameson's obstinate determination that the letter to Arnold should be forwarded notwithstanding.

André was now well on his way towards Arnold—and freedom. The recalling order came almost too late. Not until Allen and his squad were upon the hill north of Peekskill, close to the ancient St. Peter's Church, were they overtaken by the messenger,[3] "bloody with spurring, fiery-red with haste."[4]

Once more the unfortunate prisoner was turned back[5] to danger, when little more than an hour would have saved him. It was his last chance, and he was now to progress steadily towards the inevitable end. The return to Sands' Mills was about eight or nine o'clock Sunday morning,[6] the twenty-fourth.

---

[5] **Solomon Allen** was born in Northampton, Mass., February 23, 1751, and died in New York January 28, 1821. He had three brothers in the army, one the Rev. Thomas Allen, first pastor of the Congregational Church of Pittsfield, Mass., who was present at the battles of Bennington and Saratoga. Solomon served several short enlistments, and, after the close of the war served also in suppressing Shays' rebellion. Afterwards he studied theology, was ordained, and became distinguished as a Methodist pastor, chiefly in Western New York. Finally settling in New York City, he died there in 1821. See *Allen-Witter Genealogy*, and J. N. Danforth's *Sketch of Last Days of Solomon Allen*.
For his portrait and autograph I am indebted to his great grandson, Mr. Theodore L. Allen, of Pittsfield.

[1] From the quick time made, all the party must have been mounted. The *Allen-Witter Genealogy* says André's arms were bound behind him by a strap, a soldier holding the end, and orders given the squad to shoot him if he attempted to escape. Lieutenant Allen rode in the rear. The compiler of the genealogy does not give his authority for any statements, and the papers of Rev. Solomon Allen, though supposed to be somewhere in New York City (if anywhere) have never been discovered by his descendants.

[2] The order recalling Allen reads:
"From some circumstances which I have just discovered, I have reason to fear that a party of the enemy is above; and as I would not have Anderson re-taken or get away, I desire that you will proceed to Lower Salem with him, and deliver him to Captain Hoogland. You will leave the guard with Captain Hoogland also, except one man whom you may take along. You may proceed to West Point to deliver the letter to General Arnold. You may also show him this, that he may know the reason why the prisoner is not sent on."

[3] Allen's route was to New Castle Corners—really the North Castle of the Revolution—thence over Crow Hill to Pine's Bridge. Thence by the same road André had travelled in the morning—past Strang's tavern and Miller's house to the present Locust Avenue, thence to Cortlandville, near the Hollman house, and towards Continental Village.

[4] The *Allen Genealogy*, which is somewhat diffuse on this point, and in other particulars is at variance with general history, says the escort were almost mutinous at the recall, and that André encouraged them, so that it required all Allen's authority to compel them to return.

[5] Why did Allen return to Sands' Mills, instead of going to Lower (now South) Salem, as ordered? This has never been explained. [6] Authorities differ, page 38.

Benjamin Tallmadge was born in Setauket, Long Island, February 25, 1754, and died in Litchfield, Connecticut, March 7, 1835.
He was a Yale graduate, and a classmate of the unfortunate Nathan Hale. Joining the patriot army in 1775, he served throughout the war, attaining the rank of Colonel, and enjoying the especial favor of Washington. He is supposed to have been the Chief's only confidant in some of the important details of his employment of spies. After the war he was a merchant in Litchfield, and from 1801 to 1817 was a member of Congress. In this capacity he was vehemently opposed to the increasing of the André captors' pensions, claiming that they were not actuated by any motives of patriotism. Although really a native of the state of New York, his identification with Sheldon's, a Connecticut regiment, and his long residence at Litchfield, have usually caused him to be regarded as a native of Connecticut.
Among his many important services during the Revolution, none was attended with greater results than his securing the recall of André when almost in reach of Arnold.

André was once more put in the barn's "annex," and met Tallmadge for the first time. From his military walk and manner, the latter felt sure he was a soldier, and prevailed on Jameson to order him sent to Sheldon's[1] headquarters at South Salem. Accordingly, an escort of twenty dragoons, under Tallmadge, was told

---

[6] Authorities differ, some putting it as early Monday morning, but Tallmadge says Sunday. He should be good authority. Allen returning, did not reach Arnold until early Tuesday, the twenty-fifth. Tallmadge, writing to Sparks in 1834, ascribes this to the distance travelled—back to South Salem and thence to the Robinson House.

[1] The fact that Arnold had notified both Tallmadge and Sheldon, September 13th, that if a man named Anderson should come within the lines he was to be sent to headquarters, now naturally tended to strengthen Tallmadge's suspicions of the Department Commander.

Arnold wrote:

Robinson House,
7 September.

Since I saw you, I have had an opportunity of transmitting a letter to the person in New York of whom I made mention, and am in expectation of procuring a meeting at your quarters. If I can bring this matter about, as I hope, I shall open a channel of intelligence that will be regular and to be depended upon.

André had also written to Sheldon proposing a meeting at Dobbs' Ferry:

New York, the 7th Sept.

Sir,—I am told that my name is made known to you, and that I may hope your indulgence in permitting me to meet a friend near your outposts. I will endeavor to obtain permission to go out with a flag, which will be sent to Dobbs' Ferry on Monday next, the 11th instant, when I shall be happy to meet Mr. G. Should I not be allowed to go, the officer who is to command the escort—between whom and myself no distinction need be made—can speak in the affair. Let me entreat you, Sir, to favor a matter so interesting to the parties concerned, and which is of so private a nature that the public on neither side can be injured by it. I shall be happy on my part in doing any act of kindness to you in a family or property concern of a familiar nature. I trust I shall not be detained, but should any old grudge be a cause for it, I shall rather risk that than neglect the business in question or assume a mysterious character to carry on an innocent affair, and, as friends have advised, get to your lines by stealth.

I am, Sir, with all regard, your most obedient humble servant,
JOHN ANDERSON.

The meeting he thus proposed was that which Arnold failed to attend, as previously noticed (see Chap. I.). It was this letter which Lossing observes puzzled Sheldon, and which he referred to Arnold on the 9th. It was found among Arnold's papers. In Arnold's private memorandum book, was afterwards found by Varick, his aid, entries showing that he had written to "Anderson," June 7, July 13 and 17, August — and 30 (the Heron letter, which André never received), Sept. 3, 15 and 18 (a duplicate).

Sheldon replied to Arnold:

Lower Salem, 9 September.

Dear Sir,—Enclosed I send you a letter which I received last evening from New York, signed John Anderson. If this is the person you mentioned in your favor of yesterday, he must have had his information by your letter, as I never heard his name mentioned before I received this letter. I hope you will not fail meeting him at Dobbs' Ferry; if you cannot meet him yourself, pray send some person that you can confide in. I am so much out of health that I shall not be able to ride that distance in one day.

Arnold replied:

10th September.

I received last night your favor of yesterday. You judge right. I wrote Mr. Anderson on the 3rd inst. requesting him to meet me at your quarters, and informed him I had hinted the matter to you, and that you would send any letter to me, or inform me of his arrival. I did not mention his name in my letter to you, as I thought it unnecessary. I was obliged to write with great caution to him, my letter was signed *Gustavus* to prevent any discovery in case it fell into the hands of the enemy.

From the tenor of Mr. Anderson's letter (in particular that part where he says, "The officer who commands," etc., I am led to conjecture my letter *has* been intercepted. There are several things in the letter which appear mysterious. As you are unwell and I want to go to Verplanck's Point to give directions in some matters there, I am determined to go as far as Dobbs' Ferry and meet the flag. If Mr. Anderson should not be permitted to come out with the flag, and should find means to come to your quarters, I wish you to send an express to let me know; and send two or three horsemen to conduct him in the way to meet me, as it is difficult for me to ride so far.

(On account of his wounded leg.)

If your health will permit, I wish you to come with him. I am convinced of his inclination to serve the public; and if he has received my letter and in consequence thereof should come to your quarters, I make no doubt to fix on a mode of intelligence that will answer my wishes.

If General Parsons has arrived I wish you to show him my letter, and tell him my request is to have Mr. Anderson escorted to meet me. Please write me, by return of the express, through what channel you received Mr. Anderson's letter, and if your emissary has returned.

off to take him there. For a part of the way they were accompanied by Paulding, Williams and Van Wart,[1] who seem to have been hanging around headquarters. The route was by Coman's Hill, Bedford Village and Cross River, to Lower Salem, arriving at the house of 'Squire John Gilbert at about eight in the morning. The house stood on the west side of the road leading north from Lower Salem, between the present dwellings of Mrs. Abby Hoyt and John I. Bouton. It no longer exists—the illustration being taken from a water-color sketch[2] in the collection of Dr. Thomas Addis Emmet.

The account of André's arrival, given by Lieutenant (afterwards General) Joshua King, of Sheldon's, is so graphic that I insert it in full:

> He looked somewhat like a reduced gentleman. His smallclothes were nankeen, with handsome white-top riding boots—in fact his undress military clothes. His coat [was] purple, with gold lace, worn somewhat threadbare, with a small-brimmed tarnished beaver on his head. He wore his hair in a queue, with long black beard,[3] and his clothes somewhat dirty. In this garb I took charge of him. After breakfast my barber came in to dress[4] me, after which I requested him to go through the same operation, which he did. When the ribbon was taken from his hair, I observed it full of powder; this circumstance, with others that occurred, induced me to believe that I had no ordinary person in charge. He requested permission to take the bed while his shirt and smallclothes might be washed. I told him that was needless, for a shirt was at his service, which he accepted. We were close pent-up in a bedroom, with a vidette at the door and window. There was a spacious yard before the door, which he desired he might be permitted to walk in with me. I accordingly disposed of my guard in such a manner as to prevent an escape. While walking together, he observed he must make a confidant of somebody, and he knew not a more proper person than myself, as I had appeared to befriend a stranger in distress. After settling the point between us, he told me who he was, and gave me a short account of himself from the time he was taken at St. Johns in 1775.

(This looks like an attempt on Arnold's part to discover whether Sheldon had a spy in New York. His endeavor to find out the same thing about Lafayette is historic.)

About August 27 William Heron, a member of the Connecticut Legislature from Redding, and well-known to the officers of the Connecticut Line, requested General Parsons to assist him in procuring a flag of truce for the purpose of going to New York, that he might collect money due him there. Parsons accordingly gave him a note to Arnold, who, instead of granting the flag immediately detained Heron until the 30th, and then brought from his private room a letter which he said was from a friend of his own, that he had examined it, and at the same time pointing out to Heron that it had been sealed with a wafer which he had broken and afterwards sealed with wax, desired him to be careful to deliver it with his own hand if he went to New York.

Heron did go, but Arnold's extraordinary precautions led him to inspect the seal, and, finding the wafer had not been broken as Arnold said, his suspicions were excited, and instead of delivering the letter as promised, he brought it back with him, and on September 10 gave it to Parsons. As it seemed to relate merely to trade, Parsons, preferring to state the facts privately to Washington instead of making a formal communication, rode over to camp (Tappan) for the purpose—but found Washington was just leaving for Hartford. So, as Parsons expresses it, "it was left to the ripening of the horrid event to detect this unsuspecting instrument." (Parsons' letter is printed in Sargent.)

It is an interesting speculation as to how much history would have been changed, had the letter been delivered in New York, or had Parsons succeeded in bringing the matter to Washington's attention. It was the letter signed "Gustavus," and dated August 30.—CHARLES S. HALL, *Hall Ancestry*, N. Y., 1896.

1 Williams.

2 By the late Dr. Andrew Anderson, the father of American wood-engraving. It is probably the only original view existing. The late John Jay bought the house in 1856, hoping that public interest might be sufficiently awakened to preserve it; but his effort failed, and the site is now a cultivated field. It is marked 17 on the map.

3 As no gentleman of that period wore a beard, King probably means a beard of several days' growth. André could not have shaved for four days. 4 Shave.

See plate 35: The Gilbert House, South Salem
See plate 36: Portrait of Joshua King

It was in the room occupied by Dr. Bronson,[1] the "surgeon's mate" or assistant surgeon, of Sheldon's regiment, that the prisoner who so impressed King wrote at three o'clock that Sunday, his celebrated letter to Washington,[2] which Hamilton justly says is "conceived in terms of dignity without insolence, and apology without meanness:"

Salem, September 24th, 1780.

Sir,—What I have as yet said concerning myself was in the justifiable attempt to be extricated. I am too little accustomed to duplicity to have succeeded. I beg your Excellency will be persuaded that no alteration in the temper of my mind, or apprehension for my safety, induces me to take the step of addressing you, but that it is to rescue myself from an imputation of having assumed a mean character for treacherous purposes or self-interest; a conduct incompatible with the principles that actuate me, as well as with my condition in life. It is to vindicate my fame that I speak, and not to solicit security. The person in your possession is Major John André, adjutant general to the British army.

The influence of one commander in the army of his adversary is an advantage taken in war. A correspondence for this purpose I held, as confidential (in the present instance) with his Excellency Sir Henry Clinton. To favor it, I agreed to meet, upon ground not within the posts of either army, a person who was to give me intelligence. I came up in the *Vulture* man-of-war for this effect, and was fetched by a boat from the ship to the beach. Being here, I was told that the approach of day would prevent my return, and that I must be concealed until the next night. I was in my regimentals, and had fairly risked my person.

Against my stipulations, my intention, and without my knowledge beforehand, I was conducted within one of your posts. Your Excellency may conceive my sensation on this occasion, and must imagine how much more must I have been affected by a refusal to re-conduct me back the next night as I had been brought. Thus become a prisoner, I had to concert my escape. I quitted my uniform, and was passed another way in the night, without the American posts, to neutral ground, and informed I was beyond all armed parties, and left to press for New York. I was taken at Tarrytown by some volunteers. Thus, as I have had the honor to relate, was I betrayed (being adjutant general of the British army) into the vile condition of an enemy in disguise within your posts.

Having avowed myself a British officer, I have nothing to reveal but what relates to myself, which is true on the honor of an officer and a gentleman. The request I have

---

[1] **Isaac Bronson** was born in Breakneck (now Middlebury), Conn., March 10, 1760. He studied medicine, and in November, 1779, was appointed Junior Surgeon of Sheldon's regiment, where he saw much hard service under many difficulties. A single instance gives an idea of the lack of modern conveniences in Washington's army—that at times there was hardly a tent in the regiment. In 1783 he relinquished his profession and went abroad for some years, returning in 1789. From 1792 to 1794 he lived in Philadelphia, but in 1796 went to Bridgeport, Conn., and engaged in banking. He was very successful, and his advice in financial matters was often sought by Hamilton and other distinguished men. He died at Greenfield Hill, Conn., May 19, 1839. André gave him a humorous sketch, showing himself escorted by the four militia, under Lieutenant Allen. I regret not being able to trace it.

[2] This was given to Tallmadge to read, then sealed and sent to Washington by the messenger who had previously been despatched to meet him on his return from Hartford. He had gone almost to Danbury before learning that the Chief had already left Hartford on his way to Fishkill. Returning to Sands' Mills he took André's letter to the Robinson House. He did not arrive there until two on Monday afternoon, when he gave it, as well as Jameson's letter to Washington, with the Arnold papers, to Hamilton. Washington was then at West Point, and hence did not get them until his return at four o'clock. (See Chap. IV.)

See plate 37: Portrait of Isaac Bronson

to make to your Excellency, and I am conscious I address myself well, is, that in any rigor policy may dictate, a decency of conduct may mark that, though unfortunate, I am branded with nothing dishonorable, as no motive could be mine but the service of my king, and as I was involuntarily an impostor. Another request is, that I may be permitted to write an open letter to Sir Henry Clinton, and another to a friend for clothes and linen.

I take the liberty to mention the condition of some gentlemen at Charleston, who, being either on parole or under protection, were engaged in a conspiracy against us. Though their situation is not similar, they are objects who may be set in exchange for me, or are persons whom the treatment I receive might affect. It is no less, Sir, in a confidence of the generosity of your mind, than on account of your superior station, that I have chosen to importune you with this letter.

I have the honour to be, with great respect, Sir,

Your Excellency's most obedient and most humble servant,

JOHN ANDRÉ, *Adjutant General.*

While those at South Salem are waiting to hear from Washington, we may return to Smith and Arnold.

While Jameson's second messenger was riding towards the Robinson House, Smith, all unconscious of the important events of Saturday and Sunday, was dining at Fishkill, in Washington's company. Before the messenger arrived Lieutenant Allen had reached headquarters, at about nine on Monday morning.

On the way from Fishkill — Monday — Washington and his staff stopped to examine some fortifications. The Chief sent Hamilton and Major Samuel Shaw,[1] Third Continental Artillery (or Major James McHenry),[2] to notify Arnold of the cause of delay — the party being expected to breakfast with him.

Washington's servant had already started on the same errand, and so arrived first, just after Allen had delivered Jameson's letter.

Even at the tremendous news of André's arrest, the wonderful self-command Arnold had so often manifested did not forsake him. Though evincing some emotion[3] he did not give way to any great degree, but telling Allen not to say anything about the letter,[4] he returned to the breakfast room,

---

[1] **Samuel Shaw** was born in Boston, October 2, 1754. He joined the patriot army January 1, 1776, and served throughout the Revolution, becoming Captain in the Third Artillery. From 1784 to 1794 he was engaged in mercantile pursuits in Canton, China, where he was U. S. Consul (the first) from 1786 to 1790. In 1794 ill-health obliged him to leave China, and he took passage on a ship bound for Boston, but died on the voyage, May 30, 1794, and was buried at sea, while the vessel was off the Cape of Good Hope.

[2] **James McHenry** was born in Ballymena, Ireland, in November, 1753, and died in Baltimore, May 3, 1816. He came to America in 1771, and began the study of medicine, in Philadelphia, under the celebrated Dr. Rush. In July, 1775, he was appointed an assistant surgeon in the army, then at Cambridge. In 1776 we find him Surgeon of the Fifth Pennsylvania Battalion, Colonel Robert Magaw. Taken prisoner with him at Fort Washington, he was not exchanged until March, 1778. In May he became Washington's secretary, and Surgeon to the Flying Camp Hospital. In August, 1780, he was appointed Aid to Lafayette. From 1796 to 1800 he was Secretary of War.

Thacher and Lafayette agree that he — not Hamilton — went with Shaw, and as he was Lafayette's Aid, this would seem conclusive, unless Lafayette's memory in 1824 had become untrustworthy. He also says McHenry was at breakfast with the others when Allen arrived.—(Letter to Luzerne, *Memoirs*, vol. I., p. 367.)

[3] See Washington's letter, page 52.

[4] Franks' testimony at his court martial.

told the assembled officers[1] the letter required his immediate presence at West Point, but that he would return to meet Washington, ordered a horse[2] to be saddled at once, and went upstairs to bid his wife[3] farewell.[4]   At this moment, Major Franks came up, to tell him of the arrival of Washington's servant. Naturally supposing that the Chief would arrive at any moment, Arnold fled[5] precipitately[6] from the house, by a short cut down the hill, since known as Arnold's Path, to Beverly Dock,[7] where his eight-oared barge was waiting, the boatmen having been hastily summoned. He ordered the cockswain, James Larvey,[8] to push off, telling him that it was necessary he should reach the *Vulture* at once, so that he might return and meet Washington at his quarters. Showing his handkerchief as a flag of truce as the boat passed Verplanck's, he was soon aboard the *Vulture*.[9] Most historians agree that he escaped Washington by about half an hour, though Thacher says the latter did not arrive until noon,[10] while the breakfast party were assembled at ten. On his arrival, Major Franks apologized for Arnold's absence, and Dr. Eustis[11] reported his wife's illness. The Chief breakfasted, and then went to West Point, where of course he did not find Arnold, and where Colonel Lamb was as much surprised to meet him as he was not to be received with the proper salute of cannon. Thus it was not until his return to the Robinson House, at four o'clock, that he met Hamilton and learned

---

[1] Sargent says Major Burnet (see Chap. V.) was one. Thacher says Shaw and McHenry. (If so, where was Hamilton?) Franks, one of Arnold's aids, was present, but not Varick, who was sick upstairs.

[2] One belonging to Varick or Franks.—*Lafayette.*

[3] Sargent says she noticed his agitation, and followed him from the dining room.
    Lafayette (probably quoting McHenry) says he sent a servant to call her upstairs. He left the dining-room by the door seen above the screen on the right (the doors either side of the mantelpiece are of cupboards).

[4] At the abrupt announcement of the news that he must fly for his life, and they might never meet again, she fainted.

[5] Franks, astonished as he was at his abrupt departure, had to think of Mrs. Arnold, who came out of her swoon only to fall into strong convulsions.
    Dr. Eustis, surgeon of Knox's artillery, and who was hospital physician of the post, was hastily summoned to attend her.

[6] The (supposed) approach of his Excellency left him hardly an instant to take measures for his own safety, or it is likely he would have attempted (to secure) that of André, and the matter might have remained in obscurity.—*Hamilton.*
    That trivial arrival of the servant upset once more any last chance for André's safety. Even a half-hour might have been priceless to him at that juncture. A delay to that extent would not have endangered Arnold's safety, for no one suspected him except Tallmadge, who was miles away. Allen could have been immediately sent back with orders which would have sent André down to Dobbs' Ferry, or insured his safety in some other manner.

[7] This was a small affair, only 10 x 20 feet. It long ago disappeared.

[8] He was a soldier in the Fifth Massachusetts, Colonel Rufus Putnam.

[9] Dr. Eustis, in a letter printed in the *Collections* of the Mass. Historical Society, Vol. XIV, p. 52, says he retained his barge, the rowers returning in one furnished by the *Vulture's* captain.
    He also says that on Arnold's trying to persuade the men to enter the British service, two did so, who had been British deserters.
    This, I think, must be a mistake, as the British invariably hung all of their deserters whenever they fell into their hands.

[10] The Allen *Genealogy* says Lieutenant Allen dined at the house, and returned to Jameson early next morning. No mention of this is found in any other record. He was not a witness at either André's trial or Smith's.
    As to the hour of Washington's arrival, see his own letter, page 51. "Some hours" would bring it to at least noon.   [11] William Eustis was, page 43.

See plate 38: Portrait of Col. John Lamb
See plate 39: The Robinson House

the astounding news of the conspiracy. Its effect was stunning, and he despondently asked Knox and Lafayette: "Whom can we trust now?" By this time Arnold had been some time safe aboard the *Vulture*, and the hurried ride of Hamilton and Shaw (or McHenry) to Verplanck's, sixteen miles, was fruitless, except for their presence when a flag of truce arrived from her, bringing a letter[1] from Arnold to Washington, which enclosed one for Mrs. Arnold.[2] Amid the universal consternation and mutual distrust caused by these extraordinary events, Washington, his first ebullition of despair over, remained calm, and acted promptly and vigorously. As he had reason to suppose the British fleet might at any moment be sighted in the distance, on its way to capture West Point in pursuance of the plot, his first thought was for the security of the post. Colonel Lamb, who had crossed with him from the Point, and whom he promptly detached from its command by this letter —

> Sir,—It is my wish to see Colonel James Livingston[3] to-night, and I write him by you on the occasion. In his absence you will take command of the posts at Stoney and Verplanck's Points till further orders.
>
> I am, Sir, (etc., etc.,)
>
> Head Quarters, Robinson's House   G. WASHINGTON.
> in the Highlands, September 25, 1780,
> —— o'clock p. m.
> To Col. John Lamb of the Artillery.

---

[1] **William Eustis** was born in Cambridge, Mass., June 10, 1753, and died in Boston, February 6, 1825. He was graduated at Harvard, studied medicine and became associated with Dr. Joseph Warren. He attended the wounded after Bunker Hill, was appointed as an army surgeon, and was stationed at the Robinson House two or more years. From 1788 to 1794 he was a member of the Massachusetts Legislature, from 1801 to 1805, a member of Congress. In 1807 to 1813 he was Secretary of War, from 1814 to 1818 Minister to Holland; 1820 to 1823 he was again in Congress, and in 1823 elected Governor of his native state, dying in office. Several of his family have been distinguished as soldiers. The late Senator James B. Eustis, of Louisiana, who was in the Confederate army, and afterwards Ambassador to France, was his grand-nephew, as were also Brigadier General Abraham Eustis, Colonel of the First U. S. Artillery, Captain William Eustis, of the Third Infantry and First Dragoons, and Brigadier General Henry L. Eustis, Colonel Tenth Massachusetts Volunteers.

On board the Vulture,
Sept. 25, 1780.

Sir,—The heart which is conscious of its own rectitude cannot attempt to palliate a step which the world may censure as wrong. I have ever acted from a principle of love to my country, since the commencement of the present unhappy contest between Great Britain and the Colonies; the same principle of love to my country actuates my present conduct, however it may appear inconsistent to the world, who very seldom judge right of any man's actions. I have no favour to ask for myself. I have too often experienced the ingratitude of my country to attempt it; but from the known humanity of your Excellence, I am induced to ask your protection for Mrs. Arnold, from every insult and injury that the mistaken vengeance of my country may expose her. It ought to fall only on me; she is as good and as innocent as an angel, and is incapable of doing wrong. I beg she may be permitted to return to her friends in Philadelphia, or to come to me, as she may choose; from your Excellency I have no fears on her account, but she may suffer from the mistaken fury of the country. I have to request that the enclosed letter may be delivered to Mrs. Arnold, and she be permitted to write to me. I have also to ask that my cloaths and baggage, which are of little consequence, may be sent to me; if required, their value shall be paid in money.

I have the honour to be with great regard and esteem,
Your Excellency's most obedient and humble servant,

His Excellency   B. ARNOLD.
     General Washington.

P. S. In justice to the gentlemen of my family, Colonel Varick and Major Franks, I think myself in honor bound to declare that they, as well as Joshua Smith, Esq. (whom I know is suspected), are totally ignorant of any transactions of mine, that they have reason to believe were injurious to the public.
[2] There is in the possession, [3] When Washington had, page 44.

may have proposed the capture of Arnold by means of a boat attack on the *Vulture*. At any rate, such an inference is warranted from the letter he wrote to Colonel Nathaniel Wade,[1] commanding one of the Massachusetts militia regiments at the Point, and his successor in the command of the post. This has never before been published, and was evidently written very soon after the return of Washington to Arnold's quarters:

> Robinson's House,
> 25th Sept'r, 1780.
>
> Dear Sir,—Immediately on Receipt of this, send Ten Boats properly Manned, to Nelson's Point, where they are to remain till further Orders. You will pay particular attention to this matter, as it is indispensably necessary.
>
> I am, dear Sir, your obedient servt,
>
> JOHN LAMB,
> Colo. Commandant.

The *Vulture's* sailing down the river prevented any attack on her, and Lamb's letter was soon followed by a letter from the Chief himself to Wade:[2]

> Sir,—General Arnold is gone to the Enemy. I have just received a line from him, inclosing one to Mrs. Arnold, dated on board the *Vulture*. From this circumstance, and Colo. Lamb's being detached on some business, the command of the garrison for the present devolves upon you. I request you will be as vigilant as possible, and as the Enemy may have it in contemplation to attempt some enterprise, even to-night, against these Posts, I wish you to make, immediately after receipt of this, the best disposition you can of your force, so as to have a proportion of men in each work on the west side of the River. You will see or hear from me further to-morrow.
>
> I am, Sir,
> Your most obt. servt.,
>
> G. WASHINGTON.[3]

---

[2] There is in the possession of a gentleman in New York an interesting letter of Varick's to his sister Jane. It is dated soon after these events, and gives a graphic description of Mrs. Arnold's pitiable condition.

As to her possible complicity with her husband, I own to disbelieving it. Burr is the only authority for crediting it, and if it were a fact, would Arnold have left her alone—or would he have allowed her to be at the Robinson House at all, instead of remaining in Philadelphia?

[3] When Washington had finished giving Livingston the orders which he had sent for him to receive in person, he added: "It is a source of gratification to me that the post was in the hands of an officer so devoted as yourself to the cause of your country."—*Lossing.*

[1] **Nathaniel Wade** was a native of Ipswich, Mass., where he was born February 27, 1749, and where he died October 26, 1826. He was a captain of the Ipswich minute-men at Bunker Hill, and saw service, as a captain in the Twelfth Massachusetts, Colonel Little, at the siege of Boston, the battles of Long Island, Harlem Heights, White Plains and Trenton. In February, 1778, he became colonel of a militia regiment, raised in Essex and Suffolk counties, and served as such throughout the war. A singular fact in connection with his West Point experience is his statement of a conversation with one of Arnold's aids—apparently Franks—shortly before the 23rd. He was returning to the boat, after dining with Arnold. The Major, accompanying him, said impressively: "There is something going on here that I do not understand and cannot find out. I say this to put you on your guard at the Fort" (West Point) "I fear there is something brewing about us, and all I can say is, look out!" With this, he abruptly left Wade. Yet if this was really Franks, the treason was something very different from what he had anticipated, for it almost upset his reason when the revelation really came.   [2] On Lafayette's visit.   [3] This letter, page 45.

The Stearns' orderly-book, from which I have before quoted, contains an interesting statement of the composition of the garrison and the orders issued on the occasion:

Sept. 25, 8 p. m. After-orders: One captain, one subaltern, three sergeants and fifty rank and file to be turned out immediately with arms and blankets. The captain will wait on Colonel Wade for orders.

2 A. M., Sept. 26.

The following disposition of the troops to take place immediately, and officers commanding regiments and corps will be careful to have their men completed with arms and ammunition, and everything in the most perfect order for immediate action. Officers commanding regiments will take, with their own regiments, those regiments that are divided by the field officers of the same, agreeably to seniority.

Positions:

Colonel Ward's (Wade's?) regiment at Fort Arnold.[1]

Colonel Bartlet's at Fort Putnam.

Colonel Murray to send one hundred men to Fort Willis (Wyllys) and the regiment to Fort Webb.

Colonel Rand's regiment to be divided equally between Redoubts Nos. 1 and 2.

Colonel Thayer's at Nos. 3 and 4.

All the draughted artificers to join their respective regiments immediately. Major Bauman will have everything in his department in order for immediate action.

The next day Washington wrote:

Sir,—Under the present situation of affairs, I think it necessary that the respective works at West Point and its dependencies be supplied with provisions and water. You will therefore be pleased to have a proper quantity distributed to each of them, without any loss of time.

I am Sir,

Your most obedt. servt.,

G. WASHINGTON.

Head Quarters,

26 Sept. 1780. Colonel Wade.

---

[2] On Lafayette's visit to the United States in 1824, he met Colonel Wade, and recalling their Revolutionary experiences, he said: "When General Washington first heard of the defection of Arnold, he asked 'Who has the immediate command?' (Of West Point.) "Learning it was you, he said, 'He is a true man; I am satisfied.'"

[3] This letter is quoted by Sparks (*Writings of Washington*, vii., pp. 212-213) but has never before appeared in *facsimile*. For permission to use it, and the Lamb letter opposite, I am indebted to Mr. F. H. Wade, through Mr. Stuart C. Wade, of New York.

[1] All these were three months' militia, raised by drafts from various State regiments, and formed into provisional organizations. The commanders and organizations appear thus in the Massachusetts and New Hampshire records:

New Hampshire:
Col. Thomas Bartlet (at West Point).
Col. Moses Nichols (on the east bank of the Hudson).
Massachusetts:
Col. Seth Murray (the Hampshire County regiment to which Lieutenant Solomon Allen belonged).
Col. John Rand—a regiment of Worcester county.
Col. Ebenezer Thayer—a Suffolk county regiment.
Nichols' regiment had 420 men,
Bartlet's 525
———
945

See plates 40-42: Letters of Col. Lamb and George Washington to Col. Wade

To this Wade replied that pickled fish was about all the available provision, but that the water supply was abundant — a realistic picture of the poverty of the Revolutionary commissariat, even at a permanent post like West Point.

As reinforcements for West Point were likely to be needed if the British moved up the Hudson, Greene, commanding the left wing of the army, at Tappan, was ordered to march to West Point. At three in the morning of Tuesday, the twenty-sixth, the order reached Tappan, and the drums beat the alarm throughout the camp. An officer afterwards described the scene as very impressive — the non-commissioned officers hurrying through the company streets and turning out the men, lights flitting here and there through the camp, and a general sense of vague alarm and apprehension pervading. Two Pennsylvania brigades and the Sixth Connecticut, Colonel Meigs, marched at once, and the rest of the army was held ready to follow. The news of Arnold's defection created intense excitement, and Greene issued an address to the army:

> Treason of the blackest dye was yesterday discovered. General Arnold, who commanded at West Point, lost to every sense of honor, of private and public obligation, was about to deliver up that important post into the hands of the enemy. Such an event must have given the American cause a dangerous, if not a fatal wound ; but the treason has been timely discovered, to prevent the fatal misfortune. The providential train of circumstances which led to it, affords the most convincing proof that the liberties of America are the object of Divine protection. At the same time that the treason is to be regretted, the general cannot help congratulating the army on the happy discovery. Our enemies, despairing of carrying their point by force, are practising every base art, to effect by bribery and corruption what they cannot accomplish in a manly way. Great honor is due to the American army that this is the first instance of treason of the kind, where many were to have been expected from the nature of the dispute. The brightest ornament in the character of the American soldiers is their having been proof against all the arts and seductions of an insidious enemy. Arnold has made his escape to the enemy, but Major André, the Adjutant General in the British Army, who came out as a spy, is our prisoner.
>
> His Excellency the Commander in Chief has arrived at West Point from Hartford, and is no doubt taking proper measures to unravel fully so hellish a plott.

By Greene's order, the address was read by the adjutants to their respective regiments.[1]

Arnold's letter from the *Vulture* was soon followed by one from Robinson,[2] and was followed in its turn by one from Clinton himself.[3] To Robinson,

---

[1] The civil authorities also took cognizance of the fortunate escape. Governor Clinton issued a proclamation, setting apart November second as a day of thanksgiving, and the occasion was universally observed.

[2]
Vulture, off Sinsink, September 25, 1780.

Sir,—I am this moment informed that Major André, Adjutant General of his Majesty's army in America, is detained as a prisoner by the army under your command. It is therefore incumbent on me to inform you of the manner of his falling into your hands. He went up with a flag at the request of General Arnold, on public business with him, and had his permit to return by land to New York. Under these circumstances Major André cannot be detained by you without the greatest violation of flags, and contrary to the custom and usage of all nations ; and as I imagine you will see this matter in the same point of view that I do, I must desire you will order him to be set at liberty and allowed to return immediately. Every step Major André took was by the advice and direction of General Arnold, even that of taking a feigned name, and of course not liable to censure for it. I am, Sir, not forgetting our former acquaintance,

Your very humble servant,

BEV. ROBINSON, Col. Loyal Americans.

His Excellency General Washington.   [3] Letter of H. Clinton, page 47.

Washington vouchsafed no answer, but the reply to Clinton was written on the thirtieth. It will be found on page 63. The enclosure of which Clinton speaks was a letter from Arnold[1]—a good specimen of effrontery and special pleading.

While the Tappan camp was thus rudely awakened, Smith, who but a day before had been received in Washington's company, was now to meet him under very different circumstances. On Monday at midnight, Colonel Jean Baptiste Gouvion, Rochambeau's chief of artillery, came with a platoon of soldiers to Colonel Hay's house at Fishkill, where Smith was asleep with his wife. Surrounding the house with his men, he burst open the bedroom door, arrested Smith, and, refusing to allow his servant to procure his horse for him, marched him on foot eighteen miles to the Robinson House.[2] Here the weary and angry man was confronted with one who could also be terribly angry on the rare occasions when he did give way to indignation. The news of discovery was thundered in his ears, and he was threatened with hanging from the same tree with André,[3] as soon as the latter should have arrived under guard.[4]

To return to South Salem, while Greene's men are hastening to West Point, and Smith is at headquarters: About midnight of Monday, a messenger arrived from Washington, with this order to Jameson:

---

[3]
New York, Sept. 26, 1780.

Sir,—Being informed that the King's Adjutant General in America has been stopt under Major General Arnold's passports, and is detained a prisoner in your Excellency's army, I have the honor to inform you, Sir, that I permitted Major André to go to Major General Arnold at the particular request of that general officer. You will perceive, Sir, by the enclosed paper, that a flag of truce was sent to receive Major André, and passports granted for his return. I therefore can have no doubt but your Excellency will immediately direct that this officer has permission to return to my orders at New York.

I have the honor to be Your Excellency's most obedient and most humble servant,
H. CLINTON.

His Excellency
General Washington.

[1]
New York,
September 26, 1780.

Sir,—In answer to your Excellency's message respecting your Adjutant General, Major André, and desiring my idea of the reasons why he is detained, being under my passports, I have the honor to inform you, Sir, that I apprehend a few hours must return Major André to your Excellency's orders, as that officer is assuredly under the protection of a flag of truce sent by me to him, for the purpose of a conversation which I requested to hold with him relating to myself, and which I wished to communicate through that officer to your Excellency.

I commanded at the time at West Point, had an undoubted right to send my flag of truce for Major André, who came to me under that protection, and having held my conversation with him, I delivered to him confidential papers in my own handwriting, to deliver to your Excellency; thinking it much properer he should return by land, I directed him to make use of the feigned name of John Anderson, under which he had by my direction come on shore, and gave him passports to go to the White Plains on his way to New York. This officer cannot therefore fail of being immediately sent to New York, as he was invited to a conversation with me, for which I sent him a flag of truce, and finally gave him passports for his safe return to your Excellency; all of which I had a right to do, being in the actual service of America, under the orders of General Washington, and commanding general at West Point and its dependencies.

I have the honour to be Your Excellency's most obedient and very humble servant,
B. ARNOLD.

His Excellency
Sir Henry Clinton.

[2] Smith's *Narrative.* He says Colonel Hay accompanied him—probably not on foot.

[3] Smith.

[4] Smith's own account—but I see no great reason for doubting its accuracy. Washington, or any one else, under similar circumstances could not be expected to mince matters.

Headquarters,
Robinson House, 7 p. m.,
25th September, 1780.

Sir,—I wish every precaution and attention to be paid to prevent Major André from making his escape. He will without doubt make it if possible ; and in order that he may not have it in his power, you will send him under care of such a party and so many officers as to protect him from the least opportunity of doing it.

That he may be less liable to be recaptured by the enemy, who will no doubt make every effort to regain him, he had better be conducted to this place by some upper road, rather than by the route of Crompond. I would not wish André to be treated with insult ; but he does not appear to stand upon the footing of a common prisoner of war ; and therefore he is not entitled to the usual indulgence which they receive, and is to be most closely and narrowly watched. * * * * * *

The escort, consisting of one hundred dragoons,[1] under four officers, was soon ready, and started in a pouring rain.[2] The officers were Tallmadge, Captains Hoogland[3] and Rogers and Lieutenant King. From South Salem the route was north and west over Long Pond Mountain, west of Lake Waccabuc to the church at North Salem. Just before this was reached the squadron was met by a courier from Washington, bearing an order for a change of route for fear of the enemy[4] on the present one. The new way led them past the premises occupied in 1889 by Isaac H. Purdy, thence to Croton Falls and by the "old road" to Lake Mahopac[5] and the Red Mills[6]—now Mahopac Falls—in Putnam County.

At the mill a short halt was made, and the prisoner was taken into the house of Major James Cox, of the Ordnance Department of the army. In later

---

[1] Smith.

[2] Gaine's weather prediction—see page 6—was fulfilled that night. As there was no moon the night must have been of inky blackness, and the journey intensely depressing.

[3] **Jeronimus (Jerome) Hoogland,** of Flushing, New York, was born in 1757. He was Lieutenant and Adjutant of Colonel John Lasher's First New York Minute Men, or Volunteer Infantry, in 1776, was promoted to Captain in it, captured at the battle of Long Island and imprisoned in one of the prison ships. He appears as Adjutant of Sheldon's in 1777, was a Captain in 1779, and served as such through the war, dying in Lansingburgh, N. Y., 179—.
"The history of poor Hoogland, his self-sacrificing, devoted patriotism and ill-requited services, had many a parallel in the lives of the officers of the Revolution. When I first knew him, in 1774, he was a handsome, high-spirited, facetious youth of eighteen. Three years after, I met him, a sun-burnt veteran, who had already seen much hard service. In 1788, fourteen years after, I again saw him, in Lansingburgh. He was then, although young in years, old in suffering. He appeared like an old man, hobbling on crutches. Thus he lingered a few years longer, and sunk into a premature grave, a martyr in the cause of Liberty. Posterity can never estimate the sacrifices and sufferings of the patriots of the Revolution."— *Men and Times of the Revolution* (Memoirs of Elkanah Watson), by Winslow C. Watson, N. Y., 1856.
His companion was probably Jedediah Rogers, of Norwalk. He was Lieutenant in 1778, but no record of his promotion is discoverable.

[4] This was probably the same band of Cowboys against whom Boyd had warned Smith, who had driven off the Underhill cows at Yorktown, and killed Pelham in Pound Ridge, and of whom Jameson had been apprehensive. They had apparently been four days at least—Friday to Monday night—within the Neutral Ground.

[5] Dykman.

[6] So called from the color of the building. The land on which the mill stood was taken by the City of New York a few years ago and the mill was torn down. The illustration has never before been engraved.

See plate 43: The Red Mills, Mahopac Falls

years it was known as the Odell or Johnson house. It met the fate of most old frame buildings, in being destroyed by fire, in 1896. While André was inside, two sentries were posted at each door and window.[1] Phoebe, the infant daughter of the Major, was asleep in her cradle, but awoke on André's entrance. He looked at the baby and said, "Happy childhood—we know its pleasures but once. I wish I were as innocent as you."[2] He also surveyed himself in a mirror, and noticing a hole or rip, under one arm of his coat, smiled and said : "I presume General Washington will give me a new coat." Like the house, the Mills are now but a memory. I am fortunately able to give a view of them,[3] showing the building essentially as in 1780.

THE CAPTORS' MEDAL.

Resuming its march after a short halt, the squadron passed through Shrub Oak Plains, over Gray's Hill to St. Peter's Church—not far from the place whence Allen had been recalled by Jameson's order, the preceding Saturday. The church is still standing, and in good condition, though seldom used. It is a frame building, plain to ugliness, with nothing in its exterior to indicate its character. (Beverly Robinson was one of its wardens in 1780.) Built in 1767, it is one of the oldest in the State. Near it, in front, is the marble monument to Paulding.[4] At the foot of the hill the road forks, one branch south to Peekskill, the other northwest over Gallows Hill, past Continental Village, to the present village of Garrison's.

[1] The statement that he spent the night here is clearly absurd—on a par with the story that on the way from Sands' Mills to South Salem Tallmadge tied him to a tree, at night, to prevent his escape! Such are some instances of the chaff the historian has to sift out to get the real facts.

[2] *History of Putnam County*, by Wm. J. Blake, 1849. As this book also prints a spurious "Defence," attributed to André, this item may be taken with reservation, as also that about the coat.

[3] I am indebted for this to Mr. Charles L. Austin, of Mahopac Falls.

[4] The inscriptions are :

    North side.—Here repose the mortal remains of JOHN PAULDING, who died on the 18th day of February, 1818, in the 60th year of his age.

    South.—The Corporation of the City of New York erected this tomb as a memorial sacred to public gratitude.

    West.—On the morning of the 23d of September, 1780, accompanied by two young farmers of the County of Westchester (whose names will one day be recorded on their own deserved monuments), he intercepted the British spy, André.

    Poor himself, he disdained to acquire wealth by the sacrifice of his country. Rejecting the temptation of great rewards, he conveyed his prisoner to the American camp; and by this act of noble self-denial the treason of Arnold was detected; the designs of the Enemy baffled, West Point and the American Army saved; and these United States, now by the grace of God Free and Independent, rescued from most imminent peril.

    On the East side is a representation of the medal presented by Congress to each of the three captors.

Van Wart's monument in the cemetery of the old Presbyterian church, at Elmsford, in the town of Greenburgh, is similar. In 1876 a monument was erected to Williams at Old Fort, Schoharie County.

See plate 44: The Odell-Johnson House, Mahopac Falls
See plate 45: St. Peter's Church, North Peekskill

In the triangle thus formed stands the dwelling known as the Hollman house (the name of its 1780 occupant being unknown). It is shaded by huge trees, seemingly old enough to have witnessed the scenes we are considering.

The squadron here made a second halt, and André entered the right-hand room, according to tradition. The house is said to date from 1750, that is, the right-hand part, which, as shown, is clearly the original building. Just across the road is the brick dwelling known as the Van Cortland mansion house, built in 1773, and which Washington occupied for a brief period in 1777. Here occurred the incident of Smith and Webb's valise.[1] The halt was probably brief, and the squadron went on again by the road over Gallows Hill, where Putnam hanged Edmund Palmer, the spy, in 1777, to Continental Village, over another hill to the old Gay place, down Iron Rock Hill to the gate near the old Nelson place[2] (then known as Mandeville's), turned into and down Beverly Lane to the Robinson House,[3] arriving just at dawn of Tuesday, the twenty-sixth.

[1] See page 14.

John Webb, younger brother of Samuel B. Webb, was born at Wethersfield, Conn., February 18, 1759, and died April 18, 1828.

He was Lieutenant in the Second Dragoons — Sheldon's — in January, 1777, and Captain a year later. He was present at the battle of Springfield, N. J. (1780), as Aid to General Greene. In 1781 he was Aid and Secretary to General Robert Howe. He served throughout the Revolution, and was one of the original members of the Cincinnati. After the war he removed to Georgia, where he engaged in business in Camden County, where he became Colonel of the militia. Returning to Connecticut he spent the remainder of his life there. In a letter to one of his sons, he says: "I got the rheumatism for my seven years' service in the Revolutionary War, and that is all I got!"

For the portrait, and these particulars of his life, I am indebted to his great-grandson, Henry Randall Webb, Esq., of Washington.

[2] Garrison's was then called Nelson's Point. I quote Judge Dykman's words.

[3] This interesting building was burnt in 1892, and many valuable relics with it. For my two illustrations I am indebted to Mr. H. A. Wright, of Springfield, Mass. They are taken from probably the last photographs made of it.

See plate 46: The Hollman House, North Peekskill
See plate 47: Portrait of John Webb

CHAPTER IV

The Robinson House to Tappan—Suspense.

Uncertainty!
Fell demon of our fears! The human soul,
That can support despair, supports not thee.—MALLET.—*Mustapha*.

OFFICER'S BUTTON,
54TH BRITISH REGIMENT.

THE historic dwelling in which Arnold had had his head-quarters since August, when he assumed command of the West Point district, was built about 1750, and was one of the landmarks of the region. It stood on the east bank of the Hudson, one-quarter of a mile from the water's edge, and two miles below and southeast of West Point itself. Its builder and occupant until 1776 was Beverly Robinson, a man of note and wealth, and Washington's personal friend until the Revolution separated them. He removed to New York and raised a regiment, known as the "Loyal Americans," for the British cause. The confiscation of his property followed, and was the prime cause of the correspondence with Arnold which has been noted. By a singular and sinister coincidence his regiment formed part of Arnold's force, almost exactly a year later, when the traitor captured Fort Griswold, butchered many of its garrison, and burnt New London. Robinson left for England with the British at the end of the war, and never returned.[1]

After his long night ride of thirty miles, added to the fatiguing experiences of the two preceding days, André must have been thoroughly wearied, besides being probably wet from the heavy rain. Though Smith was also in the house, they did not meet. There is some variance between the different accounts as to the events of Tuesday, but most agree that—at least until evening—the day passed quietly for both the prisoners. It was doubtless a welcome rest for each of them. That day Washington notified Congress of the events of the preceding four days, in this characteristic despatch :

Robinson's House, in the
Highlands, September 26.

To the President of Congress :

Sir,—I have the honor to inform Congress that I arrived here yesterday at about twelve o'clock on my return from Hartford. Some hours previous to my arrival General Arnold went from his quarters, which were this place, and, as it was supposed, over the

---

[1] It is believed Robinson knew of Arnold's plan even before Clinton did. He had, about the 15th September, written to Arnold, enclosing a letter for Putnam, about his estate, and the traitor sent the letter we have already noticed on page 5 to the *Vulture* openly, under a flag of truce.—*Lossing*.

See plate 48: The Robinson House, Arnold's Headquarters

river to the garrison at West Point, whither I proceeded myself, in order to visit the post. I found General Arnold had not been there during the day, and on my return to his quarters he was still absent. In the meantime a packet had arrived from Lieut. Col. Jameson, announcing the capture of a John Anderson who was endeavoring to go to New York with several interesting and important papers, all in the handwriting of General Arnold. This was also accompanied with a letter from the prisoner, avowing himself to be Major John André, Adjutant to the British army, relating the manner of his capture, and endeavoring to show that he did not come under the description of a *spy*. From these several circumstances, and information that the General seemed to be thrown into some degree of agitation, on receiving a letter a little time before he went from his quarters, I was led to conclude immediately that he had heard of Major André's captivity, and that he would, if possible, escape to the enemy, and accordingly took such measures as appeared the most probable to apprehend him. But he had embarked in a barge and proceeded down the river, under a flag, to the *Vulture* ship of war, which lay at some miles below Stony and Verplank's Points. He wrote me a letter after he got on board. Major André is not arrived yet, but I hope he is secure, and that he will be here to-day.

I have been and am taking precautions which I trust will prove effectual, to prevent the important consequences which this conduct on the part of General Arnold was intended to produce. I do not know the party that took Major André, but it is said that it consisted only of a few militia, who acted in such a manner upon the occasion, as does them the highest honor, and proves them to be men of great virtue. As soon as I know their names, I shall take pleasure in transmitting them to Congress. I have taken such measures with respect to the gentlemen of General Arnold's family,[1] as prudence dictated; but, from everything that has hitherto come to my knowledge, I have the greatest reason to believe they are perfectly innocent. I early secured Joshua H. Smith, the person mentioned in the close of General Arnold's letter, and find him to have had considerable share in this business.

I have the honor to be, etc.,

Though Washington and his staff were occupying the Robinson House, the Chief avoided seeing André.[2] By Wednesday morning, the twenty-seventh, the *Vulture*, with Arnold aboard, had reached New York, and Sir Henry Clinton knew of the complete failure of his plans and the capture of his favorite. The same day, Jameson wrote to Washington a regretful letter,[3] in which it is not hard to recognize the self-reproach of an honorable man who finds he has made an extraordinary error:

Sept. 27.

* * * I am very sorry that I wrote to General Arnold. I did not think of a British ship being up the river, and expected that, if he was the man he has since turned out to be, he would come down to the troops in this quarter, in which case I should have secured him.

In the evening of Tuesday André and Smith met, as they were escorted to a boat which was to take them to West Point. Smith says he himself was under

---

[1] Colonel Varick and Major Franks. Both were put under arrest, and on November 2d tried by court martial. Both were acquitted of complicity with Arnold, or knowledge of his plans.

[2] It is a singular fact, for which Tallmadge is authority, that he never saw him at all, living or dead.

[3] This was taken to Washington by Paulding.

charge of "Captain Sheppard,"[1] of the New Jersey Continentals. Tallmadge refused to allow any communication between the prisoners.

Though all Wednesday was spent at West Point, no authority has heretofore decided the place of André's confinement. I am now able to state positively that it was Fort Putnam.[2] The officer in charge of him was the same whom we shall meet later at Tappan—Captain Ebenezer Smith, Thirteenth Massachusetts—and the statement was made by him to his son, David—himself a patriot soldier the last year of the war—(who lived to the age of ninety-six, dying in 1862) and whose grandson, Dr. H. Lyle Smith, of Hudson, N. Y., is my informant, he having received the details from David.

This explains how André was able, the next day, to minutely describe to Tallmadge, as the boat left West Point (or possibly Beverly Dock), how he had expected to ascend the steep height "at the head of a body of picked troops."—(Tallmadge's Memoirs.)

Smith says he himself was imprisoned in the provost-marshal's hut, and was there visited by the "Rev. Mr. Mason, a Presbyterian clergyman of New York."[3]

That day Washington thus wrote to Greene, at Tappan:

> I have concluded to send to camp to-morrow Major André, of the British army, and Mr. Joshua H. Smith, who has had a great hand in carrying on the business between him and Arnold. They will be under an escort of horse, and I wish you to have separate houses in camp ready for their reception, in which they may be kept perfectly secure ; and also strong, trusty guards, trebly officered, that a part may be constantly in the room with them. They have not been permitted to be together, and must be still kept apart. I would wish the room for Mr. André to be a decent one, and that he may be treated with civility, but that he may be so guarded as to preclude a possibility of his escaping, which he will certainly attempt to effect, if it shall seem practicable in the most distant degree. Smith must also be carefully secured and not treated with asperity.

---

[1] This was First Lieutenant Samuel Shippard, of the First New Jersey (Colonel Dayton). I regret not being able to secure any detailed information about him.

[2] I am indebted to Judge J. O. Dykman for a very interesting letter addressed to him in 1887 by the late William D. Garrison, of the Grand Union Hotel, New York. The writer says: " I well remember the cell (casemate) in Fort Putnam, on the arch of which appeared André's name. It was the northerly cell looking east, and had an inside dark cell. The larger (outside) cell had a fireplace, and a grated opening looking east. On the north side of this cell (on the arch or roof) was, in letters nearly three feet high, done with a burnt stick or charcoal, MAJOR ANDRÉ. The lime had struck through from the mortar, so as to cover the inscription, and it would not have been seen unless attention were drawn to it. This was prior to 1858 or '59, when the cell was demolished to build a battery on North Dock."
(Mr. Garrison was a native of the village of Garrison's, opposite West Point, and entirely familiar with the scenes of West Point itself. Yet, since receipt of the letter, I have had an interview with Colonel P. S. Michie, the veteran Professor of Mathematics at West Point, who says none of the casemates have ever been destroyed. Mr. Garrison may have stated this particular point from hearsay.)

[3] This was Rev. John Mason, page 54.

See plate 49: Ruins of Fort Putnam, West Point

54

Accordingly, on the morning of Thursday, the twenty-eighth, both prisoners were taken by boat to Stony Point — the King's Ferry landing. They were in separate boats, and Major Tallmadge commanded the party.

The sight of the place where he had crossed as a free man, only the previous Friday, must have caused André the most painful reflections, intensified by the conversation while in the boat, which Tallmadge records. On the way down André had pointed out the precise spot where he was to have landed, at the head of a body of picked troops, if all had gone well with the conspiracy.[1] In the ensuing conversation he pressed Tallmadge for an opinion as to his fate. The latter at first avoided a direct reply, but finally referred to the fate of Nathan Hale, who had been his classmate at Yale College. "But you surely do not consider his case and mine alike?" "Yes, precisely similar, and similar will be your fate," prophetically replied Tallmadge — and the solemn warning had its natural effect on the spirits of his companion, though he seems not to have fully believed it, for Tallmadge has left on record: "I never discovered any fear respecting his future destiny before I reached Tappan."

Crossing the road from Grassy Point, near what is now the Stony Point post-office,[2] the dragoon escort,[3] with Smith in the van and André in the rear, passed by Smith's house[4] to the next corner. Thence by the right-hand road, through or near what is now Garnerville, then a southwest course around Long Clove mountain to a point called the Clove, but originally known as Kakiat, and now as Hempstead,[5] at the house (or tavern) of John Coe.[6] It stands opposite

---

[3] This was **Rev. John Mason, D. D.,** the first pastor of the Presbyterian church in Cedar Street, New York, afterward known as the Scotch Church, and now situated far uptown.
He was born in Scotland in 1734, and died in New York in 1792, but the New Jersey records show that he was appointed to the army from that State. He was a trustee of Princeton College, and many years chaplain of the St. Andrew's Society of New York.
He was appointed chaplain to the Third (Gansevoort's) New York Continentals, November 21, 1776, and later was made chaplain to the posts along the Hudson. West Point seems to have been his residence in 1780. He was adverse to having his portrait taken, and the only one known to exist, from which that on page 53 is made, was made by Kosciuszko while the Doctor was at a public dinner. (It will be seen he holds a glass in one hand.) It has never before been published, and I am indebted to Mr. John Mason Knox, of New York, for its use.
Smith speaks of the Doctor as "that truly good old man," and adds that he himself was visited that day by many inquisitive people, and that Major Tallmadge displayed uncommon kindness in his treatment of him.

[1] Some historians have queried as to what André did during the time he was at Smith's — between breakfast and dinner, or dinner and the time of his leaving — and have believed the absurd story that Arnold took him to West Point; but the whole business may be dismissed by remembering that he could not possibly have had time to go there, and return to Smith's, by sunset. The other inherent impossibilities need not detain us.

[2] Dykman.

[3] A large escort had been sent from Tappan.

[4] One authority says Tallmadge allowed Smith to stop there for a while. It may here be noted, as a singular instance of the way in which families were divided by the Revolution, that Tallmadge and Smith were second cousins — the Major being grandson of Rev. John Smith, Joshua Hett's uncle, whose daughter Susanna married Rev. Benjamin Tallmadge, of Brookhaven, Long Island.

[5] The station on the New Jersey and New York railroad is Summit Park, about three-fourths of a mile west.

[6] **John Coe** was a lieutenant in the Haverstraw militia. He was a member of the New York Provincial Congress in 1775, and Judge of Orange County 1775-78, and a member of the New York Assembly from 1778 to 1780. In 1776-77 he was Deputy Chairman of the Orange County Committee of Safety.

the " English " (Presbyterian)[1] church, about ten miles west of the Hudson. Here a halt was made for dinner, guards and pickets being posted around meanwhile.

The house—now very shabby—stands close to the highway, unfenced. There are but few houses near—I do not recall any in sight—and in 1780 the place must have been very lonely, although, as two roads cross, it was doubtless a fit site for a house of public entertainment.[2] Never since that time has it received a visitor of equal historic importance with him who was the centre of attraction that September Thursday. As shown in our view, it is probably larger than in 1780, and is somewhat modernized, but the dining-room is probably very little changed, barring the substitution of carpet for bare floor and wall-paper for paint. The room, which is on the left of the entrance, is not large, and must have been well filled by the diners—probably seven or eight, besides Major Tallmadge. It is remarkable that of this occasion, the only one during his whole experience (up to this time) when the prisoner could have been in the company of so many American officers, no recollection or reminiscence has been handed down from any of them. In fact, with the exception of Tallmadge's, no names of any of them have been preserved. Dinner being over, André for the first time referred to the undignified appearance he felt he must present, in the borrowed coat, which Lieutenant King had before noticed as shabby. On this, Tallmadge promptly offered the loan of the dragoon cloak he was wearing, which was accepted after a little hesitation. (The light-blue cloak André wore up to the time of capture seems to have disappeared, as King does not mention it at South Salem.) The march was resumed, towards what is now New City, the present County seat, by the road extending almost due east from Coe's. If it was then as now it was extremely picturesque, bordered by woodland for a long distance, and crossing two or three pretty brooks, which make a charmingly diversified landscape. The stranger who to-day visits the interior of Rockland County is impressed by the exceedingly quiet and secluded aspect it presents. Although traversed by three railroads it is difficult to realize it is so near crowded cities and the great highway of the Hudson River, and the modern settlements on the east bank. The population is still very largely descended from the original Dutch settlers, and very many of the patronymics of the Revolution are still common. " Turning to the right, they passed over the road leading south to the highway near the corner of the road where the present railroad crosses the same, then wheeling to the left, they went nearly east, crossing a small stream, one of the branches of the Hackensack River. Continuing on to the Four Corners they turned to the right and passed through Clarkstown.

---

1 So called, apparently, to distinguish it from the Dutch (Reformed) Church.

2 It is commonly referred to, in contemporary records, as Coe's " Tavern."

See plates 50-51: The Coe Tavern, Hempstead, Rockland Co.

Pursuing the road south from Clarkstown to the point where it is crossed by the railroad, they crossed the Hackensack and continued on the road now crossed by the railroad near the bridge, then south again over another point crossed by the railroad, then over a small stream east of what is now Blauveltville they continued south in a direct road to Tappan."[1]

1 Dykman.

CHAPTER V.

At Tappan—Death.

And die with decency.—OTWAY—*Venice Preserved*, Act v., sc. 3.

The original U. S.
Army Button.

ON arrival, Smith was put in the church, while his companion in misfortune was taken to the stone tavern of Casparus (Jasper) Mabie. This is still standing, though built in 1755. It was for many years—and up to about 1857—a noted house of entertainment, and is a two-story edifice, about 50 x 40, built of large grey stone blocks, the corners of rough brownstone. Had the roof been slate, the place might still be habitable. As it is, the mossy roof has collapsed and the elements are working havoc with the interior, which has been closed to visitors for many years.[1] The tall weeds grow rampantly around it, and its aspect is forlorn in the extreme. The owner admitted me by a rear door, and showed me over the building. In 1800 it passed into the hands of Philip Dubey, who owned it in 1818, when Captain Alden Partridge, U. S. A., who was Superintendent of West Point in 1816-17, visited it. His account has some professional details of interest:

> André's room is 18 feet 6½ inches, by 11 feet 7½ inches, and 7 feet 5 inches high. There is but one window, in the west wall, and one door, in the south.

Since then the two rear rooms have been made into one,

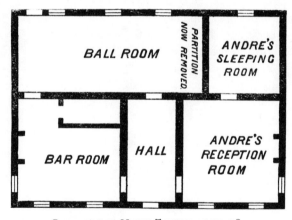

PLAN OF THE MABIE TAVERN AS IN 1780.

From *Magazine of American History*, by permission.
The "Ball-room" was enlarged in 1848 by taking down the partition, as marked. The "Bar-room" was used by General Greene as his headquarters' office.

For the interesting relic from which the sketch heading this chapter was made, one of the Continentals' buttons of the Revolution, I am indebted, as I am also for the three "André regiment" buttons heading Chapters II., III., and IV., to Mr. William L. Calver, of New York, who has a large and varied collection of such, found chiefly on the sites of the British camps on the ridge forming the north end of New York City, just below Spuyten Duyvil Creek. It may here be noted that the Massachusetts troops did not wear this button, but a State one.

1 This was written in 1897—since when the house has been opened.

See plate 52: Major Andre's Prison, Tappan
See plate 53: The Mabie Tavern, Tappan

the sordid owner of 1848 making a ballroom of them, and boasting to Lossing of having received " a whole dollar " for the lock of the door.

The street door of the building is the same as opened to admit the man whose brief sojourn within was to make the house famous; but the window-shutters are modern, or the modernity of about 1830. The piazza was originally the orthodox Dutch stoop, of just sufficient length for a seat on each side, and six steps[1] to the ground. No other building can boast of more historic interest for the same period than can this plain, heavy Dutch tavern. Almost, if not quite, every general officer of the left wing of the army (and possibly Washington also) was a visitor to it while it was Greene's headquarters, during the autumn of 1780. The Commander in Chief was the only exception during the momentous five days we are considering.

It is greatly to be regretted that neither our patriotic societies nor the Rockland County Historical Society feel able to buy and maintain it. A few more years, at most, will reduce it to ruins.[2] The old Dutch church, in which both prisoners were tried, stood at the head of the street, but was demolished in 1786, to make way for a larger, which in turn gave place (1836) to a third, the present structure, which is on the original site. The only known representation of the first church is on a seal, from which was made the cut given here.

THE OLD DUTCH CHURCH, TAPPAN, N. Y.
(Demolished 1786.)
The prison of Joshua Hett Smith, and place of trial of Major André.

The worthy Dutchmen of 1780[3] knew not the fame their sleepy village was to acquire from that September week, or surely the quaint old sanctuary would have been carefully preserved.

The order, issued by Colonel Alexander Scammell,[4] Adjutant General, to

[1] Van Dyk.

[2] Just as this was written (November, 1897,) the news arrived that a heavy gale had blown down part of it. Shortly afterwards it was sold to a purchaser who repaired the damage, but proposes to degrade the building by opening it as a saloon. *Sic transit gloria*—revolutionensis!

[3] Tappan is still very Dutch. Hundreds who speak the tongue still live within a radius of five miles from the church. To my great regret I have been unable to trace a painting—known to exist in 1897—of the trial itself. It is the only one of the scene, to my knowledge, and I will be grateful to any reader who can put me on its track.

[4] **Alexander Scammell** was born in Mendon (now Milford) Massachusetts, in 1744, and died at Williamsburg, Virginia, October 6, 1781. Graduated from Harvard in 1769, he taught school, surveyed land, and studied law until the battle of Bunker Hill, where he served with credit. His patriotism had before this been manifested by his participation in Sullivan's capture of Fort William and Mary, at Newcastle, N. H., December 14, 1774, where he personally pulled down the British flag. He accompanied Sullivan on the Canada expedition, and was taken prisoner at the battle of Long Island, but soon exchanged. He crossed the Delaware in the same boat with Washington, on the expedition to Trenton, was with him at Princeton, and was in command of the First New Hampshire battalion when ordered to raise another regiment, the Third, of which he was commissioned Colonel. He served with credit at Saratoga, though wounded a few days before. In 1778 he was promoted to be Adjutant General of the army, and of his conduct at the battle of Monmouth Washington said afterwards: "he was the man who inspired us all to do our full duty."

See plate 54: Portrait of Col. Alexander Scammell

See plate 55: Portrait of Col. Jedediah Huntington

the officers of André's special guard, was an amplification of Washington's letter to Greene on the subject (given on page 53):

> Major André, the prisoner under your guard, is not only an officer of distinction in the British army, but a man of infinite artfulness, and address, who will leave no means unattempted to make his escape[1] and avoid the ignominious death which awaits him. You are therefore, in addition to your sentries,[2] to keep two officers constantly in the room with him, with their swords drawn, whilst the other officers who are out of the room are constantly to keep walking the entry and round the sentries, to see that they are alert.[3]

Washington arrived at Tappan on the same day as the prisoners, and made his headquarters at the house of John De Windt, on the road directly east of the Mabie tavern, and about an eighth of a mile distant. It is still standing, in good condition, but its north side is entirely transformed by the addition of a wooden front. From it he issued an order convening a Court of Inquiry[4] to which André's case was referred, and which met the next day. The order reads:

> Gentlemen,—Major André, Adjutant to the British army, will be brought before you for examination. He came within our lines in the night, on an interview with Major General Arnold, and in an assumed character, and was taken within our lines in a disguised habit, with a pass under a feigned name, and with the enclosed papers concealed upon his person. After a careful examination, you will be pleased as speedily as possible, to report a precise statement of his case, together with your opinion of the light in which he ought to be considered, and the penalty which ought to be inflicted. The Judge-Advocate will attend to assist in the examination, who has sundry other papers relative to this matter, which he will lay before the board.
>
> I have the honour to be, gentlemen, your most obedient, humble servant,
>
> GEORGE WASHINGTON.

The Board was thus constituted:

General Greene, President.

Lord Stirling, Lafayette, Steuben, St. Clair, Robert Howe, [5]	Major Generals.	James Clinton, Glover, Hand, Huntington, Knox,[6] Parsons,[7] Paterson, Stark,	Brigadier Generals.

On September 30, 1781, while reconnoitering at Yorktown, he was surprised by two Hessian officers, made prisoner, and wounded after his surrender (Dr. Thacher, who attended him, so states). At Washington's request, Cornwallis allowed him to be removed to Williamsburg for treatment. There he died and was buried, a tablet being erected to his memory. Dr. Matthew Thornton, the member of Congress whose signature was the last affixed to the Declaration of Independence, wrote a dirge on hearing of his death, which may be found in an interesting sketch of Colonel Scammell's life, by William O. Clough, in the *Granite Monthly*, of Concord, N. H., September, 1892. The portrait I give is taken from that in the New Hampshire Representatives' Hall, Concord.

[1] This conclusion was natural, but hardly warranted by André's conduct. He never seems to have had any idea of escape.

[2] There were six constantly on post.

[3] The guard outside the house consisted of a captain, five subalterns, and forty rank and file.—*Bowman*.

[4] Commonly known as the Board of General Officers.

[5] The omission of Wayne has been remarked by all historians. Sparks, in 1834, asked Tallmadge the reason, and got the incisive reply: "None durst ask him (Washington) the reason why A. was appointed and B. omitted." Johnson (*Life of Greene*) says Wayne declined.   [6] It is of interest, [7] Was Parsons, page 60.

Jedediah Huntington was born in Norwich Conn., August 4, 1743, and died in New London, September 25, 1818. He came of a family distinguished for patriotism, his father, General Jabez Huntington, and his four brothers, taking an active part in the Revolution. He himself raised a regiment, in which he was a captain, which joined Washington's army at Cambridge; and from that time until the end of hostilities he took an active part in its campaigns, attaining the rank of Brevet Major General. After peace was declared he held various positions of trust and honor in his native state, culminating in the Collectorship of New London, to which he was appointed by Washington, in 1789, and which he retained until 1815. He was one of the original members of the Cincinnati.

(As the portraits of most of the members of the André court-martial are well known, I have not thought it necessary to reproduce them. General Huntington's, however, is very scarce, and I am indebted to Dr. Emmet for it. Of General Parsons I believe no portrait exists.)

John Laurance was Judge Advocate.[1] At the same time a Court was convened to try Smith. It consisted of a number of line officers, mostly of Connecticut regiments, with Colonel Henry Jackson, Sixteenth Massachusetts, as president.

As before noticed, Smith was acquitted, after the case had dragged along with frequent postponements for four weeks from September thirtieth. The report of the case is interesting. Smith, realizing his danger and able to see from his window, if he cared to, the gallows erected for his unfortunate companion, conducted his own defence with a degree of courage which compels admiration. He cross-examined every witness (of whom he complains Hamilton and Lafayette were unjust to him) and won. His liberty, however, was brief, as he was soon arrested by the civil organization styled "Commissioners of Conspiracy," taken to Goshen, and imprisoned until May 22, 1781, when he escaped to New York.[2]

While imprisoned, André was visited by a number of general officers, and was treated with the utmost consideration—in marked contrast to the treatment of Nathan Hale by Howe in 1777. He was allowed to write to Clinton[3] and

[6] It is of interest to note that Knox had met André before, at the capture of St. John's, in 1775. Knox was of the victorious force, and allowed André to share his quarters for a night.

[7] Was Parsons at that very time holding treasonable relations with Clinton? The question is one requiring more space for discussion than I can give it, but I do not credit it. A very full and interesting paper on the subject, by Congressman George B. Loring, of Salem, Mass., will be found in the *Magazine of American History*.

[1] **John Laurance** (1750-1810) was an Englishman, born in Cornwall. He was afterwards a judge of the New York District Court, a member of the first Federal Congress, and of the Senate (1796-1800). He held the rank of Colonel in the Continental Army. His wife was a daughter of General Alexander McDougall.

[2] Anxiety had undermined his wife's health, and she was unable to accompany him when he left New York with the British troops, in November, 1783, but died there January 1, 1784. At the time of his departure he owned No. 7 William Street, which was sold by his order in December. He lived in London, receiving a small pension from the British Crown—6s. a day, in 1783-4; it had been $1 per day while in New York—until 1801, when he returned to the United States, and (as I am informed by an old resident) opened a school in his old house in Haverstraw. Public opinion, however, was against him, and he soon withdrew, went South, then returned to England, where he seems to have lived at Shepton Mallet, Somersetshire. In 1808 he published his celebrated book: "An Authentic Narrative of the Causes which led to the death of Major John André." It was reprinted in New York the next year, and attracted general attention, as all three of André's captors, and most of those who had witnessed his death, were still alive. In spite of the generally unfavorable opinion which historians have entertained of it, I (as noted elsewhere) can but think its statements credible on minor points. He married a second time, whether while living in England or in the South is not determinable, though the lady's name, Anna Middleton, is common in South Carolina. By his will, dated December 31, 1817, and proved in New York, October 15, 1818, he gives her an estate in Shepton Mallet. He returned to New York, some time after 1808, and died there October 10, 1818. He was buried in a vault of either the Middle or North Dutch Church, New York.
The portrait given is the only known one of him, and is owned by a private collector in New York. It has never been copied before. Trumbull met Smith in London, and the portrait is endorsed in his handwriting: "Joshua H. Smith, who was a very smart (?) man. Arnold and André met in his House. I met him in England, 1808, and after in N. York, and were the best of friends. J. T."

[3]   Tappan, Sept. 29.
His Excellency
General Sir Henry Clinton, K. B., etc.
      Sir,—Your Excellency is doubtless already apprised of the manner in which I was taken, and possibly of the serious light in which my conduct is considered and the rigorous determination that is impending.
      Under these circumstances, I have obtained General Washington's permission to send you this letter; the object of which is to remove from your breast any suspicion that I could imagine I was bound by your Excellency's orders to expose myself to what has happened. The events of coming within an Enemy's posts, and of changing my dress, which led me to my present situation, were contrary to my own intention, as they were to your orders; and the circuitous route which I took to return was imposed (perhaps unavoidably) without alternative, upon me.

See plate 56: Portrait of John Laurence

others in New York, and to have his servant,[1] Peter Laune, come thence with clothing for his use, on Friday, the twenty-ninth. A surgeon, Dr. Nathaniel Gardiner, First New Hampshire Continentals, was detailed to attend him.[2]

On his examination by the Board André made the explicit statement:

That the boat in which he came ashore carried no flag.

In reply to the question whether he considered himself under the protection of a flag, he replied:

That it was impossible for him to so consider; and that if he had he certainly might have returned under it,[3] adding: I leave them (his detailed statements, as given in the Appendix) to operate with the Board, persuaded that you will do me justice.

After he had been returned to his prison[4] he remarked:

I foresee my fate, and though I pretend not to play the hero or to be indifferent about life, yet I am reconciled to whatever may happen, conscious that misfortune, not guilt, will have brought it upon me.

Regarding his treatment by the Board, he said:

I flatter myself that I have never been illiberal, but if there were any remains of prejudice in my mind, my present experience must obliterate them.

The Board deliberated, but it was obvious that they could come to but one decision,[5] and accordingly reported:

I am perfectly tranquil in mind, and prepared for any fate, to which an honest zeal for my King's service may have devoted me. In addressing myself to your Excellency on this occasion, the force of all my obligations to you, and of the attachment and gratitude I bear you, recurs to me. With all the warmth of my heart I give you thanks for your Excellency's profuse kindness to me, and I send you the most earnest wishes for your welfare which a faithful, affectionate and respectful attendant can frame.

I have a mother and three sisters, to whom the value of my commission would be an object, as the loss of Grenada has much affected their income. It is needless to be more explicit on this subject; I am persuaded of your Excellency's goodness.

I receive the greatest attention from his excellency General Washington, and from every person under whose charge I happen to be placed.

I have the honour to be, with the most affectionate attachment, your Excellency's most obedient and most humble servant,

JOHN ANDRÉ,
Adjutant-General.

[1] Two servants.—*Dewees.*

[2] **Nathaniel Gardiner** was son of Colonel Abraham Gardiner, of Gardiner's Island, Long Island, N. Y. He was born January 11, 1759, and died March 25, 1804. On the 28th June, 1780, he was appointed surgeon of the First New Hampshire, which appointment he resigned December 17, 1782. He was several times a member of the New York Legislature, and, after 1790, resided in New York City, where he was a member of the firm of Gardiner, Thompson and Co., shipping merchants.

A singular coincidence may be noticed in this connection. In 1776, the British had possession of the east end of Long Island, and André was quartered in the Gardiner house. Dr. Gardiner had ventured to return for a secret visit to his home. André afterwards told his father that he had known of his presence, but as he had not actually met him, had forborne to have him arrested, as would have otherwise been his duty to do. On leaving East Hampton, André presented Colonel Gardiner with a wine glass in exchange for one of the Colonel's which he took with him. The glass is still preserved by the family, who have also kindly furnished me with the portrait and autograph of the Doctor.

[3] Lafayette told Sparks that Greene asked the prisoner: "When you landed, did you consider yourself acting as a British officer, or as a private individual?" "As a British officer," was the unhesitating reply.

[4] During the trial he wore the clothes in which he had been captured, but on its termination he resumed his uniform.

[5] Lafayette told Sparks that Greene alone wished to hang him. He contended that the laws of war required that a spy be hung; the adoption of any less rigorous mode of punishment would excite the belief that palliatory circumstances existed in the case of André, and the decision might thereby be brought into question. He carried his point with the others of the Board.—*Gordon* (and L. M. Sargent).

This, however, is evidently a mistake. Witness Steuben's words: "It is not possible to save him. He put us to no proof, but in an open, manly manner confessed everything but a premeditated design to deceive."—Kapp's *Life of Steuben.*

See plate 57: Portrait of Nathaniel Gardiner

The Board of General Officers appointed to examine into the case of Major André report :

1st. That he came on shore from the *Vulture* sloop of war in the night of the 21st September last, on an enterprise with General Arnold, in a private and secret manner.

2d. That he changed his dress within our lines, and under a feigned name and in a disguised habit passed our works at Stony and Verplank's Points the evening of the 22d September last, and was taken the morning of the 23d September last, at Tarrytown, in a disguised habit, being then on his way to New York, and when taken he had in his possession several papers which contained Intelligence for the Enemy.

The Board having maturely considered these facts, do also report to his Excellency General Washington, That Major André ought to be considered as a spy from the enemy, and that agreeably to the law and usage of nations, it is their opinion he ought to suffer death.

The report and finding were thus approved:

Headquarters, Tappan, Sept. 30, 1780.

The Commander in Chief approves of the opinion of the Board of general officers respecting Major André, and orders that the execution of Major André take place to-morrow at five o'clock P. M.[1]

---

[1] Captain Ebenezer Smith, of the Thirteenth Massachusetts, commanded the execution guard for this day, and has left on record a graphic picture which shows André not to have been unmoved by the sentence : "The agony of his mind as he walked the room was most distressing, and it seemed to me that his very flesh crawled upon his bones."

The order postponing the execution arrived before five, to the Captain's great relief. The next morning he was a witness to the tears of Laune, André's servant.—*Sparks*, Am. Whig Review, Vol. V.

From Judge Dykman I have received the following interesting item, the authority for which he is unable to name, but which it may be legitimately surmised from Captain Smith's statement, must have been himself, or one of the other officers on guard that night : During the night previous to his death, André said : "I am in a deplorable state : just about to be launched into the presence of my God."

Ebenezer Smith was born in Lebanon, Connecticut, January —, 1764, and died in New Marlborough, Massachusetts, September —, 1816. In 1775 he was living in New Marlborough. When the "Lexington Alarm" was sounded, within two hours of the news, his company of Minute Men assembled, and the next day they marched for Boston and fought at Bunker Hill. He was commissioned Ensign, and soon after Captain. From that time on he was in service, only retiring when peace was established in 1783, when he was the oldest captain of the Massachusetts Line. During his whole service — eight years, eight months and nine days — he was on furlough only six months. At Ticonderoga, Monmouth, Long Island, Saratoga, Valley Forge, in Rhode Island, his regiments (Thirteenth and Sixth Massachusetts) were in the front rank. They froze at Valley Forge (where for two days his sole food was an old beef-bone, pounded and boiled) and parched at Monmouth, where, nearly dying of heat and thirst, he bore off the field one of his wounded sergeants, and where his own life was saved from a British dragoon by a comrade. His witness to the fearful heat of that day was his description to his son, David, (himself a soldier at sixteen,) of counting nine British soldiers, lying close beside a spring, without a wound on any of them, all dead from the heat. He was stationed at West Point when André was brought there, and his son is the authority for the positive statement received from the Captain, that André was under his charge in old Fort Putnam. He went to Tappan, and being an especial favorite with Washington (at whose request he thrice withdrew his offered resignation from the army), was again his guard there. Neither he, his widow nor any of his children ever asked or received a pension, nor were any of the family repaid the losses he sustained by the depreciation of Continental money in which he was paid.

A proof of Washington's confidence in him appears from this incident, told by his son to his grandson, the late E. Goodrich Smith, of Washington : The evening of October 1st the Chief sent for Captain Smith, and warned him that he was fearful lest the food or drink which might be offered him that night, be drugged, in order to make André's escape possible ; adding, "Treachery is all around me, and I hardly know whom to trust, but I know I can trust you — you must mount guard over him to-night." "My life shall answer for his safety," was Smith's reply, and he did not leave André that night. After hostilities ended, Captain Smith was a member of the Massachusetts Legislature, and one of the original members of the Cincinnati. He was a man of exemplary religious life, and universally honored by all who knew him.

(Though I have given more space to the record of this officer, and to those of some others, than their comparatively slight connection with André might seem to require, they present such remarkable instances of endurance and patriotic service that nothing less extensive could pretend to do them justice. It was by the devotion of such men that our Republic was made a possibility.)

That same day he wrote Clinton in such terms as effectually prevented any repetition of the latter's ridiculous "flag of truce" plea, to which André's own explicit testimony had just given its quietus:

Head Quarters,
September 30.

Sir,—In answer to your Excellency's letter of the 26th instant, which I had the honour to receive, I am to inform you that Major André was taken under such circumstances as would have justified the most summary proceedings against him. I determined, however, to refer his case to the examination and decision of a Board of General Officers, who have reported on his free and voluntary confession and letters.—(Here follows the sentence: "That he came on shore from the *Vulture*," etc., as on page 62, and the finding of the Board.)

From these proceedings it is evident that Major André was employed in the execution of measures very foreign to the objects of flags of truce, and such as they were never meant to authorize or countenance in the most distant degree; and this gentleman confessed, with the greatest candor, in the course of his examination: "That it was impossible for him to suppose he came on shore under the sanction of a flag."

I have the honour to be, etc., etc.,
G. WASHINGTON.

(With this was enclosed André's letter to Clinton.)

That day the Chief received a letter from an officer high in Clinton's confidence, and at the time Commandant of New York:

New York, 29th September, 1780.

Sir,—Persuaded that you are inclined rather to promote than to prevent the civilities and acts of humanity which the rules of war permit between civilized nations, I find no difficulty in representing to you, that several letters and messages sent from here have been disregarded, are unanswered, and the flags of truce that carried them, detained. As I ever have treated all flags of truce with civility and respect, I have a right to hope that you will order my complaint to be immediately redressed. Major André, who visited an officer commanding in a district, at his own desire, and acted in every circumstance agreeable to his direction, I find is detained a prisoner; my friendship for him leads me to fear he may suffer some inconvenience for want of necessaries; I wish to be allowed to send him a few, and I shall take it as a favor if you will be pleased to permit his servant to deliver them.

In Sir Henry Clinton's absence it becomes a part of my duty to make this representation and request.

I am, etc., etc., etc.,
JAMES ROBERTSON,
Lieut. General.

It is remarkable that a man holding such an office as Washington's found time to write—frequently with his own hand—as often and at as much length as he did. The prompt reply to Robertson is an instance:

Tappan, September 30, 1780.

Sir,—I have just received your letter of the 29th. Any delay which may have attended your flags, has proceeded from accident, and the peculiar circumstances of the occasion—not from intentional neglect or violation. The letter that admitted of an answer, has received one as early as it could be given with propriety, transmitted by a flag this morning.   As to messages, I am uninformed of any that have been sent.

The necessaries for Major André will be delivered to him,[1] agreeable to your request.

I am, Sir, etc., etc.,

GEORGE WASHINGTON.

That night the prisoner made a sketch of the Hudson, showing Smith and himself going ashore from the *Vulture*, and also one of West Point from the river,[2] and gave them to Laune to take to New York.   The guard officer who was constantly in the room with him, told Dr. Thacher that when the sentence and the hour fixed—noon—were announced to him[3] he received the news without emotion, merely replying: "I avow no guilt, but am reconciled to my fate." "While all present were oppressed with silent gloom, he retained a firm countenance, with calmness and composure of mind."[4]

It is not clear who hinted to him that he might suggest to Clinton to surrender Arnold, but the suggestion was instantly repelled.[5]

But his friends were not idle.   Thacher records:

October 1.   I went this afternoon to witness the execution—a large concourse of people had assembled and the gallows was erected, but a flag of truce arrived from Clinton, in consequence of which the execution is postponed till to-morrow at noon.

The suggestion about Arnold was carried further.   Captain Aaron Ogden, of Lafayette's light infantry corps, was sent on the preceding day—September thirtieth—to Paulus Hook—now Jersey City—with a package of papers for Clinton.   This contained an official account of the trial, the report of the Board, and a letter from André.   Ogden, following his orders, communicated to the commander at Paulus Hook, where he spent the night, his belief that André might be saved by the surrender of Arnold.[6]   This was instantly transmitted to Clinton, but, as might have been expected under the circumstances, he refused to entertain the idea.   Ogden reached Tappan again on the morning of October first,[7] accompanied by a British flag of truce bearing this letter from Clinton:

---

[1] That day Tallmadge wrote to Colonel Webb, who was out on parole, either at Flatbush or Wethersfield: "I never saw a man, whose fate I foresaw, whom I so sincerely pitied.   Though he knows his fate, he seems to be as cheerful as if he were going to an assembly."

[2] Anburey.   Of the second sketch I can find no trace, but the other, which was about 12 x 7 inches, was sent to New York, and engraved in mezzotint.   The self-control which would enable a man within a day of death to sketch with such ease and dexterity, has no parallel in history so far as I know.

[3] Two officers came the first day for the purpose, one being Major Robert Burnet, Aid to Greene.   While the other is not named, it was probably Scammell.   Major Burnet was the last survivor of the original members of the Society of the Cincinnati, dying in Newburgh in 1854.

[4] This may have been on the morning of October second.   The various authorities differ about events of the two days.

[5] Hamilton wrote on this point: "The moment he had been guilty of so much frailty I should have ceased to esteem him.   It was proposed to me to suggest it, but I knew I should have forfeited his esteem by doing it, and therefore declined it.   As a man of honor he could not but reject it."

[6] A very interesting but indefinite statement is made by some authorities, on the strength of statements by some unnamed British officers, on their return to England, after the war, that Arnold offered to go to the American camp and surrender himself for André.   Clinton's reply is said to have been: "Your offer, Sir, does you great honor, but if André were my own brother, I could not consent to it."   It is to be regretted that so interesting an item is not definite enough to be available as history.   [7] That night, page 65.

See plate 58: Reading the Death-Warrant

New York, Sept. 30, 1780.

Sir,—From your Excellency's letter of this date I am persuaded the Board of General officers, to whom you referred the case of Major André, can't have been rightly informed of all the circumstances on which a judgment ought to be formed. I think it of the highest moment to humanity that your Excellency should be perfectly apprized of the state of this matter, before you proceed to put that judgment in execution.

For this reason I shall send His Excellency Lieut. General Robertson, and two other gentlemen, to give you a true state (*sic*) of facts, and to declare to you my sentiments and resolution. They will set out to-morrow as early as the wind and tide will permit, and will wait near Dobbs's ferry for your permission and safe conduct, to meet your Excellency, or such persons as you may appoint, to converse with them on this subject.

I have the honour to be, etc., etc.,

H. CLINTON.

P. S. The Hon. Andrew Elliot, Esq., Lieut. Governor, and the Hon. William Smith, Chief justice of this province, will attend His Excellency Lieut. General Robertson.

H. C.

His Excellency
General Washington.

The execution was consequently postponed until the next day—October second[1]—and Robertson, Elliot and Smith arrived in a flag vessel—the schooner *Greyhound*. Robertson alone, as a soldier, was allowed to land, and met Greene, as Washington's representative, who forestalled any lengthy discussion by saying, " Let us understand our position : I meet you only as a private gentleman, not as an officer, for the case of an acknowledged spy admits of no discussion." As nothing was produced which Greene deemed material to the point, Robertson proposed that Rochambeau and Knyphausen should be appointed a committee to decide. This was naturally refused, and then, apparently as a last resort, Robertson produced a letter from Arnold, addressed to Washington :

New York, October 1, 1780.

Sir,—The polite attention shown by your Excellency and the Gentlemen of your family to Mrs. Arnold, when in distress, demands my grateful acknowledgment and thanks, which I beg leave to present.

From your Excellency's letter to Sir Henry Clinton, I find a Board of General officers have given it as their opinion that Major André comes under the description of a spy. My good opinion of the candor and justice of those Gentlemen leads me to believe

---

[7] That night, André's sister, in England, dreamed of his arrest and execution. The story is told at length in *Ainsworth's Magazine*, but has since been denied in *Notes and Queries*.

[1] On the same day Arnold's resignation of his commission was received by Washington :

New York, October 1, 1780.

Sir,—I take this opportunity to inform your Excellency that I consider myself no longer acting under the commission of Congress. Their last to me being among my papers at West-point, you, Sir, will make such use of it as you think proper.

At the same time, I beg leave to assure your excellency that my attachment to the true interest of my country is invariable, and that I am actuated by the same principle which has ever been the governing rule of my conduct, in this unhappy contest.

I have the honour, etc., etc.,

B. ARNOLD.

that if they had been made fully acquainted with every circumstance relating to Major André, that they would by no means have considered him in the light of a spy, or even of a prisoner. In justice to him, I think it my duty to declare, that he came from on board the *Vulture* at my particular request, by a flag sent on purpose for him by Joshua Smith, Esq., who had permission to go to Dobbs's ferry to carry letters, and for other purposes not mentioned, and to return. This was done as a blind to the spy-boats; Mr. Smith at the same time had my private directions to go on board the *Vulture*, and bring on shore Colonel Robinson or Mr. John Anderson, which is the name I had requested Major André to assume. At the same time I desired Mr. Smith to inform him, that he should have my protection, and a safe passport to return in the same boat, as soon as our business was completed. As several accidents intervened to prevent his being sent on board, I gave him my passport to return by land. Major André came on shore in his uniform (without disguise) which with much reluctance, at my particular and pressing instance, he exchanged for another Coat. I furnished him with a horse and saddle, and pointed out the route by which he was to return, and as commanding officer in the department, I had an undoubted right to transact all these matters; which if wrong, Major André ought by no means to suffer for them.

But if, after this just and candid representation of Major André's case, the Board of General officers adhere to their former opinion, I shall suppose it dictated by passion and resentment; and if that Gentleman should suffer the severity of their sentence, I shall think myself bound by every tie of duty and honour to retaliate on such unhappy persons of your army as may fall within my power, that the respect due to flags, and to the law of nations may be better understood and observed. I have further to observe, that forty of the principal inhabitants of South Carolina have justly forfeited their lives, which have hitherto been spared by the clemency of His Excellency Sir Henry Clinton, who cannot in justice extend his mercy to them any longer, if Major André suffers; which in all probability will open a scene of blood at which humanity will revolt.

Suffer me to entreat your Excellency, for your own and the honour of humanity, and the love you have of justice, that you suffer not an unjust sentence to touch the life of Major André.

But if this warning be disregarded, and he suffer, I call heaven and earth to witness, that your Excellency will be justly answerable for the torrent of blood that may be spilt in consequence.

I have the honour to be, etc., etc.,

B. ARNOLD.

His Excellency
     General Washington.

Surely a more remarkable jumble of brazen avowal of treason, pleading, threats and hypocrisy, was never written — and this by the man who had attacked Quebec, saved the day at Saratoga, nearly captured Tryon at Danbury (Compo), saved from want the children of Warren, and for five years been intimately associated with the very men he now declares to be "actuated by passion or resentment!"

If he really expected it to help André, he was singularly deficient in knowledge of the man he addressed.[1] Sparks well says: "It is hardly possible that

---

[1] Sargent thinks it did not reach Washington until after the execution.

See plate 59: Portrait of Benedict Arnold

it could have been read by Clinton, although written at his request with a view of operating on the judgment and clemency of Washington." Marbois says Greene contemptuously let it fall on the ground at Robertson's feet. Notwithstanding, the shrewd Scotchman told him he would stay aboard the *Greyhound* all night, and expressed his hope that André would be released the next day, or at any rate saved from death, on Greene's statement to his chief of Robertson's arguments. The sincerity of his belief, unfounded as it was, appears in the letter he wrote Clinton that very day.[1] While these efforts were making to save him, André, recalling Tallmadge's warning of his fate, wrote to Washington the letter which N. P. Willis afterwards paraphrased in verse,[2] and which remains to this day a model of manly feeling,[3] tersely and forcibly expressed by one who, feeling himself within one day of death, was yet only solicitous about its mode :

---

[1]
Off Dobbs' Ferry,
1 October.

Sir,—On coming to anchor here, I sent Murray on shore, who soon returned with notice that General Green was ready to meet me, but would not admit a conference with the other two gentlemen.

I paid my compliments to his character, and expressed the satisfaction I had in treating with him in the cause of my friend, the two armies, and humanity. He said he could not treat with me as an officer— that Mr. Washington had permitted him to meet me as a gentleman, but the case of an acknowledged spy admitted no opportunity of discussion. I said that a knowledge of facts was necessary to direct a General's judgment ; that in whatever character I was (received) I hoped he would represent what I said candidly to Mr. Washington. I laid before him the facts and Arnold's assertion of Mr. André's being under a flag of truce and disguised by his order. He showed me a low-spirited letter of André's saying that he had not landed under a flag of truce, and lamenting his being taken in a mean disguise. He expresses this in language that admits it to be criminal. I told him that André stated facts with truth, but reasoned ill upon them ; that whether a flag was flying or not, was of no moment. He landed and acted as directed by their General. He said they would believe André in preference to Arnold. * * * *

Green said one thing would satisfy them—they expected if André was set free, Arnold should be given up. This I answered with a look only which threw Green into confusion. I am persuaded André will not be hurt.

Believe me, Sir, etc., etc., etc.,
JAMES ROBERTSON.

(The omitted portions correspond with the general narrative, hence are omitted as repetitions.) His assertion about surrendering Arnold is almost certainly pure invention. Greene repelled his intimation that Lieut. Governor Gadsden and other South Carolina prisoners might be retaliated upon.

[2] Willis wrote :

It is not the fear of death
    That damps my brow ;
It is not for another breath
    I ask thee now.
I can die with a lip unstirred
    And a quiet heart—
Let but this prayer be heard
    Ere I depart.

I can give up my mother's look—
    My sister's kiss ;
I can think of love—yet brook
    A death like this !
I can give up the young fame
    I burn'd to win ;
All—but the spotless name
    I glory in.

Thine is the power to give,
    Thine to deny ;
Joy for the hour I live,
    Calmness to die.
By all the brave should cherish,
    By my dying breath,
I ask that I may perish
    By a soldier's death.

[3] Sargent says, page 68.

October 1.

Sir,—Buoyed above the terror of death by the consciousness of a life devoted to honourable pursuits, and stained with no action that can give me remorse, I trust that the request I make to your excellency at this serious period, and which is to soften my last moments, will not be rejected. Sympathy towards a soldier will surely induce your excellency, and a military tribunal, to adopt the mode of my death to the feelings of a man of honour. Let me hope, Sir, if aught in my character impresses you with esteem towards me, if aught in my misfortunes marks me as the victim of policy and not of resentment, I shall experience the operation of these feelings in your breast by being informed I am not to die on a gibbet.[1]

I have the honour, etc., etc.,

JOHN ANDRÉ.

From Washington's silence in regard to it André must have inferred a refusal, at first, as is shown by his letter to his friend Lieutenant Colonel William Crosbie, 22d Regiment, in New York :[2]

The manner in which I am to die at first gave me some slight uneasiness; but I instantly recollected that it is the crime alone that makes any mode of punishment ignominious — and I could not think an attempt to put an end to a civil war, and to stop the effusion of human blood, a crime.

From his subsequent words, it would seem that the impression had given place to a belief that his request would be granted.

The morning of the eventful second of October brought no message of comfort to the waiting Robertson, but a note from Greene conveyed the news that the execution would not be further delayed :

Camp, Tappan,

2 October.

Sir,—Agreeably to your request, I communicated to General Washington the substance of your conversation, with all the particulars, as far as my memory served me. It made no alteration in his opinion and determination. I need say no more, after what you have already been informed.

Robertson, as a last hope, wrote again to Washington :

Greyhound Schooner,
Flag of Truce,
Dobbs's Ferry,
October 2, 1780.

Sir,—A note I had from General Greene leaves me in doubt if his memory had served him, to relate to you with exactness the substance of the conversation that had passed between him and myself on the subject of Major André. In an affair of so much

---

[3] Sargent says he remarked : "Since it is my lot to die, there is still a choice in the mode which would make a material difference to my feelings, and I would be happy, if possible, to be indulged with a professional death."

[1] On the morning of the second, Hamilton wrote to Miss Schuyler :

Everything that is amiable in virtue, in fortitude, in delicate sentiments, and accomplished manners, plead for him ; but hard-hearted policy calls for a sacrifice. He must die. I must inform you that I urged a compliance with his request to be shot, and I do not think it would have had an ill effect, but some people are only sensible to motives of policy, and sometimes, from a narrow disposition— mistake it.

[2] This was taken to New York by Laune, after the execution.

consequence to my friend, to the two armies, and humanity, I would leave no possibility of a misunderstanding, and therefore take the liberty to repeat the substance of what I said to General Greene.

I offered to prove by the evidence of Colonel Robinson and the officers of the *Vulture*, that Major André went on shore at General Arnold's desire, in a boat sent for him with a flag of truce; that he not only came ashore with the knowledge and under the protection of the General who commanded in the district, but that he took no step while on shore but by direction of General Arnold, as will appear by the enclosed letter from him[1] to your Excellency.

Under these circumstances I could not, and hoped you would not, consider Major André as a spy, for any improper phrase in his letter to you.

The facts he relates correspond with the evidence I offer; but he admits a conclusion that does not follow. The change of cloaths and name was ordered by General Arnold, under whose direction he necessarily was, while within his command.

As General Greene and I did not agree in opinion, I wished that disinterested gentlemen of knowledge of the law of war and nations, might be asked their opinion on the subject; and mentioned Monsieur Knyphausen and General Rochambault.

I related that a Captain Robinson had been delivered to Sir Henry Clinton as a spy, and undoubtedly was such; but that it being signified to him that you were desirous that this man should be exchanged, he had ordered him to be exchanged.

I wished that an intercourse of such civilities as the rules of war might admit of, might take off many of its horrors. I admitted that Major André had a great share of Sir Henry Clinton's esteem, and that he would be infinitely obliged by his liberation; and that if he was permitted to return with me, I would engage to have any person you would be pleased to name, set at liberty. I added that Sir Henry Clinton had never put to death any person for a breach of the rules of war, though he had, and now has, many in his power. Under the present circumstances, much good might arise from humanity,[2] much ill from want of it. If that could give any weight, I beg leave to add, that your favorable treatment of Major André will be a favor I should be ever intent to return to any you hold dear. My memory does not retain with the exactness I could wish, the words of the letter General Greene showed me from Major André[3] to your Excellency. For Sir Henry Clinton's satisfaction, I beg you will order a Copy of it to be sent me at New York.

I have the honour, etc., etc.,

JAMES ROBERTSON.

His Excellency
General Washington.

The signing of André's death warrant is said to have cost Washington great distress, and as the hour of noon approached he ordered the window blinds

---

[1] This is vague, but most probably refers to the Arnold letter refused by Greene.

[2] The efforts made to save André did credit to his friends, but the writers of the several letters, in their frequent references to "humanity" seem to have altogether forgotten a fact which none of their antagonists ever could—that thousands of American prisoners were then languishing and dying of starvation in the prisons—and particularly the prison ships—of New York and Charleston. Of the persons we have met during our story, Paulding had twice been a prisoner, and was soon to be such for the third time; Captains Boyd, Van Dyk and Foote also, had been prisoners; Adjutant Hoogland had been captured at the battle of Long Island, and had suffered on one of the prison ships; and doubtless others of whom I have less information, had had more or less taste of British jails. While such facts could not affect the treatment of André, references to "humanity" were in singularly bad taste at a time when Cunningham was almost nightly hanging prisoners without trial, and the *Jersey* was a floating hell.

[3] That of October 1st, asking that he might be shot.

of his room to be closed, that he might not see the hill, where a large crowd had already assembled.[1] Never since has Tappan had an assemblage of equal size. "Many hundreds, if not thousands"[2] were present. General Glover was officer of the day, while Colonel Joseph Cilley, of the First New Hampshire, Lieutenant Colonel Henry Dearborn, of the same regiment, Major Peter Harwood, Sixth Massachusetts, and Major Thomas Pettingill, Ninth Massachusetts, were the others

of the day's detail, as shown by Greene's orderly-book, in still perfectly distinct handwriting.

Early in the morning, without the aid of a mirror, André made the pen-and-ink sketch of himself, which is now owned by Yale College. This he gave to an officer of the guard, Ensign Tomlinson,[3] of the Ninth Connecticut (Webb's). At eight he breakfasted, and then, having apparently been a second time notified of the hour for execution, by Colonel Scammell, heard it with calmness. His servant being overcome with grief, he turned to him, saying: "Leave me until you can show yourself more manly."[4] Having shaved, dressed himself in his uniform and packed his two trunks, he gave the keys to Laune, with directions where to take them in New York, and then, turning to Ensign[5] Samuel Bowman, Third Massachusetts, and Captain John Hughes, of the Congress

---

[1] In spite of some denials, I am inclined to think André could have seen the gibbet from his window; for Greene, writing that morning to Governor William Greene, of Rhode Island, says: "The gallows is erected in full view of the place where I am writing" (presumably his headquarters). However, it is certain André did not see it until the escort, at the foot of the hill, wheeled to the left and thus came in sight of it.
  Captain Partridge also says the hill could be seen from André's room. There are too many trees now for it to be visible.

[2] Russell. See page 73.

[3] **Jabez H. Tomlinson.** (Not Jabez L., as Lossing has it.) He was born in Stratford, Conn., December 24, 1760, and died there January 14, 1849. He was graduated from Yale in 1780, and was a captive in the Old Sugar House for a long time. The cane he is shown as holding was made from wood of his prison house. I am indebted to his great-granddaughter, Mrs. A. B. Fairchild, of Bridgeport, Conn., for his portrait — the only one made, and never before reproduced.   [4] This may,   [5] Samuel Bowman, page 71.

See plate 60: Road up André Hill, Tappan
See plate 61: Portrait of Col. Joseph Cilley
See plate 71: Map of the Village of Tappan

Regiment—Second Canadian—who had been in constant attendance on him for twenty-four hours, said: "Gentlemen, I am now ready to obey your call;"[1] or, as

John Hughes - - - Capt

another authority has it, "I am ready at any time, gentlemen, to wait on you."

Jabez H. Tomlinson.

The street in front of the tavern had meanwhile been filled with about five hundred troops. Captain John Van Dyk,[2] of Lamb's (Second) Artillery, with another officer,[3] were standing on either side the stoop as the door opened, and Bowman and Hughes appeared with the prisoner, "pale as death, but tranquil and calm." Dressed, as he was, in the rich uniform of a British staff-officer,[4] he must have presented an appearance in striking contrast to the Continentals. Van Dyk walked on the left of his left-hand officer.[5] As the drums and fifes began to play,[6] he composedly said: "I am very much surprised to find your troops under so good discipline, and your music is excellent."

---

[4] This may have been on the previous day. Thacher, Sargent and others are at variance about events on these days.

[5] **Samuel Bowman** was born in Lexington, Mass., December 2, 1753. He was one of the minute-men at the Lexington fight, and in January, 1776, enlisted in the Third Massachusetts, whence he was afterwards transferred to the First, and promoted to be lieutenant. He served throughout the war, and in 1786 removed to Wilkes Barre, Penn. In 1794 he was in arms again, on occasion of the "Whiskey insurrection" —and, in 1799–1800, was a captain in the Eleventh U. S. Infantry of the "Provisional Army," which was disbanded in 1800. Singular to relate, this veteran soldier, who had passed unhurt through eight years' warfare, met his death in sight of his own house, by being gored by a savage bull, June 25, 1818. Hon. Charles Miner, the historian, of Wilkes Barre, described him as "a man simple in heart and of (as) kindly affection as *Uncle Toby* himself, yet sensible and well-informed."
Although he is usually called Captain, the records do not give him that rank in 1780.
His eldest son, Lieutenant Colonel Alexander H. Bowman, of the Engineers, was Superintendent of West Point, in 1863, and another son, Charles S., was Captain and Brevet Major of Cavalry.

[1] Bowman.

[2] **John Van Dyk** was born in New York in 1753, and died there February 28, 1840. He was a member of Colonel John Lasher's New York Minute Men (the same regiment to which Captain Hoogland—see *ante* —belonged) in 1775, and when the British fleet was confronting New York, in 1776, he assisted Alexander Hamilton to remove the cannon from the Battery. Afterwards he was appointed to Lamb's Artillery, where he remained through the war. For many years afterwards he was employed in the Custom House at New York. It is a coincidence that his old commander, Colonel Lamb, was the Collector of the Port.
For his portrait I am indebted to his great great-grandson, Dr. Harold A. Meeks, of Meriden, Conn.

[3] Probably Captain Ebenezer Smith.

[4] With the exception of sash, gorget, sword and spurs. Darley's drawing is historically wrong in showing spurs, and also, I think, in showing three-cornered hat. As a staff-officer, he would wear a cocked hat but I have been unable to find any authentic representation of one of the period.

[5] It has been, [6] Van Dyk says, page, 72.

John Hughes was born in Lancaster County, Pennsylvania, in 1759. His father, Barnabas Hughes, removed to Maryland in 1760, and built an iron foundry near Hagerstown, where in later years was cast much of the cannon and shot used by the Continental army. (The names of two Hughes, Daniel and Samuel, probably his successors, occur frequently in the Maryland records of the Revolution.) At seventeen young Hughes entered the army as lieutenant in Colonel Hazen's regiment (of Pennsylvania) the "Second Canadian," generally known as the Congress regiment, or "Congress's Own." He served with credit, particularly at Brandywine and Germantown, and resigned from the army, as captain, in 1781. He then married Miss Chamberlaine, of Talbot County, Maryland, and settled near Havre de Grace, where he died May 21, 1805, leaving three daughters. When the British captured Havre de Grace, in 1813, the Hughes homestead was burned, with all its contents, and hence no portrait of him is known to exist. He was one of the original members of the Cincinnati. Mr. John Sterett Gittings, of Baltimore, is his great grandson, and to him I am indebted for the autograph shown on page 71. Daniel and Samuel Hughes were the elder brothers of Captain John.

The road which the procession took makes a right angle to the west, a few yards north of the tavern. The whole distance to the place of execution is exactly half

John Van Dyk

a mile, and the spot is almost exactly due west of the building.[1]

Greene and the other general officers, mounted, were drawn up in line beside the road; and to them, particularly to his judges, the prisoner raised his cocked hat as he passed. Washington and his staff were alone absent, and Russell[2] notes the prisoner's appreciation of the fact. Tallmadge and Thacher walked close to him, as did also Dr. Timothy Hall,[3] of the Fifth Massachusetts, who attended professionally.

Dr. Thacher says:

I was so near, during the solemn march to the fatal spot, as to observe every movement and to participate in every emotion the melancholy scene was calculated to produce. Melancholy and gloom pervaded all ranks, and the scene was affectingly awful. The

[5] It has been very difficult to decide who were the four officers; but an exhaustive search of all authorities, and recent information received from descendants of some of those concerned, leads me to decide that Bowman and Hughes walked arm in arm with him, while Van Dyk was on Bowman's left and Smith on Hughes' right. Lieutenant King and Captain Allen were certainly present, and may have been close behind the group, where Dr. Hall also probably walked.

[6] Van Dyk says they played "lively(!) tunes"—but Dewees, who was himself a fifer, says the Dead March. Some names of the band have been preserved to us: Alexander McKinley was the Drum Major, and Benjamin Abbot (who died at Nashua, N. H., in 1851) was a drummer. "The late Dr. Horace Green, of New York, while living in Rutland, Vt., was a skilful flute-player and frequently played to please an aged Revolutionary soldier there. The veteran usually wished to hear a simple but plaintive air known as the 'Bluebird,' which he said he had heard played on the occasion."—*Henry J. Raymond, 1880.*

Following this clue, I have been able, through the kind assistance of Dr. Green's daughter, Mrs. Anna G. Loveland, of Proctor, Vt., and of the officials of the Lenox Library, New York, to find a part of the "Bluebird." I am not aware that it has been published before.

For the other tune, "Roslin Castle," I am indebted to Mrs. Arthur H. Dyer, of Brooklyn, N. Y., great great-granddaughter of Colonel Benjamin Hinman, who was a spectator of the execution, and handed down the tune to his descendants. It is stated (Harvey, *History Lodge 61, F. and A. M., Wilkes Barre, Pa.*) that "Roslin Castle" was usually played as a funeral or dead march, in Washington's army, and was especially appropriate when Washington's Farewell Address was read to the troops at Newburgh, on their disbandment in 1783.

Benjamin Hinman was born in Woodbury, Conn., in 1729, and died there March 22, 1810. He was Colonel of the Fourth Connecticut in 1775, and took part in the capture of St. John's—where he may have met André. Arnold quarrelled with him at Crown Point because ordered by Massachusetts to obey him. Subsequently he was Colonel of the Thirteenth Connecticut, and left the army, on account of age and ill-health, in January, 1777. He was present at Tappan as a spectator.

[1] Sargent makes, [2] Benjamin Russell, [3] Timothy Hall, page 73.

eyes of the immense multitude were fixed on him who, rising superior to the fears of death, appeared as if conscious of the dignified deportment he displayed. Not a murmur or a sigh ever escaped him, and the civilities and attentions bestowed on him were politely acknowledged.

"Baldwin's" account says the guard marched in single file (probably hollow square is meant), the mounted officers first, next the baggage-wagon with the black-painted coffin,[1a] next the officers on foot, then André himself with his immediate bodyguard. At the spot where the troops wheeled to the left and quitted the highway leading to Old Tappan to  enter the field to the south, Clinton's unfortunate Adjutant for the first time saw the gallows, and realizing that his request for a "professional death" had thus been denied, and an ignominious end awaited him, involuntarily stopped short for an instant, overcome by the shock. The captain of the guard[2b] asked: "Why this emotion, Sir?" Thacher's version of his reply is the usually-received one: "I am reconciled to my death, but detest the mode." Bowman, however, who was certainly nearer to him than was Thacher, told Tallmadge in 1816, that his reply was:

> I have borne everything with fortitude, but this is too degrading! As respects myself it is a matter of no consequence,[3c] but I have a mother and sister who will be very much mortified by the intelligence.

By the kindness of Miss Ella M. Bowman, of Wilkes Barre, Pa., a great great-granddaughter of Ensign Bowman, I am permitted to reproduce an exact copy of his letter to Tallmadge, which differs slightly from that in print, and from which I have heretofore quoted:

---

1 Sargent makes a singular mistake in saying the procession passed Washington's headquarters. The De Windt house was east of the Mabie, and it was impossible to pass it unless a *détour* was made for the purpose, which the narratives of spectators prove was not done. See the map. Winsor repeats the error.
The two little daughters of Mr. De Windt were among the spectators. In old age one of them told Lossing that she gave André a peach, which he carried awhile and then gave to one of his guard. As he was surrounded by troops, the account would be justly regarded as an invention, had it not come from the one concerned in it.

2 **Benjamin Russell** was born in Boston, September 13, 1761, and died there January 4, 1845. At seventeen, while an apprentice to Isaiah Thomas, a printer of Worcester, the latter was drafted for military service. The youth volunteered in his stead, and was present at André's execution, as a private in the Worcester militia.
He was the first American "war correspondent," as he supplied news to the Worcester *Spy* during his six months' enlistment. After the war he founded the *Columbian Centinel*, of Boston, and was for many years a member of the Legislature, and the chief spirit of the Massachusetts Charitable Mechanic Association. He was the originator of the word "Gerrymander."

3 **Timothy Hall** was born in North Brookfield, Mass., June 4, 1758. In 1776 he enlisted as a private in the Connecticut militia, and was in the battles of Long Island, Harlem Heights and White Plains. His enlistment expiring with 1776, he seems to have studied medicine during the ensuing three years, as in February, 1780, we find him commissioned as Surgeon's Mate of the Fifth Massachusetts, Colonel Rufus Putnam. He served as such to January, 1781, and afterwards settled in East Hartford, Conn., where he practised his profession with great distinction for many years, and where he died August 6, 1844.

1a Considering the humanity with which André had been treated, it would have been inconsistent to have paraded his coffin before his face; hence I doubt this statement, which I call "Baldwin's" to identify it. Its author was an unnamed private in Colonel Jeduthan Baldwin's Massachusetts regiment of Artificers (Artillery).

2b "An officer by his side."—*Thacher*. Probably Hughes or Smith, as Bowman does not mention it. Another account says he asked: "Must I die in this manner?"

3c It must be confessed that this conflicts with his request to be shot.

See plate 62: Portrait of Timothy Hall

74

He was reprieved until the 2d (October). His guard was then relieved by Captain John ——[1] of the Congress regiment. * * * We relieved Captain Allen[2] of Rhode Island, by whom we were all introduced to Major André. He requested Captain Hughes and myself to remain with him, to which we consented. * * * Not a murmur escaped during the time I was with him; but on the contrary he expressed himself in the warmest terms for the indulgence he received from the court before whom he was tried and from all the officers under whose care he had been placed, particularly Major Tallmadge. On the morning of the fatal day he early put on his morning-gown, and appeared very sociable, conversed on different subjects, never mentioning his own situation, but when he saw us dull would take a glass, saying, "Come, let us take a glass of wine. It only makes me feel the worse to see your feelings hurt." Then he would commence some other conversation evidently with intention to take our thoughts from the situation. * * * He took his hat, put it on the table, and said, "Gentlemen, I am now ready to obey your call," with as much composure as if he had dressed for a party of pleasure. I said I was sorry we had to separate so soon, and he said it would be the sooner over. * * * When we came in sight of the gallows, I had never before seen him disturbed, but there was now evidently excitement, asking us earnestly whether we knew the mode of death. We told him we did not, and seeing you (Tallmadge) at some distance he asked if that were you. I answered him it was. He requested (leave) to speak to you, and you can recollect the observation, "I have borne everything with fortitude," etc.

Van Dyk says no reply was made, but other accounts represent the officer as saying: "It is unavoidable, Sir." "How hard is my fate!" replied the prisoner. He paused an instant, and added: "It will soon be over"[3]—the march was resumed, and the gallows reached. This had been made by setting up two forked trees, with a third laid across. It was unusually high, and under it stood the cart, or two-horse army baggage-wagon,[4] in which was the coffin. André waited a moment, "betraying some emotion, putting one foot on a small stone, and rolling it over and choking in his throat as if attempting to swallow.[5] He bowed his head and looked at himself from the feet upward, for an instant, before attempting to get on the wagon by the tail-board. His first attempt failing, he said a few words to his servant, who was standing by overcome with

---

[1] This must be Hughes.

[2] **William Allen.** He was born at Rehoboth, Mass., March 27, 1752, and died at Providence, R. I., August 17, 1815. He was Ensign of the Second Rhode Island, June 28, 1775; Captain, January 1, 1777; was transferred to the First, January 1, 1781, and was honorably discharged, December 25, 1783. In 1786 he was appointed Major of the Third U. S. Infantry, and was Brigadier General of the Rhode Island militia, 1799-1801. His son, William Henry Allen, was a naval officer, and was mortally wounded in the action between the *Argus* and the British brig *Pelican*, August 14, 1813.

[3] Tallmadge. His behaviour was becoming an officer and a gentleman, and such in his last moments as drew tears from many eyes.—*Heath.*

[4] Even this has its history. Such were then rare in the county, and the local Committee of Safety had the duty of procuring them—sometimes forcibly—when needed by the army. A farmer—Van Ostrand—hid his under the hay in his barn. Hendrick Oblenis, president of the Committee, found and seized it. At the close of the war, the owner refused to send for it, sued Oblenis for its value, was defeated, and then left it to decay under a tree behind the Oblenis homestead in Clarkstown.—*C. M. Oblenis, Nyack.*

[5] Thacher.

See plate 63: On the Way to Death

grief, and then, putting one hand on the wagon body, made a determined spring and succeeded.[1]

Stepping on his coffin he deliberately surveyed the scene, surrounded by the five hundred and fifty infantry on guard,[2] a great number of additional soldiers and civilian spectators, including, unfortunately, women and children.

Colonel Scammell, as Adjutant, read the order for execution, in a loud voice, then the commanding officer[3]—Glover—said: "Major André, if you have anything to say you can speak, for you have but a short time to live." Standing with hands on hips, the prisoner bowed to him and replied in clear, unfaltering tone:[4]

> I have nothing more to say, gentlemen, than this: I pray you to bear witness that I meet my fate like a brave man.

One account:

> All I request of you, gentlemen, is that you will bear witness—

The *Continental Journal*, Boston:

> I have said all I had to say, before; all I request of you—

The hangman, a Tory named Strickland, who was under arrest, and had been promised liberty for performing the odious office, had disguised himself by smearing his face with stuff like shoe-blacking, producing a hideous effect. Some of the stuff probably adhered to his hands, for on approaching André he was repulsed with the sharp command: "Take off your black hands." Removing his gold-laced cocked-hat, and handing it[5] and his watch[6] to his servant, who stood by the wagon, he next took off his white neck-cloth, and put it in his coat-pocket,[7] unbuttoned his shirt-collar and turned it down. Taking the noose from Strickland's hands he put it over his head and drew it close around the throat; then, taking a handkerchief from his pocket, he bandaged his eyes, and stood awaiting death. The hangman fastened the rope to the cross-beam,[8] when the commanding officer suddenly ordered André's hands to be tied. André immediately

---

1 Among the extraordinary circumstances that attended him in the midst of his enemies, he died universally esteemed.—*Hamilton*.

2 Colonel Israel Shreve, Second New Jersey, commanded the detachment.—*Shreve*.

3 Baldwin—but Thacher says it was Scammell.

4 He appeared as little daunted as John Rogers is said to have been when about to be burnt at the stake.—*Baldwin*.

Poor André was executed yesterday; nor did it happen without a tear on my part. He was a rare character. From the time of his capture to his last moments, his conduct was such as did honor to the human race. I mean by these words to express all that can be said favorable of man. The compassion of every man of feeling and sentiment was excited for him, beyond your conception.—*Lieutenant Colonel Richard K. Meade* to Colonel Theodoric Bland, Jr., October 3.

(Meade was one of Washington's Aids, and grandfather of Commodore R. W. Meade, U. S. N.)

Joel Barlow, who was then chaplain of General Poor's brigade of the Massachusetts line, was a spectator, and says: "A politer gentleman, or a greater character of his age, perhaps is not alive. He suffered with calmness and cheerfulness."

5 L. M. Sargent.

6 J. R. Simms.

7 These trivial details serve to illustrate how eye-witnesses' accounts differ. One says the hat and "stock" were laid on the coffin. 8 This fact, page 76.

pushed the handkerchief from his eyes, took a second one[1] from a pocket, and handed it to Strickland, first replacing the one over his eyes. The hangman having bound his arms behind him with the handkerchief, for an instant the slight figure, attired in coat of bright scarlet ,faced with green, waistcoat and breeches of buff, and top-boots, stood bareheaded, sharply outlined against the clear sky and the forest covering the distant hills.[2] The multitude was perfectly silent, overcome with emotion.[3] Then Colonel Scammell signalled the wagoner, by dropping the point of his sword — the horses were led forward, and the pinioned figure swung violently[4] at the end of the rope ———

There was happily hardly any struggle — it seemed in truth, as he had anticipated, "only a momentary pang."[5] For possibly half an hour the body oscillated, during which time the assembled multitude remained quiet. "The chambers of death were never· stiller,"[6] said one spectator, in unconsciously felicitous phrase. Then the rope was cut by the commanding officer himself, while two soldiers on either side bore up the body, that it might not fall. Laid on the ground beside the open grave, the uniform was taken off and handed to Laune, who, with the other servant, stood by. The guard was finally withdrawn, the multitude allowed to come forward[7] and gaze on the unconscious clay of the "darling of the British Army" — he who barely a fortnight earlier had left New York on the mission which was to, and so nearly did, insure the ruin of the patriot cause. "Thus died," says Thacher, "in the bloom of life, the accomplished Major André, the pride of the royal army, and the valued friend of Sir Henry Clinton."

By degrees the crowd lessened, and when but a few remained,[8] the body was wrapped in a shroud[9] and decently buried, near the gallows. Washington thus reported the event to Congress:

---

[8] This fact, mentioned only by Captain Van Dyk, probably accounts for Shreve's statement that the execution was from a ladder. The height of the gallows probably obliged Strickland to use a short ladder to reach the cross-piece from the wagon.

[1] Dr. Hall, who stood close to the wagon, says it was a piece of blue ribbon. Thus, again, do eye-witnesses differ about details.

[2] His personal accomplishments, appearance and behaviour, gained him the good wishes and opinion of every person who saw him. He was perhaps the most accomplished officer of the age—he met his fate in a manner which did honor to the character of a soldier.—*Scammell* to *Colonel Nathaniel Peabody*, October 3.

[3] The three captors were among the spectators. In after years Van Wart often shed tears when describing the scene.
I walked with him to the place of execution, and parted from him under the gallows, entirely overwhelmed with grief that so gallant an officer and so accomplished a gentleman should come to such an ignominious end.—*Tallmadge.*
When I saw him swinging under the gibbet, it seemed for a time as if I could not support it. All the spectators seemed to be overwhelmed by the affecting spectacle, and many were suffused with tears. There did not appear to be one hardened or indifferent spectator in all the multitude.—*Thacher.*

[4] Baldwin describes it as "a most tremendous swing," due to the height of the gallows.

[5] Thacher.

[6] Baldwin.

[7] The tears of thousands fell on the spot where he lay.—*Thacher.*　　[8] A French soldier, [9] Simms, page 77.

To the President of Congress. Paramus, 7 October.

Sir,—I have the honour to enclose to Congress a copy of the proceedings of a board of General officers in the case of Major André, adjutant general to the British army.

This officer was executed in pursuance of the opinion of the Board, on Monday, the 2d instant, at twelve o'clock, at our late camp at Tappan. He acted with great candor, from the time he avowed himself after his capture, until he was executed. Congress will perceive by a copy of a letter I received from him on the 1st instant, that it was his desire to be shot; but the practice and usage of war, circumstanced as he was, were against the indulgence. * * *

I have now the pleasure to communicate the names of the three persons who captured Major André and who refused to release him, notwithstanding the most earnest importunities and assurances of a liberal reward, on his part. Their conduct merits our warmest esteem; and I beg leave to add that I think the public will do well to make them a handsome gratuity. They have prevented, in all probability our suffering one of the severest strokes that could have been meditated against us. Their names are John Paulding, David Williams and Isaac Van Wart.

I have the honour, etc., etc., G. WASHINGTON.

Congress acted on the suggestion, settling a pension of $200 on each, and giving each a farm of two hundred acres in addition. They were also offered captaincies in the army, but declined them.

Two letters, written subsequent to the event, may be quoted here, to preserve and complete the continuity of the narrative. The first is from Clinton to Washington. It was never sent, news of the execution having arrived:

New York, Oct. 4, 1780.

Sir,—I conceived I could not better or more fully express my sentiments in answer to your Excellency's letter of the 30th September respecting Major André, than by sending Lieut. Gen. Robertson to converse, if possible, with you, Sir; or at least with some confidential officer from you. I cannot think Lieutenant General Robertson's conversation with General Green has entirely answered the purpose for which I wished this meeting. General Green's letter of the second instant to General Robertson expresses that he had repeated to you, Sir, as far as memory served, the discourse that had passed between them, and that it had not produced any alteration in your opinion or determination concerning Major André.

---

8 A French soldier, Pierre Besançon, who came with Lafayette, was probably the last survivor of those present. He died at Warsaw, New York, in 1855.

9 Simms.

André has met his fate, and with that fortitude which was to be expected from an accomplished man and a gallant officer.—*Washington* (*Gordon*, Hist. Am. War, page 134).

Never did a man suffer death with more justice, or deserve it less. There was something singularly interesting in the character and fortunes of André. To an excellent understanding, well improved by education and travel, he united a peculiar elegance of mind and manners, and the advantage of a pleasing person.—*Hamilton*.

From the few days of intimate intercourse I had with him, I became so deeply attached to Major André that I could remember no instance where my affections were so fully absorbed by any man.—*Tallmadge*.

He behaved with so much frankness and courage that I could not help lamenting his unhappy fate. It is impossible to express too much respect or too much regret for Major André.—*Lafayette*.

This brave, accomplished officer was yesterday hanged—not a single spectator but pitied his untimely fate.—*Scammell*.

He was more unfortunate than criminal.—*Washington*.

The gold watch, of which he had been deprived at Tarrytown, and which we have noticed had been restored at Tappan, was now sold by the captors to Lieutenant Colonel Wm. S. Smith, Thirteenth Massachusetts (one of Washington's Aids), for £30. It was intended to be sent to the family in England, but it seems never to have reached them.

I have, Sir, most carefully re-perused your letter of September thirtieth, which contains indeed an opinion of a Board of your General Officers, but in no respect any opinion or determination of your Excellency.

I must remain therefore, altogether at a loss what they may be, until you are so good as to inform me, which I make no doubt of your Excellency's doing immediately. I will, Sir, in the meantime very freely declare my sentiments upon this occasion, which positively are, that under no description Major André can be considered as a spy; nor by any usage of nations at war, or the customs of armies, can he be treated as such. That officer went at Major General Arnold's request from me to him, at that time in the American service and Commanding officer at West Point. A flag of truce was sent to receive Major André with which he went on shore and met General Arnold.

To this period he was acting under my immediate orders as a military man. What happened after was from the entire direction and positive orders of Major General Arnold, your officer commanding at West Point: and Major André travelled in this way to New York, with pass-ports from that American General Officer who had an undoubted right to grant them. And here it may be necessary to observe that Major André was stopped upon the road, and on Neutral Ground, and made a prisoner two days prior to Major General Arnold's quitting the American service at West Point.

From all of which I have a right to assert, that Major André can merely be considered as a messenger, and not as a spy. He visited no Posts, made no Plans, held no conversation with any person save Major General Arnold; and the papers found upon him were written in that General officer's own hand-writing, who directed Major André to receive and deliver them to me.

From these circumstances, I have no doubt but you, Sir, will see this matter in the same point of view with me, and will be extremely cautious of producing a precedent which may render the future progress of this unhappy war liable to a want of that humanity which I am willing to believe your Excellency possesses, and which I have always pursued.

I trust, Sir, to your good sense and to your liberality, for a speedy release of Major André who, I am free to own, is an officer I extremely value and a Gentleman I very sincerely regard.

I enclose to you, Sir, a list of persons, among whom is a Gentleman who acted as the American Lieutenant-Governor of South Carolina. A discovered conspiracy and correspondence with General Gates's army, have been a reason for removing these persons from Charleston to St. Augustine. Being desirous to promote the release of Major André upon any reasonable terms, I offer to you, Sir, this Lieutenant Governor, Mr. Gadson,[1] for my Adjutant General, or will make a military exchange for him should you, Sir, prefer it. Lieutenant General Robertson in his report to me, mentions his having requested from your Excellency a copy of Major André's letter to you, Sir, upon which seems grounded great matter of charge against him — given, as if that letter might be considered as confession of his guilt as a spy. I have waited until this evening with some impatience for the copy of the Letter I mention, not doubting but your Excellency will send it to me.

I have now to request you will, Sir, do so, and I shall pay it every due consideration and give your Excellency my answer upon it immediately.

I have the honour to be, etc.,

H. CLINTON.

---

1 Christopher Gadsden.

Vulture, off Spiken Devil,

October 5, 1780,

Sir,—The account Colonel Robinson has given your Excellency of our transactions during our late excursion, is so full and just in all its particulars that there is very little left for me to add.

But as they have been attended with such fatal consequences to Major André, I hope it will not be held improper if I beg leave to submit my own observations on the subject :—at least so far as they relate to his leaving the *Vulture* and the light I then saw him in. Your Excellency has already been informed that on the night of the 21st September a Mr. Smith came on board with a flag of truce. The substance of his order was for himself and two servants to pass to Dobbs' Ferry and back again. He likewise had a written permission to bring up with him a Mr. John Anderson and boy, and a letter addressed to Colonel Robinson: all of these papers signed B. Arnold. Most of these circumstances I had been previously taught to expect ; and I had also been informed that Major André was the person understood by John Anderson, and that he was to go on shore under that name, to hold a conference with General Arnold. Mr. Smith's powers appeared to be of sufficient authority, and as Major André's going under a fictitious name was at the particular request of the officer from whom they were derived, I saw no reason for supposing he, from that circumstance, forfeited his claim to the protection they must otherwise have afforded him. Clear I am that the matter must have appeared in the same light to him ; for had it not, measures might have been concerted for taking him off whenever he pleased, which he very well knew I, at any time, was enabled to accomplish. I am likewise persuaded that Mr. Smith's ideas perfectly coincided with ours ;—for when on the point of setting off Colonel Robinson observed, that as they had but two men in a large boat, they would find some difficulty in getting on shore,—and proposed that one of ours should tow them in some part of the way : to which he objected, as it might, in case of falling in with any of their guard-boats, be deemed an infringement of the flag.

On my first learning from Major André that he did not intend going on shore in his own name, it immediately occurred to me, that an alteration of dress might likewise be necessary ; and I offered him a plain blue coat of mine for that purpose, which he declined accepting, as he said he had the Commander in Chief's direction to go in his uniform, and by no means to give up his character, adding, at the same time, that he had not the smallest apprehension on the occasion, and that he was ready to attend General Arnold's summons when and where he pleased.

The night the flag was first expected, he expressed much anxiety for its arrival ; and all next day was full of fear lest anything should have happened to prevent its coming. The instant it arrived on the ensuing night, he started out of bed, and discovered the greatest impatience to be gone : nor did he in any instance betray the least doubt of his safety or success. I own I was equally confident. Nor can I now, on the most mature consideration of circumstances, find the least reason for altering my opinion. What, therefore, could possibly have given rise to so tragical an event as has unhappily befallen Major André is a matter of the utmost surprise and concern to me.

I have the honour, etc., etc.,

A. SUTHERLAND.

To His Excellency

Sir Henry Clinton.

While the army was subsequently encamped at Verplanck's Point, the captors were asked to dinner by Washington, and the silver medals awarded by Congress were presented to them. Washington also gave each a sword and pair of pistols, telling them they "might expect to be hunted like partridges." It is said their lives were more than once attempted by Tories, but all died in their beds—Paulding at Peekskill, February 18, 1818; Van Wart at Greenburgh, May 1, 1828, and Williams at Broome, Schoharie County, August 2, 1830. (A monument was erected to his memory at Old Fort, where he is buried.)

A curious incident in connection with Van Wart's funeral is found in a letter from Edward G. W. Butler, published in the New York *Sun*, October 10, 1879. Butler was a West Point graduate and served in the Mexican War. His statement was that while a cadet, he was one of a party sent to bury Van Wart with the honors of war. He further says his own mother was a cousin of André, "being a daughter of the British grenadier officer who three times led the forces up Bunker Hill."[1]

Captain Partridge, on his visit in 1818, found the grave marked by head and foot stones, neither inscribed. These had disappeared in 1850, and a small boulder, lettered: "André Executed, Oct. 2, 1780," had replaced them,[2] but this too, disappeared in the course of time before the Vandal's hammer and chisel, and for many years the spot was unmarked, save by a heap of stones.

The news of the execution produced a great effect on Clinton and his army.[3] Clinton thus announced the event:

Head Quarters, New York, October 8.

The Commander in Chief does with infinite regret inform the army of the death of the Adjutant General, Major André. The unfortunate fate of this officer calls upon the Commander-in-chief to declare that he ever considered Major André a gentleman as well as, in the line of his military profession, of the highest integrity and honor, and incapable of any base action or unworthy conduct. Major André's death is very severely felt by the Commander-in-chief, as it assuredly will be by the army; and must prove a real loss to the country and to His Majesty's service.

André's commission was sold, as he had requested, by Clinton, for the benefit of his mother and sisters. George III. gave £1,000 to his mother and a pension of £300 was settled on his sisters (the last of whom died single in 1845). The King also ordered the army to wear mourning, and caused a monument[4] to be erected in the South Aisle of Westminster Abbey, near the Poets' Corner, and in 1821 André's remains were buried nearby.

While stationed in New York in 1777, André had made his will. It reads:

---

[1] Who was this? I cannot identify him.

[2] Lossing (*Two Spies*) says this was set up by James Lee, a merchant, of New York.

[3] Simcoe had, [4] Peter Van Schaack says, page 81.

See plate 64: John Paulding's Monument
See plate 65: André Monument, Westminster Abbey

The following is my last Will and Testament, and I appoint as Executors thereto, Mary Louisa André, my Mother; Andrew Giraudot, my Uncle; John Lewis André, my Uncle. To each of the above Executors I give Fifty Pounds. I give to Mary Hannah André my Sister, Seven Hundred Pounds. I give to Ann Marguerite André my Sister, Seven Hundred Pounds. I give to Louisa Katharine André, my Sister, Seven Hundred Pounds. I give to William Lewis André my Brother, seven Hundred Pounds. But the conditions on which I give the above-mentioned Sums to my four Sisters and brother, are that each of them shall pay to Mary Louisa André, my Mother, the sum of Ten Pounds yearly during her Life. I give to Walter Ewer, Jun'r, of Dyer's Court, Aldermanbury, One Hundred Pounds. I give to John Ewer, jun'r, of Lincoln's Inn, One Hundred Pounds. I desire a Ring, value Fifty Pounds, to be given to my friend Peter Boissier, of the Eleventh Dragoons. I desire that Walter Ewer Jr. of Dyer's Court, Aldermanbury, have the inspection of my Papers, Letters, Manuscripts. I mean that he have the first inspection of them, with Liberty to destroy or detain whatever he thinks proper, and I desire my watch[1] to be given to him. And I lastly give and bequeath to my brother John Lewis André the residue of all my effects whatsoever.

Witness my hand and seal, Staten Island, in the Province of N. York, N. America, the 7th June, 1777.

JOHN ANDRÉ,
Capt'n in 26th Regt. of Foot.

N. B. The currency alluded to in this will is sterling money of Great Britain. I desire nothing more than my wearing apparel be sold by public auction.

J. A.

Remarks.

There were no witnesses to the will, and (so) it could not be proved, but on the 9th of October, 1780, Henry White and William Seaton,[2] Esqs., both of the city of New

---

[3] Simcoe had his legion adopt black and white cockades in mourning, and Arnold vented his chagrin in a characteristic letter to Washington:

Sir,—The wanton execution of a gallant British officer in cold blood, may be only the prelude to further butcheries on the same ill-fated occasion. Necessity compelled me to leave behind me in your camp a wife and offspring, that are endeared to me by every sacred tie.

If any violence be offered to them, remember I will revenge their wrongs in a deluge of American blood.

Yours, etc.,

New York,   B. ARNOLD.

October 5, 1780.

No reply was vouchsafed to this.—*Upcott Papers*, vi., page 65.

Mrs. Arnold was safely conveyed to Philadelphia, Major Franks escorting her.

Elias Boudinot, the American Commissary of prisoners—who was afterwards the first President of the American Bible Society—says Clinton shut himself up for three days on receipt of the news.

[4] Peter Van Schaack says he saw Arnold and his wife, visiting the Abbey, stop and view the monument.—Van Schaack's *Life of Peter Van Schaack*, page 147.

The *Gentleman's Magazine*, July, 1801, records that Arnold died in Gloucester Place, London, June 14, 1801, and on the 21st was buried at Brompton. But Mr. Everard Home Coleman, of London, informs me (1899) that he has more than once tried to find his grave, without success.

As we have seen, André had a gold and a silver one. It was the first one Colonel Smith bought, and sent to Robertson for the family in England. Yet in 1885 Bangs, Merwin and Co., of New York, sold at auction a gold watch, which they guaranteed to be the original one, to a purchaser unknown to them, giving the name of Peabody. I have been unable to trace it. It would be interesting to know how and why it never reached England. This watch was exhibited at the Philadelphia Centennial, and was later owned by Mr. Gabriel Furman, of East Orange, N. J. André's pocket-book in some unknown manner came into the hands of Joshua Barrell, of Bridgewater, Mass., and is now in the collection of the Connecticut Historical Society, Hartford.

[2] This was **William Seton,** afterwards the first cashier (1784-1794) of the Bank of New York. He was a noted loyalist, but remained in the city after the British left. He was the last person to hold the office of Notary Public under a British appointment.

See plate 66: André's Chair

York, appeared before Cary Ludlow, surrogate of the city, and declared that they were well acquainted with the handwriting of John André, formerly Capt. of the 26th Regiment, and since Adjutant General, deceased, and they believed that the before-written instrument, purporting to be his last will and testament, was his own and proper handwriting. Their declaration is signed by the Surrogate.[1]

The original will cannot now be found in the New York Surrogate's office.[2]

For forty years the grave on "André Hill" remained undisturbed. Soldiers of the Revolution, who dwelt in Tappan, and peaceful citizens who had witnessed the death of its inmate, oft told the story to the generation born after the second war with Great Britain. No spot in the county, indeed in the State, was better known or more accurately identified.[3] In 1820, the head and footstones of Captain Partridge's visit had disappeared, and but a heap of stones and a peach tree planted by the hands of a sympathizing woman, marked the spot. In 1821, at the instance of Mr. James Buchanan, British Consul at New York, the Duke of York — Queen Victoria's uncle, and Commander of the British Army — asked permission of Governor De Witt Clinton to remove the remains to England. This being granted[4] a British man-of-war, commanded by Captain Paul, conveyed the Consul and a small party of friends up the Hudson to Dobbs' Ferry, on August 10, 1821. It was a significant fact, that no British armed vessel had been in those waters since the close of the Revolution (nor has any such been there since). At Dobbs' Ferry the party disembarked and proceeded to Tappan by way of Sneeden's landing, opposite the Ferry, and were met by Rev. John Demarest, of Tappan, owner of the land where was the grave. Mr. Buchanan's account says:

> We proceeded up a narrow lane to the opening into the field, which led to an elevated spot[5] on the hill, commanding a view of the surrounding country for miles. General Washington's headquarters was fully in view. The field was cultivated, but

---

[1] *N. E. Genealogical and Antiquarian Register*, Vol. vi. (January, 1852). Collateral descendants of André are (1899) living in England. I have just read a letter from Mr. John Lewis André, the grandson of his uncle and executor, who resides at Horsham, Surrey. André's sisters lived for many years at No. 23 Circus, Bath, England, where Louisa Katharine died, on Christmas Day, 1835, eighty-one years old, and Mary Hannah, on March 3, 1845, at ninety-three (of the third sister, Ann Marguerite, I have no details). The two were buried at Bathhampton, near Bath.

Notes and Queries (London), January 15, 1870, says that André, while a prisoner at Albany (?), painted the portraits of his parents, and that this painting is in the possession of the family of Major General Cuyler, of Uitenhage, Cape Colony — that General Cuyler's father (?) had been Mayor of Albany. This cannot be verified.

[2] Mr. John Schuyler, the former Secretary of the New York Society of the Cincinnati, makes a singular error in saying the will was filed at Tappan. (History of the Society, New York, 1886.) I have copied the will from Lossing.

[3] It was reserved for an anonymous writer of 1890, in compiling a railroad guide, to gravely assure the public that "contrary to the general belief, André was not hanged, but shot" (!)—and for the Rev. S. Reynolds Hole (Canon Hole), of England, to repeat the blunder in 1898. As the latter writer visited the United States in 1893, his error is the more remarkable. Such assertions are fairly entitled to *Mr. Boffin's* characterization of "scarers in print."

[4] When it is considered that the war of 1812 had ended only six years before, and that its memories, with those of 1776, and of the kidnapping of our seamen and their cruel treatment in Dartmoor Prison, culminating in the "Dartmoor Massacre," were fresh in the minds of our people, I think this consent was magnanimous.   [5] Captain Partridge says, page 83.

around the grave the plough had not approached nearer than three or four yards, that space being covered with loose stones thrown upon and around the grave, which was only indicated by two cedar trees about ten feet high. A small peach tree had also been planted at the head of the grave. As soon as the stones were cleared away, not a tongue moved amongst the multitude[1] — breathless anxiety was depicted on every countenance. * * * * The earth was removed with the hands, as we soon discovered the coffin-lid was broken in the centre. With great care this was removed, and there lay the bones in perfect order. The roots of the peach tree had completely surrounded the skull, like a net.[2] After allowing all to pass around and view the remains as they lay, which very many[3] did, with unfeigned tears and lamentations,[4] the bones were carefully removed and placed in the sarcophagus of mahogany, lined with crimson velvet (which had been provided by order of the Duke of York). * * * * I did not find a single button, nor any article, save a leather string[5] that had tied the hair, in perfect preservation, coiled and tied as it had been on his hair at the time. This I forwarded to his sisters in England.[6] * * * * The sarcophagus was borne amid the silent and unbought regret of the numerous assemblage, to Mr. Demarest's house, with the intention of removing it to His Majesty's packet on the Tuesday following.[7]

The peach tree was dug up and taken to London, where it was replanted in the King's garden behind Carlton House. The two cedars were also sent to London, and from the wood of one the Duke of York had a snuff box[8] made,

[5] Captain Partridge says the place is 200 feet above tide in the Hudson, and 123 feet above the floor of André's room.

[1] Although Mr. Buchanan does not mention it, the pastor of the Dutch church, Rev. Nicholas Lansing, was present, and Rev. Dr. Cole informs me that he is tolerably positive that he was told, in his boyhood, that a brief religious service was conducted by Dr. L. Some writers say the Duke of York was present. This is impossible. He was never in the United States.

[2] An instance, similar to this curious circumstance, may be recalled in the fact that when, a number of years since, the grave of Roger Williams was opened in Providence, R. I., his skeleton was found entwined with the roots of an apple tree that had grown near the grave.—*Wm. L. Stone, to the Author.*

[3] There were then living in Tappan many persons who, as young people (and some also as soldiers) had witnessed the execution. Some of those to whom they told the story of 1780 are yet living. One is Rev. Dr. David Cole (now of Yonkers), son of the then pastor of the Dutch Church at Tappan. From him I have received much information.

[4] *Cf.* Thacher's words, forty-one years before, "The tears of thousands fell on the spot where he lay." As Dr. Thacher was living at this time, and until 1844, it is to be regretted he was not present on this memorable occasion.

[5] Mr. Buchanan had supposed André was buried in his uniform, and complained bitterly that the historic statement of Dr. Thacher to that effect was false. But in 1834 Dr. Thacher wrote him that, while he had so stated, he had not waited to see the actual interment, and that the subsequent statement which I credit to "Baldwin" (that the uniform was given to Laune) was doubtless correct. The Consul accepted the explanation, and had the Doctor's letter published in the *United Service Journal*, of London, and its substance in the New York *Albion*, March 7, 1834.
Why Dr. Thacher delayed writing it until 1834 is not explained.

[6] "Some locks of his hair remained, which were sent to his sisters. The string which tied his hair is in possession of the Dean of Westminster."—Stanley, *Historical Memoirs or Westminster Abbey*, II., page 93.

[7] This part of the plan seems not to have been carried out, as they were actually conveyed to Portsmouth by the frigate *Phaeton*, Captain W. C. Montague. She arrived there in October. The remains were interred in Westminster Abbey—in the presence of a representative of the War Department, and of Mr. Locker, Secretary of Greenwich Hospital (and father of the late Frederick Locker, the poet), who attended on behalf of André's sisters. In 1840 Grant Thorburn wrote in the *Knickerbocker Magazine:* "I had an ardent desire to handle the skull which had once contained such mighty projects. I obtained an order from the Consul, and boarded the frigate, taking with me a handsome myrtle plant, which I placed on the lid of the sarcophagus. This was carried to London, planted and flourished, and many persons of note had cuttings from it, as it was known as 'André's myrtle.' When I held André's skull in my hands I observed that the root of a tree had penetrated the bone on one side and come out on the other."

[8] Now owned by, page 84.

lined with gold, which he sent to Mr. Demarest in recognition of his services. André's sisters also sent him a silver cup, suitably inscribed.

After the exhumation the grave was refilled, and once more the field where the historic drama had been enacted that October day was left lonely and uncared for, save for the placing of the inscribed boulder, noted on page 80, until 1879. Ninety-nine years after André's death Dean Stanley visited the United States, and was the guest of Cyrus W. Field, at Irvington. At his suggestion Mr. Field erected a monument to mark the spot of execution.[1] Its erection, or inscription, gave offence to some Socialists, one of whom, Hendrix[2] by name, blew it up with dynamite. A second met the same fate. The inscription on it reads:

Here died, October 2, 1780,
MAJOR JOHN ANDRÉ of the British Army,
who, entering the American lines
on a secret mission to Benedict Arnold
for the surrender of West Point,
was taken prisoner, tried and condemned as a spy.
His death,
though according to the stern code of war,
moved even his enemies to pity;
and both armies mourned the fate
of one so young and so brave.
In 1821 his remains were removed to
Westminster Abbey.
A hundred years after the execution
this stone was placed above the spot where he lay,
by a citizen of the United States against which he fought,
not to perpetuate the record of strife,
but in token of those better feelings
which have since united two nations,
one in race, in language and in religion,
in the hope that the friendly understanding
will never be broken.

ARTHUR PENRHYN STANLEY,
Dean of Westminster.

He was more unfortunate than criminal.

GEORGE WASHINGTON.

Sunt lachrymæ rerum et mentem mortalia tangunt.

ÆNEID, Book I., line 462.

---

8 Now owned by Rev. John Demarest's daughter, Mrs. James I. Blauvelt, Paterson, N. J. It is also stated by Mr. Buchanan that "André's watch" was "recovered" and sent to his sisters. It is not stated from whom it was "recovered." The history of the watches is decidedly obscure.

1 Representatives of the New York and Rockland Counties Historical societies, and many other guests, were present at the unveiling of the monument. In 1878 there were living three men who had witnessed the exhumation of André's remains—David D. Brower, John J. Griffiths and John H. Outwater. Through their testimony, Mr. Henry Whittemore, Secretary of the Rockland County Society, had identified the spot where the execution took place, and the monument was placed there.

2 He met a violent death in Brooklyn in 1884.

The line from the Æneid, literally translated, is, "Here are tears for our affections, and human calamities touch the mind." In Conington's translation it is thus rendered:

E'en here the tear of pity springs
And hearts are touched by human things.

When my first visit was made, the monument, which is of polished granite 7½ x 5 x 3 feet, was lying on its side, and of its foundation only a few bricks remained, but it has since been re-erected. The whole is surrounded by an iron railing.

Aside from the historic interest of the place, the view from and around it is charming. East and north the country is well wooded, yet dotted with small farms. Northeast, across the Hudson, are the Tarrytown heights, and the Captors' Monument. Haverstraw, Stony Point and King's Ferry are a few miles above, and as the tourist stands on the scene of the last act of the tragedy, Dobbs' Ferry, where lay the *Greyhound* with Robertson and his companions aboard, that eventful October day, is directly east and almost in sight. The visitor of any sentiment instinctively recalls Dr. Johnson's words about Marathon and adapts them to the scene before him: "That man is little to be envied whose patriotism would not gain force upon the plain of "—Tappan.

See plate 67: André Monument, Tappan

APPENDIX.

THE ITINERARY.

1780.

SEPTEMBER	10.	(*Sunday*)	Arnold visits Smith at Haverstraw to arrange matters.
"	11.	(*Monday*)	Arnold goes by boat to near Dobbs' Ferry, is fired on and narrowly escapes.
"	13.	(*Wednesday*)	Writes André to meet him on the 20th.
"	18.	(*Monday*)	Writes to Robinson.
"	19.	(*Tuesday*)	The dinner to Clinton at Kip's house. Arnold spends that night at Smith's house.
"	20.	(*Wednesday*)	Arnold returns to his quarters, with his wife. André spends all day on the *Vulture*, expecting Arnold.
"	21.	(*Thursday*) (Morning)	Arnold returns to Haverstraw and coerces the Colquhoun brothers.
"	"	(Midnight)	Smith goes aboard the *Vulture*.
"	22.	(*Friday*) (Just past midnight)	Smith brings André ashore at Long Clove.
"	"	(*Friday*) (Almost dawn)	André and Arnold ride to Smith's house.
"	"	(*Friday*) (Day break)	Colonel Livingston opens fire on the *Vulture*.
"	"	(*Friday*) (Before 10 A. M.)	Arnold returns to his quarters.
"	"	(*Friday*) (Up to about 5 P. M.)	André remains at Smith's house.
"	"	(*Friday*) (5 P. M.)	André, guided by Smith, rides to King's Ferry.
		(*Friday*) (8.30 P. M.)	Being stopped by Captain Ebenezer Boyd, Second Westchester Militia, they pass the night at house of Andreas Miller, four miles east of Peekskill.
"	23.	(*Saturday*) (Dawn)	The journey resumed, they are stopped at Crompond Corner by Captain Ebenezer Foote, of the Commissary Department, but allowed to proceed.
"	"	(*Saturday*) (Daylight to 9.30)	At home of Isaac Underhill, 3½ miles from Crompond Corner, they have breakfast. Smith parts from André and goes to Arnold's headquarters. André proceeds over Pine's Bridge in direction of Dobbs' Ferry. In Chappaqua he enquires his way of Stevenson Thorne, and in Pleasantville waters his horse opposite Sylvanus Brundage's house. At house of Staats Hammond, Pleasantville, he learns of the scouts at Young's Tavern, below, and retraces his path to Mekeel's Corners.

1780.

SEPTEMBER	23.	(*Saturday*) (9.30 or 11)	Reaches Tarrytown and is captured.
"	"	(*Saturday*) (About noon)	The march towards Jameson's headquarters. First stop at the Reed Tavern, East Tarrytown, where André has bread and milk — next at Foshay house, below Kensico, and third at Reuben Wright's, at Kensico.
"	"	(*Saturday*) (About 5)	Arrival at Jameson's headquarters, Sands Mills, Armonk, twelve miles from Tarrytown. Jameson sends him on towards Arnold.
"	"	(*Saturday*) (Late at night)	Major Tallmadge returns from outpost duty, and urges that he be brought back.
"	24.	(*Sunday*) (8 A. M.)	André is returned to Sands Mills. Tallmadge meets him there.
"	"	(*Sunday*) (Uncertain hour)	He is taken to Sheldon's headquarters at South Salem, in Gilbert house, and meets Lieutenant King and Dr. Bronson.
"	"	(*Sunday*) (Noon)	Smith dines in Washington's company at Fishkill.
"	25.	(*Monday*) (Breakfast)	Arnold, at the Robinson House, receives the letter announcing André's arrest, and escapes.
"	"	(*Monday*) (4 to 6 P. M.)	Washington orders André to be sent to the Robinson House.
"	"	(*Monday*) (Midnight)	{ Smith arrested at Fishkill and taken to the Robinson House. { André taken from Sheldon's quarters, under a strong escort, during heavy
"	26.	(*Tuesday*) (At Dawn)	rain, and reaches the Robinson House. The day is passed there.
"	27.	(*Wednesday*)	André and Smith are taken to West Point.
"	28.	(*Thursday*)	Both are taken by boat to Stony Point (King's Ferry), and by land towards Tappan.
"	"	(*Thursday*) (noon)	They dine at Coe's Tavern, Hempstead, and
"	"	(*Thursday*) (afternoon)	reach Tappan.
"	"	(*Thursday*) (later)	Washington also arrives and orders a court martial.
"	29.	(*Friday*)	The court finds André guilty.
"	30.	(*Saturday*)	Washington approves the sentence, and orders André to be hung on October 1st, at 5 P. M.
OCTOBER	1.	(*Sunday*) (Noon)	Clinton's committee — Elliot, Robinson and Smith — come up to Dobbs' Ferry, and the execution is postponed one day.
"	2.	(*Monday*) (Noon)	**ANDRÉ EXECUTED.**

1821.

AUGUST	10.	His remains disinterred and taken to Halifax, N. S.
OCTOBER	—	Taken to England in the frigate *Phaeton*.
NOVEMBER	—	Interred in Westminster Abbey.

HOW STANDS THE GLASS AROUND?

THE writer and composer of this song are unknown. It appeared as a broadside in **1710**. In 1729 it was produced at a little theatre in the Hay Market, London, under the title "Why, Soldiers, why?" in "The Patron, or the Statesman's Opera." Collections made in 1775 have both words and music, and Shield introduced the song into "The Siege of Gibralter." It is usually called "General Wolfe's song," and is said to have been sung by him on the eve of the battle of Quebec. There is a story, which seems to be authentic, that as his night expedition against the city was floating down the St. Lawrence, he repeated several stanzas from Gray's "Elegy," and remarked that he "would rather have written that poem than take Quebec to-morrow." It is not unlikely that this anecdote, together with the fact that he had sometimes sung "How stands the glass around?" was what gave rise to the story which makes it his death-song.

Harmonized by Edward S. Cummings.

QUARTETTE.

1. How stands the glass a - round? For shame! ye take no care, my boys; How stands the glass a - round? Let mirth and wine a - bound! May we still be found Con - tent with our hard fate, my boys, On the cold ground!

2. Why, sol - diers, why, Should we be mel - an - cho - ly, boys? Why, sol - diers, why? Whose bus - i - ness 'tis to die! Cold, hot, wet, or dry, We're always bound to fol-low, boys, And scorn to fly!

3. 'Tis but in vain— I mean not to up - braid you, boys—'Tis but in vain For sol - diers to com - plain. But, if we re - main, A bot - tle and a kind landlady Cure all a - gain!

SOLO.

The trum - pets sound:— the col - ors they are fly - ing, boys—To fight, kill, or wound,
What! sigh - ing? fie! Don't fear; drink on; be jol - ly, boys! 'Tis he, you, or I!
Should next cam - paign Send us to Him who made us, boys, We're free from pain;

QUARTETTE.

ROSLIN CASTLE.

(So-called, but differing from the present-day air.)

THE "BLEW" BIRD.

(Written before 1800.)

(Copied from a manuscript collection in the Drexel Musical Library, belonging to the New York Public Library, Lenox Branch.)

(FOR FIFE OR FLUTE.)

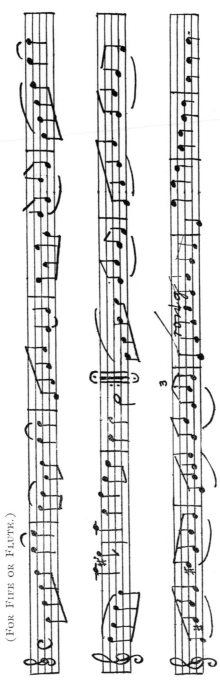

(The original copyist seems in part astray in his notation of a few notes, as is evident from the insertion of the word "rong.")

The following poem was written by Major André after the attack of Wayne upon a block-house, near Bull's Ferry. The last canto was published in Rivington's *Gazette*, on the day when André was captured at Tarrytown. I copied this from an original copy in the handwriting of André himself; and I made a facsimile of the last stanza as it appears in that copy. It is written upon small folio paper, and under the endorsement of André himself are the following lines:

—*Lossing*.

"When the epic strain was sung,
The poet by the neck was hung;
And to his cost he finds too late,
The *dung-born tribe* decides his fate."

Elizabethtown, Aug. 1, 1780.

CANTO I.

1 To drive the kine one summer's morn,
    The tanner took his way,
  The calf shall rue that is unborn
    The jumbling of that day.

2 And Wayne descending steers shall know,
    And tauntingly deride,
  And call to mind, in ev'ry low,
    The tanning of his hide.

3 Yet Bergen cows still ruminate
    Unconscious in the stall,
  What mighty means were used to get,
    And lose them after all.

4 For many heroes bold and brave
    From New Bridge and Tapaan,
  And those that drink Passaic's wave,
    And those that eat soupaan.

5 And sons of distant Delaware,
    And still remoter Shannon,
  And Major Lee with horses rare,
    And Proctor with his cannon.

6 All wondrous proud in arms they came—
    What hero could refuse,
  To tread the rugged path to fame,
    Who had a pair of shoes?

7 At six the host, with sweating buff,
    Arrived at Freedom's Pole,
  When Wayne, who thought he'd time enough,
    Thus speechified the whole :

8 "O ye whom glory doth unite,
    Who Freedom's cause espouse,
  Whether the wing that's doomed to fight,
    Or that to drive the cows ;

9 Ere yet you tempt your further way,
    Or into action come,
  Hear, soldiers, what I have to say,
    And take a pint of rum.

10 Intemp'rate valor then will string
    Each nervous arm the better,
  So all the land shall IO ! sing,
    And read the gen'ral's letter.

11 Know that some paltry refugees,
    Whom I've a mind to fight,
  Are playing h—l among the trees
    That grow on yonder height.

12 Their fort and block-house we'll level,
    And deal a horrid slaughter ;
  We'll drive the scoundrels to the devil,
    *　　*　　*　　*　　*　　*

13 I under cover of th' attack,
    Whilst you are all at blows,
  From English Neighb'rhood and Tinack
    Will drive away the cows.

14 For well you know the latter is
    The serious operation,
  And fighting with the refugees
    Is only demonstration."

15 His daring words from all the crowd
    Such great applause did gain,
  That every man declared aloud
    For serious work with Wayne.

16 Then from the cask of rum once more
    They took a heady gill,
  When one and all they loudly swore
    They'd fight upon the hill.

17 But here—the muse has not a strain
    Befitting such great deeds,
  Hurra, they cried, hurra for Wayne !
    And shouting　　*　　*　　*

CANTO 2.

18 Near his meridian pomp, the sun
    Had journey'd from the horizon,
  When fierce the dusky tribe mov'd on,
    Of heroes drunk as poison.

19 The sounds confused of boasting oaths,
    Re-echoed through the wood,
  Some vow'd to sleep in dead men's clothes,
    And some to swim in blood.

20 At Irvine's nod, 'twas fine to see
    The left prepared to fight,
  The while the drovers, Wayne and Lee,
    Drew off upon the right.

21 Which Irvine 'twas Fame don't relate,
    Nor can the Muse assist her,
  Whether 'twas he that cocks a hat,
    Or he that gives a glister.

22 For greatly one was signalized,
    That fought at Chestnut Hill,
  And Canada immortalized
    The vender of the pill.

23 Yet the attendance upon Proctor
    They both might have to boast of ;
  For there was business for the doctor,
    And hats to be disposed of.

24 Let none uncandidly infer
    That Stirling wanted spunk,
  The self-made peer had sure been there,
    But that the peer was drunk.

25 But turn we to the Hudson's banks,
    Where stood the modest train,
  With purpose firm, though slender ranks,
    Nor car'd a pin for Wayne.

26 For them the unrelenting hand
    Of rebel fury drove,
  And tore from ev'ry genial band
    Of friendship and of love.

27 And some within a dungeon's gloom,
    By mock tribunals laid,
  Had waited long a cruel doom,
    Impending o'er their heads.

28 Here one bewails a brother's fate,
    There one a sire demands,
  Cut off, alas ! before their date,
    By ignominious hands.

29 And silver'd grandsires here appear'd
    In deep distress serene,
  Of reverend manners that declared
    The better days they'd seen.

30 Oh ! curs'd rebellion, these are thine,
    Thine are these tales of woe ;
  Shall at thy dire insatiate shrine
    Blood never cease to flow ?

31 And now the foe began to lead
    His forces to th' attack ;
  Balls whistling unto balls succeed,
    And make the block-house crack.

32 No shot could pass, if you will take
       The gen'ral's word for true ;
    But 'tis a d—ble mistake,
       For ev'ry shot went through.

33 The firmer as the rebels pressed,
       The loyal heroes stand ;
    Virtue had nerv'd each honest breast,
       And Industry each hand.

34 In valor's phrensy, Hamilton
       Rode like a soldier big,
    And secretary Harrison,
       With pen stuck in his wig.

35 But, lest chieftain Washington
       Should mourn them in the mumps,
    The fate of Withrington to shun,
       They fought *behind* the stumps.

36 But ah ! Thaddeus Posset, why
       Should thy poor soul elope?
    And why should Titus Hooper die,
       Ah ! die—without a rope?

37 Apostate Murphy, thou to whom
       Fair Shela ne'er was cruel ;
    In death shalt hear her mourn thy doom,
       Och ! would ye die, my jewel?

38 Thee, Nathan Pumpkin, I lament,
       Of melancholy fate,
    The gray goose, stolen as he went,
       In his heart's blood was wet.

39 Now as the fight was further fought,
       And balls began to thicken,
    The fray assum'd, the gen'rals thought,
       The color of a licking.

40 Yet undismay'd the chiefs command,
       And, to redeem the day,
    Cry, "Soldiers, charge !" they hear, they stand,
       They turn and run away.

CANTO 3.

41 Not all delights the bloody spear,
       Or horrid din of battle,
    There are, I'm sure, who'd like to hear
       A word about the rattle.

42 The chief whom we beheld of late,
       Near Schralenberg haranguing,
    At Yan Van Poop's unconscious sat,
       Of Irvine's hearty banging.

43 While valiant Lee, with courage wild,
       Most bravely did oppose
    The tears of women and of child,
       Who begg'd he'd leave the cows.

44 But Wayne, of sympathizing heart,
       Required a relief,
    Not all the blessings could impart
       Of battle or of beef.

45 For now a prey to female charms,
       His soul took more delight in
    A lovely Hamadryad's arms,
       Than cow driving or fighting.

46 A nymph, the refugees had drove
       Far from her native tree,
    Just happen'd to be on the move,
       When up came Wayne and Lee.

47 She in mad Anthony's fierce eye
       The hero saw portray'd,
    And, all in tears, she took him by
       — the bridle of his jade.

48 Hear, said the nymph, O great commander,
       No human lamentations,
    The trees you see them cutting yonder
       Are all my near relations.

49 And I, forlorn, implore thine aid
       To free the sacred grove ;
    So shall thy prowess be repaid
       With an immortal's love.

50 Now some, to prove she was a goddess !
       Said this enchanting fair,
    Had late retired from the *Bodies*,
       In all the pomp of war.

51 That drums and merry fifes had play'd
       To honor her retreat,
    And Cunningham himself convey'd
       The lady through the street.

52 Great Wayne, by soft compassion sway'd
       To no inquiry stoops,
    But takes the fair, afflicted maid
       Right into Yan Van Poop's.

53 So Roman Anthony, they say,
       Disgraced th' imperial banner,
    And for a gipsy lost a day,
       Like Anthony the tanner.

54 The Hamadryad had but half
       Received redress from Wayne,
    When drums and colors, cow and calf,
       Came down the road amain.

55 All in a cloud of dust were seen,
       The sheep, the horse, the goat,
    The gentle heifer, ass obscene ;
       The yearling and the shoat.

56 And pack-horses with fowls came by,
       Befeathered on each side,
    Like Pegasus, the horse that I
       And other poets ride.

57 Sublime upon the stirrups rose
 The mighty Lee behind,
And drove the terror-smitten cows,
 Like chaff before the wind.

58 But sudden see the woods above
 Pour down another corps,
All helter skelter in a drove,
 Like that I sung before.

59 Irvine and terror in the van,
 Came flying all abroad,
And cannon, colors, horse, and man,
 Ran tumbling to the road.

60 Still as he fled, 'twas Irvine's cry,
 And his example too,
"Run on, my merry men all—for why?"
 The shot will not go through.

61 As when two kennels in the street,
 Swell'd with a recent rain,
In gushing streams together meet,
 And seek the neighboring drain,

62 So meet these dung-born tribes in one,
 As swift in their career,
And so to New Bridge they ran on—
 But all the cows got clear.

63 Poor Parson Caldwell, all in wonder,
 Saw the returning train,
And mourn'd to Wayne the lack of plunder,
 For them to steal again.

64 For 'twas his right to seize the spoil, and
 To share with each commander,
As he had done at Staten Island
 With frost-bit Alexander.

65 In his dismay, the frantic priest
 Began to grow prophetic,
You had swore, to see his lab'ring breast,
 He'd taken an emetic.

66 "I view a future day," said he,
 "Brighter than this day dark is,
And you shall see what you shall see,
 Ha! ha! one pretty marquis;

67 And he shall come to Paulus' Hook,
 And great achievements think on,
And make a bow and take a look,
 Like Satan over Lincoln.

68 And all the land around shall glory
 To see the Frenchman caper,
And pretty Susan tell the story
 In the next Chatham paper."

69 This solemn prophecy, of course,
 Gave all much consolation,
Except to Wayne, who lost his horse
 Upon the great occasion.

70 His horse that carried all his prog,
 His military speeches,
His corn-stalk whisky for his grog—
 Blue stockings and brown breeches.

71 And now I've clos'd my epic strain,
 I tremble as I show it,
Lest this same warrio-drover, Wayne,
 Should ever catch the poet.

And now [~~I have~~] I've clos'd my Epic Strain,
I tremble as I show it,
Lest this same warrio-drover Wayne
Should ever catch the Poet.

Finis

NOTES.

(For some of these notes I am indebted to Lossing's *Two Spies* (D. Appleton & Co., New York), but most are from his *Field-Book*, and a few are original.)

[1] Wayne had been a tanner before the Revolution.

[4] Soupaan, or suppawn, the homely dish of Indian-meal mush and milk then common in the colonies, especially New England. See reference to it on page 23.

[6] Shoes were scarce in Washington's army, at all times.

[7] Freedom's Pole was a little settlement in Bergen County.

¹⁰ In his letter to Congress, July 26, 1780, concerning this expedition, Washington spoke of the American cannon being too light to penetrate the logs of which it (the block-house) was constructed. He also attributed the great loss of the Americans to the "intemperate valor" of the men. André exercised a poetic license in putting these words in Wayne's mouth before the fight.

²¹ History commonly speaks of "the two Irvines" as though they were brothers, or at least relatives. But there is no evidence to prove this. In fact the names are widely different. James "Irvine" is really James Ewing, of Pennsylvania (probably born at Lancaster). He commanded the Flying Camp in 1776, and was distinguished in the fight at Chestnut Hill, near Philadelphia. He it was that was a hatter by trade. William Irvine, a physician, is the one who took part in the attack on the block-house.

²⁴ Lord Stirling (William Alexander) had been frustrated in his attempt to gain a Scotch estate and peerage, to which he was clearly entitled. He assumed the title of Earl of Stirling as of right.

³² Wayne reported the cannon too light for effective work.

³⁴ General Charles Lee, in his testimony at his court martial after the battle of Monmouth, spoke of Hamilton "flourishing his sword and saying, 'I will stay and we will all die here on the spot.'"
"I could not but be surprised," said Lee, "at his expression, but observed him much fluttered, and in a sort of frenzy of valor."
Richard Harrison, Washington's secretary.

³⁵ Mumps were prevalent in the patriot army.
A direct reference to the old ballad of *Chevy Chase:*

> For Witherington needs must I wayle,
> As one in doleful dumps ;
> For when his legges were smitten off,
> He fought upon his stumps.

⁵⁰ "The Bodies"—a soldier's slang word for the royal troops constituting the King's body-guard.

⁵¹ That she was a disreputable woman, who had been drummed out of camp, under guard of the provost-marshal's force. Cunningham was the notorious jailer at New York.

⁵² A dramshop.

⁶³ Rev. James Caldwell, an earnest patriot of New Jersey, pastor of a church at Connecticut Farms. His wife had been shot by a newly-enlisted soldier, in the parsonage, when the British, under Knyphausen, made a raid upon Springfield, in 1778.

⁶⁴ "Calling himself, because ordered not to do it, Earl of Stirling, though no sterling Earl." In a winter expedition to Staten Island, a large proportion of his soldiers were frost-bitten.

⁶⁶ Lafayette.

⁶⁷ Now Jersey City, where the British had a redoubt, which Major Henry Lee surprised in August, 1779, capturing 159 prisoners. (I have never seen explained the allusion to the city of Lincoln.)

⁶⁸ Miss Susannah Livingston, daughter of Governor William Livingston, of New Jersey, who was suspected of political authorship.
Chatham, was Chatham, N. J.
(By a singular coincidence, the signature under André's portrait—my frontispiece—is photographed from his official congratulatory letter, as Deputy Adjutant-General, to Cuyler, the Tory who was Colonel of the refugee corps which defended the block-house. The original letter, one of the most interesting of Revolutionary documents, is in the collection of Dr. Thomas Addis Emmet, who kindly allowed the reproduction of the signature.)

ERRATA.

This item should have appeared on page 4.

The Orderly-Book of Captain E. Stearns' company, Colonel John Rand's Massachusetts regiment, now in the possession of the Massachusetts Historical Society, records: "August 6, 1780: The Honorable General Arnold takes command in this department."

In addition to Note 4, page 9.

Ann Hawkes Hay. A letter from him to General George Clinton, dated July 14, 1776, records, that "on Friday, the 12th, a barge and cutter from the British fleet of one forty and one twenty-gun ship (the *Rose*, Captain Wallace, and *Phœnix*, Captain Parker) with four cutters, anchored opposite Nyack." Hay's regiment was called out, the barge was fired on and driven off.—*American Archives*, Vol. I., 5th Series, pp. 338, 580.

On August 10, 1776, Hay was appointed Commissary of Militia.

On November 30, 1776, General John Morin Scott, writing to Washington, refers to Colonel Hay as "a gentleman uncommonly spirited in the publick cause." (Page 929.)

In addition to Note 6, page 5.

Major Kiers is also referred to in the *American Archives*: His store (Haverstraw) is mentioned, July 19, 1776 (Vol. X., p. 452). On October 10, 1776, he is mentioned as paid £27 11s. 2d. for apprehending deserters (page 236), and the sum of £400 is acknowledged due to him for provisions for the public use (page 338).

This should have made part of Note 5, on page 35.

Samuel Youngs was born in 1760, and died in 1837. He was a well-known figure in Westchester County, and held the office of Surrogate for several terms.

It has been claimed that from him Irving drew the character of *Ichabod Crane.*—M. D. Raymond, *Souvenir*, etc., Tarrytown, 1880.

This should have appeared on page 71.

John Hughes was born in Lancaster County, Pennsylvania, in 1759. His father, Barnabas Hughes, removed to Maryland in 1760, and built an iron foundry near Hagerstown, where in later years was cast much of the cannon and shot used by the Continental army. (The names of two Hughes, Daniel and Samuel, probably his successors, occur frequently in the Maryland records of the Revolution.) At seventeen young Hughes entered the army as lieutenant in Colonel Hazen's regiment (of Pennsylvania) the "Second Canadian," generally known as the Congress regiment, or "Congress's Own." He served with credit, particularly at Brandywine and Germantown, and resigned from the army, as captain, in 1781. He then married Miss Chamberlaine, of Talbot County, Maryland, and settled near Havre de Grace, where he died May 21, 1805, leaving three daughters. When the British captured Havre de Grace, in 1813, the Hughes homestead was burned, with all its contents, and hence no portrait of him is known to exist. He was one of the original members of the Cincinnati. Mr. John Sterett Gittings, of Baltimore, is his great grandson, and to him I am indebted for the autograph shown on page 71.

This should have appeared on page 37.

Benjamin Tallmadge was born in Setauket, Long Island, February 25, 1754, and died in Litchfield, Connecticut, March 7, 1835.

He was a Yale graduate, and a classmate of the unfortunate Nathan Hale. Joining the patriot army in 1775, he served throughout the war, attaining the rank of Colonel, and enjoying the especial favor of Washington. He is supposed to have been the Chief's only confidant in some of the important details of his employment of spies. After the war he was a merchant in Litchfield, and from 1801 to 1817 was a member of Congress. In this capacity he was vehemently opposed to the increasing of the André captors' pensions, claiming that they were not actuated by any motives of patriotism. Although really a native of the state of New York, his identification with Sheldon's, a Connecticut regiment, and his long residence at Litchfield, have usually caused him to be regarded as a native of Connecticut.

Among his many important services during the Revolution, none was attended with greater results than his securing the recall of André when almost in reach of Arnold.

John Hughes: Daniel and Samuel Hughes were the elder brothers of Captain John.

This autograph should have appeared on page 19.

This should have appeared on page 59.

Jedediah Huntington was born in Norwich Conn., August 4, 1743, and died in New London, September 25, 1818. He came of a family distinguished for patriotism, his father, General Jabez Huntington, and his four brothers, taking an active part in the Revolution. He himself raised a regiment, in which he was a captain, which joined Washington's army at Cambridge; and from that time until the end of hostilities he took an active part in its campaigns, attaining the rank of Brevet Major General. After peace was declared he held various positions of trust and honor in his native state, culminating in the Collectorship of New London, to which he was appointed by Washington, in 1789, and which he retained until 1815. He was one of the original members of the Cincinnati.
(As the portraits of most of the members of the André court-martial are well known, I have not thought it necessary to reproduce them. General Huntington's, however, is very scarce, and I am indebted to Dr. Emmet for it. Of General Parsons I believe no portrait exists.)

Sutherland's letter, page 79, should be dated 1780, not 1781.

André's Statement.—On the 20th of September I left New York, to get on board the *Vulture*, in order (as I thought) to meet General Arnold there in the night. No boat, however, came off, and I waited on board until the night of the 21st. * * * * * I went into the boat, landed, and spoke with Arnold. I got on horseback with him to proceed to——† house, and in the way passed a guard I did not expect to see, having Sir Henry Clinton's directions not to go within an enemy's post, or quit my own dress. (The rest corresponds with the general narrative as given.—W. A.)

† Smith's.

This should have appeared as part of note on page 23.

Richard Varick was born in Hackensack, N. J., March 25, 1753, and died in Jersey City, July 30, 1831. Commissioned a Captain in McDougall's New York Regiment in 1775, he rose to the rank of Lieutenant Colonel in 1777 as Deputy Muster-master General. He was an ardent admirer of Arnold's military genius and became his Aid. The discovery of the treason nearly upset his reason (as it did that of Major Franks). He became Recording Secretary to Washington soon afterwards, and after the war was Recorder of New York City (1783-89), and from 1791 to 1801 he was Mayor (the first) of the city. He was many years President of the Merchants' Bank and of the American Bible Society. In all the relations of life he was most exemplary, a model man in both public and private life.

BIBLIOGRAPHY OF MAJOR ANDRÉ.

[This originally appeared in the *Magazine of American History* for January, 1882 (Vol. 8, No. 1), and is the work of Mr. Charles A. Campbell. I have re-arranged it in a form more convenient for reference, and have added a little to it.—W. A.]

BIOGRAPHY.

1. ANDRÉ, MEMOIRS OF MAJOR JOHN. Winthrop Sargent. 12mo. Boston: Ticknor & Fields, 1861.
2. ——, LIFE OF. Cr. 8vo. New York: D. Appleton & Co., 1871. Portraits of author and André. (A reprint, not a revised copy, of the first-named.)
3. ARNOLD, LIFE OF. By Isaac N. Arnold. 12mo. Chicago: A. C. McClurg & Co., 1880. Gives an account in which he endeavors to show the incentives to Arnold's treason. (I. N. Arnold was President of the Chicago Historical Society, and only very remotely connected with the traitor's family.)
4. ——, LIFE AND TREASON OF. Jared Sparks. 16mo. (Vol. 3 of *American Biography*.)
5. ——, TREASON OF. — Atwill. Northampton, Mass., 1836. (A very rare pamphlet.)
6. ——, TREASON OF. Geo. C. Hill. Boston, 1858.
   (For correspondence between Tallmadge and Sparks, see *Magazine of American History*, December, 1879, pp. 247–256. The letters are (1882) in possession of Mary E. Norwood, N. Y.

GENERAL ACCOUNTS.

7. ANDRÉ-ANA. H. W. Smith. 8vo. Phila., 1865. Contains the trial and kindred matter.
8. BANCROFT, HISTORY OF UNITED STATES, Vol. 10, p. 395. He followed "only contemporary documents, which are abundant and of the truest character, and which, taken collectively, solve every question."
9. BOLTON, Rev. R., HISTORY OF WESTCHESTER COUNTY. 1st edition, 1848; 2d edition, 1881.
10. BOYNTON. See No. 40.
11. COOPER, J. FENIMORE, THE TRAVELLING BACHELOR. Gives particulars of Arnold's own statement, from a British officer, and Lafayette's recollections (1824) (and some other matter less reliable.—W. A.).
12. DEARBORN, General H. A., Military Journal.
13. DUNLAP, WILLIAM, HISTORY OF NEW YORK, Vol. 2, ch. 13.
14. EMMET, Dr. THOS. ADDIS, of New York, has an enlarged copy of *Sargent* and *André-ana*, the two being extended to seven volumes thick 8vo, by insertion of a large number of autograph letters, portraits, etc.
15. GREENE, General NATHANAEL, LIFE OF. By Professor Geo. W. Greene. Vol. 2, p. 227.
16. HAMILTON, ALEXANDER, LIFE OF. By John C. Hamilton. Vol. 1, p. 262.

17. HARPER'S MAGAZINE. Vols. 3 and 23. Article by Lossing, May, 1876.
18. HEADLEY, WASHINGTON AND HIS GENERALS. By J. T. Headley.
19. HILDRETH, HISTORY OF UNITED STATES. Vol. 3, ch. 41, gives an outline.
20. HISTORICAL MAGAZINE (Dawson's), Morrisania, New York. August, 1859; August, 1863; Supplement of 1866; December, 1870.
21. HOLLAND, ELIHU G., ESSAYS. Contains a play, entitled "The Highland Treason." (I have not been able to find it.—W. A.)
22. HULL'S REVOLUTIONARY SERVICES. By General Wm. Hull. On André and Nathan Hale.
23. IRVING, LIFE OF WASHINGTON. Vols. 2 and 4. He made use of the MSS. of Colonel Benjamin Tallmadge.
24. LAMB, Colonel JOHN, LIFE OF. By Isaac Q. Leake.
25. LETTERS ABOUT THE HUDSON. By Freeman Hunt. 1836. Contains some traditional gossip (see p. 4.—W. A.)
26. LORD MAHON (Stanhope). See No. 63.
27. LOSSING, FIELD-BOOK OF THE REVOLUTION. By Benson J. Lossing. 2 vols. 8vo. New York : Harper & Bros., 1850. Vol. 1, chaps. 30, 31, 32, gives an account which contains much local detail, fully illustrated. His book, *The Hudson from Wilderness to Sea*, 4to, New York, 1866, gives a general account, illustrated.
28. MARBOIS, COMPLOT D'ARNOLD ET SIR H. CLINTON, etc. Par Barbe Marbois (French Secretary of Legation to the United States during the Revolution). For a translation of it, see No. 38.
29. MARSHALL, LIFE OF WASHINGTON. Vol. 4, p. 274.
30. MEMORIALS, Historical Society of Penn., Vol. 6, p. 329, and *Sargent*, p. 266, and Appendix, for opinions of Marbois. (See also Greene.)
31. NATIONAL QUARTERLY REVIEW, December, 1862.
32. NEW MIRROR FOR TRAVELLERS. By "An Amateur." New York, 1828, pp. 103–109.
33. NILES' REGISTER. Vol. 20.
34. PICTORIAL HISTORY OF ENGLAND. Gives an account from the British Tory point of view.
35. SCHARF, J. T., HISTORY OF WESTCHESTER COUNTY. 1886.
36. SHAW, Major SAMUEL, JOURNALS OF. By Josiah Quincy. 8vo. Boston, 1847, p. 77.
37. SOUTHERN LITERARY MESSENGER. Vol. 11.
38. WALSH'S AMERICAN REGISTER. Vol. 2, 1817. Gives a translation of Marbois.
39. WASHINGTON AND THE GENERALS OF THE AMERICAN REVOLUTION. Philadelphia, 1848. (Supposed to be written by Bancroft.) Gives a biography of Arnold.
40. WEST POINT, HISTORY OF. By General H. V. Boynton. 8vo. New York, 1863. Points out the military importance of the place, and gives a general account.
41. WINSOR, JUSTIN, NARRATIVE AND CRITICAL HISTORY OF THE UNITED STATES. Vol 6, Boston, 1881.

ENGLISH COMMENT.

42. ADOLPHUS, HISTORY OF ENGLAND. Vol. 3, chap. 39, takes "an adverse view of the American grounds."
43. BIDDLE. (Answer to Lord Mahon). See No. 62.
44. BIOGRAPHICAL DICTIONARY of the Society for the Diffusion of Useful Knowledge. Vol. 2.
45. CHAMBERS' BIOGRAPHICAL DICTIONARY. Article, "*Washington*."
46. CHAMBERS' ENCYCLOPÆDIA (1859 edition) unfavorable to André, and refers to No. 43, *ante*.

47. CLINTON—OBSERVATIONS ON STEDMAN (No. 73). By Sir Henry Clinton. London, 1794. Was privately reprinted in New York in 1864.
48. COKE, TRAVELS OF A SUBALTERN (in America). By E. T. Coke. London, 18—.
49. COLDSTREAM GUARDS, ORIGIN AND SERVICES OF. By MacKinnon. Vol 2, ch. 9.
50. CRITIC AND LITERARY JOURNAL. London, August 15, 1857.
51. GENTLEMAN'S MAGAZINE. London, January, 1855.
52. GEOGRAPHICAL, COMMERCIAL, ETC., VIEW OF UNITED STATES. (See No. 76, seq.) By Winterbotham. London, 1794.
53. HINTON, HISTORICAL AND TOPOGRAPHICAL HISTORY OF UNITED STATES.
54. HISTORY OF ENGLAND—Lord Mahon (afterward Earl Stanhope). Vol. 7. London, 1854. Denounces André's execution. Answered by C. J. Biddle. See No. 62.
55. HISTORY OF ENGLAND. Massey. Vol. 3, ch. 25.
56. "   "   Lord Mahon. Vol. 7. London, 1854.
57. HISTORICAL MAGAZINE. New York, July, 1857.
58. "   "   Boston, Vol. 1, No. 4, p. 102.
59. LONDON GENERAL EVENING POST, November 14, 1780.
60. LONDON DAILY NEWS (quoted in No. 62, p. 388, seq.).
61. MATHEW, Lieutenant, JOURNAL OF. This journal was communicated to Thomas Balch, Philadelphia, and published in the *Historical Magazine* (No. 57, *ante*).
62. MEMORIALS of the Historical Society of Penna. Vol. 6. ("*Contributions to American History*.") 8vo. Phila., 1858. In this is a very full statement of André's case in its relations to military law. See also Vol. 6, pp. 319–416, for summary.
63. MISCELLANIES. By Lord Mahon (Earl Stanhope). 2d Series. London, 1872. In this he states he held a correspondence with George Ticknor, the historian, on the subject of Miss Seward's statements. This led to Mr. Ticknor's searching Colonel Humphreys' papers, then (1855) in the possession of Mr. D. G. Olmstead, of New York. (See Potter's *American Monthly*, August, 1876, No. 69, *seq.*)
64. MONODY ON MAJOR ANDRÉ. Miss Seward. Potter's *American Monthly*, 1876.
65. MOORE, DIARY OF AMERICAN REVOLUTION. Frank Moore. Vol. 2, pp. 393, 484.
66. NEW YORK IN THE REVOLUTIONARY WAR. Jones. Vol. 1, chap. 18, says Arnold played "a noble and virtuous part." See also p. 737.
67. NORTH AMERICAN REVIEW. Boston, January, 1855.
68. PICTORIAL HISTORY OF THE REIGN OF GEORGE III. London, Vol. 1, p. 434.
69. POTTER'S AMERICAN MONTHLY. Philadelphia: J. E. Potter & Co., August, 1876.
70. ROMILLY, SIR SAMUEL, LIFE OF. Vol. 1, p. 104.
71. SABIN'S AMERICAN BIBLIOPOLIST. October, 1872. (Reprint *Saturday Review*.)
72. SATURDAY REVIEW. London, 1872. (Reprinted, see above.)
73. STEDMAN, HISTORY OF THE AMERICAN WAR. London, 1794. This book, according to Lowndes, was written by William Thomson, LL.D. The copy in the library of the late John Carter Brown, Providence, R. I., belonged to Sir Henry Clinton himself, and contains his MS. account of the André affair. This is printed in *Sargent*, pp. 415–419; also in New York *Tribune*, May 24, 1875, and Jones' *New York in Revolution*, Vol. 1, p. 737. A section of it is lacking in that given by Lord Mahon (*History of England*, Vol. 7), and reprinted in *Memorials*, Historical Society, etc. (see No. 62, *ante*).
74. TRIBUNE. New York, May 24, 1875.
75. UNITED STATES, CUBA AND CANADA, THE. Hon. H. A. Murray. London, 1857.
76. WINTERBOTHAM'S, Rev. GEORGE, GEOGRAPHICAL, COMMERCIAL, ETC., VIEW OF UNITED STATES. London, 1794.

THE CASE OF MAJOR ANDRÉ.

77. "The Case of Major John André, Adjutant General to the British Army, who was put to death by the Rebels, October 2, 1780, Candidly Represented: with Remarks on the said Case." New York: Rivington, 1780. 4to, pp. 27.

This is in the Brown Library, Providence. It was probably never published, for this copy, the only one known to exist, is made up of the printer's proofs. It was unquestionably drawn up under Clinton's supervision, and my own opinion, after a very careful examination of it, is that it was written by Clinton himself — intended by him to be published as an offset to the "Proceedings of a Board," issued by the Americans, but withdrawn from the press by him after the types had been set up and the first proofs taken. (See *Magazine of American History*, December, 1879, p. 742.) It is in *Sargent*, p. 274. It states that the gallows was "placed in full view of the windows of Washington's headquarters, as if the sight afforded him pleasure."

ANDRÉ'S TRIAL.

78. American Criminal Trials. P. W. Chandler. Vol. 2. Boston, 1861.
79. Boynton's History of West Point, pp. 127–147, contains *facsimile* of the proceedings. (It is rather a manifesto than a report of the trial. It does not contain André's statement, which is in *Sargent*, p. 149.)
80. Generals of the American Revolution (contains biographies of the members of the Board of Officers). Supposed to be by Geo. Bancroft.
81. Gentleman's Magazine. London, 1780, *et seq.*
82. Greene, General N., Life of. By G. W. Greene. P. 234.
83. ——, Life of. By — Johnson. Vol. 1. Note on p. 208.
84. Hamilton, Life of. By John C. Hamilton. Vol. 1, pp. 271–3. Contains André's statement to H.
85. ——, Writings of. Contains letters by Hamilton to Laurens, Sears, and Miss Schuyler.
86. International Law. Halleck. Pp. 407–9.
87. Lossing, Field-Book. Vol. 1, p. 770.
88. Memorials, Historical Society Penna. Vol. 6, pp. 341, 398, etc.
89. Proceedings of a Board of General Officers, etc. 8vo, p. 21. Philadelphia: Francis Bailey, 1780. (Reprinted in Boynton, pp. 127–147.)
90. Sargent. Pp. 347-360. Both contain Washington's letter, September 29, as well as other letters. (Also p. 380.)
91. Sparks, Life of Washington. Vol. 7.
92. Steuben, Life of. By Kapp.
93. Rhode Island Historical Collections. Vol. 6. Revolutionary Correspondence (Greene's letters).
94. —— Colonial Records. Vol. 9, p. 246.
95. State Paper Office, London — American and West Indies. Vol. 126. Contains Clinton's official despatches, his letters, October 11, 12, 16, 30. (Also used by Sparks and Sargent.)
96. Traditions of the Revolution. Johnson. Pp. 255–7.
97. Troy Morning Whig, April —, 1879, contains a letter from Tallmadge to Webb, September 30, 1780. (Part of it is in No. 88, above.)

ANDRÉ'S EXECUTION AND BURIAL.

98. BARBER AND HOWE'S HISTORICAL COLLECTIONS, NEW JERSEY. P. 77. (Also in *Sargent*, p. 396.)

99. BLAND PAPERS. Vol. 2, p. 33.

100. CHICAGO EVENING JOURNAL, August 27, 1879.

101. CHILD, Mrs. L. M., LETTERS FROM NEW YORK.

102. CHRISTIAN JOURNAL AND LITERARY REGISTER. Vol. 5. New York, 1821 (disinterment).

103. CITY AND COUNTRY, Nyack, N. Y., September 26, 1879. (C. M. Oblenis' letter.)

104. CONNECTICUT COURANT, October 24, 1780. (Reprinted in New York *World*, September 14 and 16, 1879.)

105. CONTINENTAL JOURNAL. Boston, October 26, 1780. (See *New England Magazine*, No. 122, below.)

106. COURIER, Canajoharie, N. Y., September 27, 1879.

107. DEWEES' (SAM'L) LIFE AND SERVICES. Baltimore, 1844, pp. 208–24.

108. EVANGELIST, New York, January 30, 1879, February 27, 1879.

109. EVENING POST, New York, August 11, 1831.

110. FARMER AND MOORE'S COLLECTIONS. Vol. 3, p. 288.

111. HARPER'S MAGAZINE, August, 1855.

112. HEATH'S MEMOIRS (General Wm. Heath).

113. HISTORICAL COLLECTIONS OF NEW YORK, p. 479. (Reprinted in *Sargent*, p. 396.)

114. HISTORY OF MASONIC LODGE, No. 61, WILKES BARRE, PA. By Harvey.

115. JOEL BARLOW, LIFE OF. By Todd.

116. KNICKERBOCKER MAGAZINE. Vol. 16. 1840. Editor's Table.

117. MAGAZINE OF AMERICAN HISTORY. September, 1877, p. 573; December, 1879, p. 754. (Cf. *Sargent*, pp. 408–411.) September, 1879, p. 574; July, 1880, p. 59.

118. MAGAZINE OF NATURAL HISTORY. J. C. Loudon. Vol 4. London, 1831, pp. 112–114.

119. MEMORIALS, Historical Society Penna. Vol. 6, pp. 372–5.

120. MILITARY JOURNAL. Thacher. 8vo. Boston, 1827, p. 225.

121. NATIONAL INTELLIGENCER. January 14, February 25, March 4, 1817.

122. NEW ENGLAND MAGAZINE. Boston, May, 1834. Vol. 6, p. 358.

123. NEW JERSEY HISTORICAL SOCIETY, PROCEEDINGS, 1875.

124. NEW YORK EVANGELIST. January 30, 1879; February 27, 1879.

125. —— EVENING POST. October 15, 1879; August 11, 1821 (disinterment).

126. —— TIMES. October 20 and 22, 1879.

127. —— WORLD. September 8, 14 (two), 21 (two), 10, 15, 16; August 30, September 19, and 21, September 23, September 29, October 12, 1879.

128. PENNSYLVANIA GAZETTE. October 11, 1780.

129. —— JOURNAL. October 18, 1780. (Reprinted in *Life of Hamilton*. New York, 1834. Vol. 1, p. 273.)

130. —— PACKET. October 10, 1780; October 14, 1780.

131. SHREVE, JOHN, NARRATIVE. *Magazine American History*, September, 1879, p. 574.

132. STANLEY, A. P., HISTORICAL MEMORIALS OF WESTMINSTER ABBEY. London, 1876, pp. 256–7.

133. TALLMADGE—LETTER. Reprinted in *Magazine American History*, December, 1879, p. 754.

134. TALLMADGE—MEMOIRS. New York, 1858, p. 36.
135. UNITED SERVICE JOURNAL. London, November, 1833 (disinterment).
136. WILKES BARRE (PA.) GLEANER. February 21 and 29, 1817. (Reprinted in *National Intelligencer*, March 4, 1817.)
137. —— DAILY UNION LEADER. June 16, 1880. (Reprint of June 21, 1870.)
138. YONKERS GAZETTE. March 24, 1866.

ANDRÉ'S WATCH.

139. AMERICAN HISTORICAL RECORD. October, 1874, p. 470. See also for March, 1874.
140. ARNOLD, LIFE OF. Sparks. P. 230.
141. GRAPHIC, New York, July 25, 1876.
142. EVENING POST, New York, October 20, 1879; October 15, 1879.
143. SUNNYSIDE PRESS, Tarrytown, N. Y., September 18, 1880.
144. VINDICATION OF THE CAPTORS, ETC. Benson. New York, 1817.

ANDRÉ'S WILL.

145. Recorded in Surrogate's Office, New York; probated October 12, 1780 (Seaton and White, witnesses). Potter's *American Monthly*, September, 1876, p. 172; Sabine's *American Loyalists*, Vol. 2, pp. 273, 418 (Seaton and White).
146. STEVENS' COLLECTION OF RECORDS OF NEW YORK CHAMBER OF COMMERCE. 8vo. New York, 1867. (Notice of H. White.)

JOSHUA HETT SMITH.

147. ARNOLD. Sparks. Preface.
148. AUTHENTIC NARRATIVE, ETC. By Smith. London, 1808; New York, 1809.
149. GENTLEMAN'S MAGAZINE. London, 1780, supplement, p. 610; July, 1801.
150. HERALD, New York, 1842.
151. HISTORICAL MAGAZINE, 1866; supplements 1 and 2.
152. MAGAZINE OF AMERICAN HISTORY. Vol. 6. July, 1880; April, 1881, p. 279.
153. RECORD OF THE TRIAL OF J. H. SMITH. Edited by Henry B. Dawson. 8vo. Morrisania, New York, 1866. (See No. 310 for Smith's pedigree.)

THE CAPTORS.

154. AMERICAN HISTORICAL RECORD. September, 1872, p. 407; December, 1873, Vol. 3, pp. 471, 515.
155. AMERICAN LOYALISTS. Sabine. Vol. 2, p. 194.
156. ANALECTIC MAGAZINE. Vol. 10.
157. ARNOLD. Sparks. Pp. 222–6.
158. BOLTON, HISTORY OF WESTCHESTER COUNTY. Vol. 1, pp. 80–213.
159. CENTENNIAL SOUVENIR. M. D. Raymond. Tarrytown, N. Y., 1880.

160. CITY AND COUNTRY, Nyack, N. Y., October 10, 1879.
161. FIELD-BOOK OF THE REVOLUTION. Lossing. Vol. 1, p. 755.
162. GRAPHIC, New York, October 6, 1879.
163. GREENPOINT (N. Y.) GLOBE, October 11, 1879.
164. HISTORICAL MAGAZINE. November, 1857 ; June, 1865.
165. HISTORY OF SCHOHARIE CO. Simms. 8vo. New York, 1845, p. 646.
166. HOUSE OF REPRESENTATIVES JOURNALS, 1817 (Tallmadge's Speech).
167. MAGAZINE OF AMERICAN HISTORY. February, 1887, page 168.
168. NEW YORK IN THE REVOLUTION. Jones. Vol. 1, p. 734.
169. NEW YORK COMMERCIAL ADVERTISER. August 30, October 3, 1879.
170. ———— COURRIER DES ÉTATS-UNIS. October 4, 1879.
171. ———— EVENING EXPRESS. October 3, 1879.
172. ———— EVENING MAIL. October 4, 1879.
173. ———— EVENING POST. January 8, 1879 ; September 16, 1879 ; October 1, 3, 4, 20, 1879 ;
    November 21, 1879.
174. ———— EVENING TELEGRAM. October 4, 1879.
175. ———— HERALD. October 3, 1879.
176. ———— STAR. October 3, 1879.
177. ———— SUN. September 29 ; October 1, 2, 3, 4, 6, 12, 13, 15, 1879.
178. ———— SUNDAY MERCURY. October 5, 1879.
179. ———— TIMES. October 3, 4, 1879 ; November 23, 1879 ; September 23, 1880.
180. ———— TRIBUNE. October 3, 7, 1879.
181. ———— WORLD. September 23, October 7, 8, 1879.
182. POTTER'S AMERICAN MONTHLY. August and September, 1876.
183. PUCK, New York. October 22, 1879.
184. ROCKLAND COUNTY JOURNAL, Nyack, N. Y. October 11, 1879.
185. SHAW, SAMUEL, JOURNALS OF. Edited by Josiah Quincy. Boston, 1847.
186. SUNNYSIDE PRESS, Tarrytown, N. Y. September 11, 1880.
187. TELEGRAPH, Pittsburgh. June 11, 17, 25, 1879.
188. VINDICATION OF THE CAPTORS OF MAJOR ANDRÉ. Benson, N. Y., 1819. Reprinted,
    (Sabin reprints, No. 3) New York, 1865, and elsewhere.

POEMS AND BALLADS.

189. BRAVE PAULDING AND THE SPY. In Moore's *Songs and Ballads of the American Revolu-
    tion*, p. 316. (Various others may be found in *Sargent*.)
190. BRITISH HERO IN CAPTIVITY, THE. Puddicombe. 4to. 1783.
191. INCIDENT OF ANDRÉ'S CAPTURE, AN. John Banvard (*Commercial Advertiser*, New York,
    September, 1880).
192. JOURNAL OF ORIGINAL AND AUTHENTIC OCCURRENCES DURING THE AMERICAN WAR.
    By Sergeant R. Lamb, Royal Welch Fusiliers. Dublin, 1809, p. 338.
193. MEMOIRES, COUNT DE MORÉS. Paris, 1828. (Contains some French verses.) See Pont-
    gibaud, No. 218.
194. POEM. — Miller. (Not found.—W. A.)
195. ————. N. P. Willis. (See Chapter V.)
196. POTTER'S AMERICAN MONTHLY. August, September, 1876. Contains the *Monody*, by
    Miss Seward.

DRAMAS.

197. ANDRÉ. By William Dunlap. London, 1799.
198. ——. (5 acts). 1798. Believed to be by Dr. Elihu H. Smith.
199. ARNOLD, A TRAGEDY. By ——.
200. ARNOLD AND ANDRÉ. By Geo. H. Calvert. 1840.
201. HIGHLAND TREASON. By Elihu G. Holland. (In his *Essays*.)

FICTION.

202. ANDRÉ. (Theodore S. Fay is said, on authority of the *New York Mirror*, to have been engaged, in 1838, on a novel so-called.) It does not appear to have been published.
203. HUGH WYNNE. Dr. S. W. Mitchell. Philadelphia, 1897. (Introduces André.)
204. PEMBERTON. By Henry Peterson. Philadelphia, 1873. (Reprinted with illustrations, 1898.)
205. SIR HENRY'S WARD—A TALE OF THE REVOLUTION. Mrs. Ann S. Stephens, in *Graham's Magazine*, 1846.

THE COW-CHACE.

206. Originally printed in Rivington's *Royal Gazette*, New York, 1780. Canto I., August 16; Canto II., August 30; Canto III., September 23.

After his death, it was published by Rivington in book-form, 8vo, pp. 69, and by Fielding, London, 1781, 4to, pp. 32, with "explanatory notes by the Editor."

It also appears in Dunlap's *André* (London, 1799) in Lossing's *Field-Book*, Vol. 2, p. 684, and *Hudson from the Wilderness to the Sea*, Moore's *Songs and Ballads of the Revolution*. It was also published in Cincinnati, 1869, 8vo, pp. 32.

An original MS. copy, in André's writing, dated Elizabethtown, August 1, 1780, is in the Sprague (Albany, N. Y.) collection of autographs. Lossing reprints it.

Another autograph copy seems to be extant, for Sargent does not mention the above. (See pp. 234 and 235.)

CONTEMPORARY RECORDS.

207. ALBANY DAILY ADVERTISER. 1839. (See Potter's *American Monthly*, September, 1876.)
208. ALMON'S REMEMBRANCER, London, 1780. Vol. 10, pp. 76, 77. (André at Charleston.)
209. AMERICAN HISTORICAL RECORD. March, 1874, p. 115; Vol. 1, p. 436.
210. ARNOLD. Sparks. Pp. 233, 235, 255.
211. BARBER & HOWE'S HISTORICAL COLLECTIONS OF NEW JERSEY.
212. —— HISTORICAL COLLECTIONS OF NEW YORK.
213. BLAKE'S HISTORY OF PUTNAM COUNTY, N. Y. 1849. 12mo.
214. BOLTON'S WESTCHESTER COUNTY. Vol. 1, pp. 215–223.
215. BOYNTON'S WEST POINT. 110–120.
216. CASE OF MAJOR ANDRÉ. P. 18.
217. FIELD-BOOK. Lossing. Vol. 1, pp. 721, 764, 765.

218. French Volunteer in War of Independence.   Pontgibaud or Morés.   Paris, 1821 : New York, 1898.
219. Historical Magazine, New York.   October, 1857 ; November, 1862, p. 293.
220. Hours With Living Men and Women of the Revolution.   Lossing.
221. Lafayette's Memoirs.   American Edition.   Vol. 1, pp. 253–257, 264, 349.
222. Magazine of American History.   Vol. 3, pp. 748, 756 ; December, 1879, p. 758. Vol. 5, pp. 57, 58, 105–112, July, 1880.
223. New York Evening Post.   September 16, 1879.
224. —— Star.   October 12, 1879.
225.   Times.   October 3, 1879.
226. —— World.   September 28, 1880.
227. Original and Authentic Journal of Occurrences During the Late American War.   Sergeant R. Lamb, Royal Welch Fusiliers.   Dublin, 1809.
228. Pennsylvania Magazine of History and Biography.   Vol. 4, p. 61.   (H. Lee's letter, about capture and execution.)
229. Potter's American Monthly.   September, 1876.
230. Proceedings Board of General Officers.   (Boynton's *West Point*, p. 149.)
231. Recollections.   S. G. Goodrich.   New York, 1856.
232. Sabine's American Loyalists.   1864.   Vol. 2, p. 355.
233. Sparks' Life and Writings of Washington.   Vol. 7.
234. St. Clair Papers.
235. Sunday Herald, Boston.   September 14, 1879.
236. Sunnyside Press, Tarrytown, N. Y.   September 18, 1880.
237. Tallmadge's Memoirs.
238. Tarleton's Campaigns.   London, 1787.   (André in South Carolina.)
239. Washington, Irving's Life of.   Vol 4, chap. 11.
239a. Webb, Samuel B., Life and Correspondence of.   Edited by W. C. Ford, N. Y., 1886.
239b. —— Journals and Reminiscences.   By his son, J. Watson Webb.
240. Women of the Revolution.   Mrs. Ellet.   1849.   Vol. 2.
241. Writings of Hamilton.
242. Yonkers Gazette.   June 7, 1865.

MAPS, PLANS AND VIEWS.

243. Arnold.   Sparks.   P. 177.   (Not fully accurate.)
244. Atlas New York and Vicinity.   New York : Beers, Ellis & Soule, 1868.
245. Battles of the Revolution.   Carrington.   P. 512.
246. Battles of the United States.   Dawson.
247. Bolton's History of Westchester County.
248. Boynton's West Point.   *First* edition.
249. Complot d'Arnold.   Marbois.
250. Field-Book.   Lossing.
251. Harper's Magazine.   May, 1876.
252. History of Orange County.   Ruttenber.
253. Magazine of American History.   February, 1880 ; March, 1880, p. 200 ; July, 1880.
254. Magazine of Natural History.   J. C. Loudon, Vol. 4, p. 112 ; London, 1831.

255. NEW YORK HERALD. September 23, 1880.
256. MANUAL COMMON COUNCIL NEW YORK. D. T. Valentine. 1861, pp. 496–498; also, for 1852 and 1858.
257. OLD NEW YORK. Dr. J. W. Francis. New York, 1866.
258. POTTER'S AMERICAN MONTHLY. September, 1876.
259. WASHINGTON ATLAS. Guizot.

RELICS OF ANDRÉ.

260. His silver spur is at Washington's Headquarters, Newburgh, N. Y.; his pocket-book at rooms of Connecticut Historical Society, Hartford; his MS. account of the Mischianza, in possession of the Howard family of Maryland; silhouettes, etc., cut by him, were owned (1880) by the Foxhall Parker estate, New York; a wine glass is owned by the Gardiner family, Gardiner's Island, L. I., N. Y.

MISCELLANEOUS.

261 AMERICAN CITIZEN, Tarrytown. August 25, 1801. Notice of the tulip tree. (Reprinted *Magazine of American History*, December, 1880.)
262. AMERICAN HISTORICAL AND LITERARY CURIOSITIES. Smith and Watson.
263. ATLANTIC MONTHLY. December, 1860.
264. BLAKE'S HISTORY OF PUTNAM COUNTY, N. Y., contains a spurious "defence," said to have been offered by André. (See also Potter's *American Monthly*, April, July and August, 1876.)
265. BOTTA, CHARLES, HISTORY OF THE WAR OF INDEPENDENCE. New Haven, Ct., 1840.
266. CHRONICLES OF EAST HAMPTON, L. I. David Gardiner, 1871.
267. DEALINGS WITH THE DEAD. L. M. Sargent.
268. DRAPER'S BATTLE OF KING'S MOUNTAIN. Pp. 37–9.
269. DUKE OF SAXE-WEIMAR, TRAVELS IN AMERICA. Philadelphia, 1828.
270. GALAXY, N. Y. February, 1876.
271. HOURS WITH LIVING MEN AND WOMEN OF THE REVOLUTION. Lossing. (Mrs. Beekman.)
272. GENTLEMAN'S MAGAZINE. London, July, 1801. (Arnold's death.)
273. HISTORY OF THE SOCIETY OF THE CINCINNATI, STATE OF NEW YORK. By John Schuyler. New York, 1886.
274. LOYALIST POETRY OF STANSBURY AND ODELL. Sargent. Albany, 1860.
275. MAGAZINE OF AMERICAN HISTORY. Vol. 8. (Long article about Colonel Varick and the treason, etc.) Vol. 5, p. 57 (Partridge, about Mabie Tavern), p. 20 (Campbell, about Smith's house); December, 1879, p. 758, July, August, December, 1880 (Itinerary André's journey.)
276. MASSACHUSETTS HISTORICAL SOCIETY COLLECTIONS. Vol. 2, p. 195; Vol. 14, p. 52.
277. MEMOIRS OF THE AMERICAN REVOLUTION. John Drayton.
278. MEMORIALS AND LETTERS OF S. B. WEBB. Edited by Worthington C. Ford. New York, 1886.
279. MEN AND TIMES OF THE REVOLUTION (Elkanah Watson). Winslow C. Watson. New York, 1856.

280. MEDALLIC HISTORY OF UNITED STATES. Loubat.
281. MEMORABLE DAYS IN AMERICA. William Faux. 8vo. London, 1823.
282. MILITARY JOURNAL. Simcoe. 8vo. New York, 1844.
283. NAVAL AND MILITARY MEMOIRS. — Beatson. London. Vol. 6, p. 203.
284. NIGHT SIDE OF NATURE. Mrs. Crowe. Vol. 1, chap. 3. (Dream of André's death.)
284b. NEWELL, Rev. E. F., LIFE AND OBSERVATIONS OF. By C. W. Ainsworth. Worcester, Massachusetts, 1847.
285. NEW YORK CHRISTIAN ADVOCATE. December 30, 1880.
286. —— EVENING POST. October 2, 1879.
287. —— SUN. June 3, 1854 ; October 20, 1879.
288. NOBLE DEEDS OF AMERICAN WOMEN. J. Clement.
289. NORTH AMERICAN REVIEW. July, 1861.
290. NORTHERN INVASION. F. B. Hough.
291. NOTES AND QUERIES. London, December 31, 1853. January 15, 1870.
292. PAPERS CONCERNING THE CAPTURE AND DETENTION OF MAJOR ANDRÉ. Dawson.
293. PAPERS. A letter of Elliot to Eden (Lord Auckland) is in the *Auckland MSS.* at Cambridge University, England.
294. PATTISON PAPERS, THE, (General Pattison of the British Army,) *New York Historical Society Publications, 1875*, contains some official letters to André.
295. POLITICAL MAGAZINE. London, March, 1781.
296. REED'S LIFE OF GENERAL JOSEPH REED.
297. RELIQUARY. Vol. 4, p. 60.
298. REMINISCENCES OF SAMUEL B. WEBB. By J. Watson Webb.
299. REVOLUTIONARY MEMORIALS. Rev. Wheeler Case. New York, 1852.
300. ROCHAMBEAU'S MEMOIRS. Vol. 1.
300b. PROCEEDINGS OF THE MASSACHUSETTS HISTORICAL SOCIETY, 1861–2 (Vol. 19, p. 385), contains extract from Stearns' orderly-book.
301. PROCEEDINGS OF THE NEW JERSEY HISTORICAL SOCIETY, 1876.
302. SABIN'S AMERICAN BIBLIOPOLIST. 1869–70.
303. SCRIBNER'S MONTHLY. Vol. 4. (Article about West Point.)
303b. SOCIETY OF THE CINCINNATI. Memorial volumes, List of Members, etc., of the different State Societies.
304. SOUVENIR OF REVOLUTIONARY SOLDIERS' MONUMENT AT TARRYTOWN, 1880. M. D. Raymond, Tarrytown.
305. SPARKS' MSS. 49, No. 14, 53. (At Cornell University.)
306. TRUMBULL'S AUTOBIOGRAPHY.
307. VAN SCHAACK'S LIFE OF PETER VAN SCHAACK. P. 147.
308. WASHINGTON IN DOMESTIC LIFE. Rush.
309. WHITING'S REVOLUTIONARY ORDERS. Pp. 109, 112. (Greene's proclamation and the Board's decision.)
310. WILLS OF THE SMITH FAMILY OF NEW YORK AND LONG ISLAND. By W. S. Pelletreau. New York, 1898.
311. YONKERS (N. Y.) GAZETTE. May 6, 1865, to April 14, 1866.

Index.

PAULDING Monument, 49.
PEEKSKILL, 19, 37.
PELHAM, —, 27.
PETTINGILL, Major THOMAS, 70.
Phaeton FRIGATE, 83.
PINE'S BRIDGE, 24, 31.

RAND, Colonel JOHN, 45.
RAYMOND, HENRY J., 72.
RED MILLS, 48.
REED HOUSE, 27, 33.
REQUA, ABRAHAM, 20.
—— Amos C., 20.
—— EDMUND, 20.
ROBBINS' MILLS, 21, 23, 34.
ROBERTSON, General JAMES, 63, 65, 67, 68.
ROBINSON, BEVERLY, 5, 6, 46, 50.
—— HOUSE, 23, 41, 47, 50, 51.
ROCHAMBEAU, General COUNT, 65.
ROGERS, Lieutenant JEDEDIAH, 48.
ROMER, JAMES, 27.
—— JOHN, 33.
—— Mrs. JACOB, 27, 33.
ROSSELL'S CORNERS, 25.
RUSSELL, BENJAMIN, 72, 73.

ST. CLAIR, General ARTHUR, 59.
ST. PETER'S CHURCH, 37, 49.
SANDS MILLS, 35, 36, 37.
SARGENT, WINTHROP, 13, 14, 31, 66, 68, 73.
—— L. M., 61.
SCAMMELL, Colonel ALEXANDER, 58, 64, 70, 75, 76, 77.
SCOTT, JOHN MORIN, 23.
SEATON, WILLIAM, 81.
SEE, ISAAC, 27.
SHAW, Major SAMUEL, 41.
SHELDON, Colonel ELISHA, 35, 38.
—— DRAGOONS, 21, 23, 32.
SHIPPARD, Lieutenant SAMUEL, 53.
SHREVE, Colonel ISRAEL, 75, 76.
SIMCOE, Colonel J. G., 20, 81.
SKINNERS, 26.
SMITH, CLAUDIUS, 27.
—— DAVID, 53.
—— Captain EBENEZER, 53, 62.
—— JOSHUA HETT, 4, 5, 8, 9, 10, 11, 14, 15, 19, 20, 23, 47, 51, 60.
—— RICHARD, 27.
—— THOMAS, 12.

SUPPLEMENT TO
THE CRISIS OF THE REVOLUTION

—

JUNE 1, 1909

—

Since the publication of this work, some additional facts and a few trifling *errata* have been discovered which seem to make it advisable to issue this as a supplement.

But it is a matter of congratulation to the author that no serious error has as yet been detected by any critic—a newspaper discussion of a few years ago regarding the number of André's captors failing to upset his statement that there were eight of them instead of the commonly-received seven.

CHANGES AND ADDITIONS

Page 4. The South Carolina *Genealogical and Historical Magazine* of July, 1902, says: *Belvedere* was only the name of a plantation, not a town, and her father was John Gordon, of Charleston.

Page 13. (Map opposite.) Note 14. The cannon-ball is now in the possession of Dr. R. B. Coutant, of Tarrytown.

Page 39. John I. Bouton should be John F.

Page 39. Note 2. "Andrew" Anderson should be Alexander.

Page 48. James Cox should be Cock.

Page 49. One of the André captors' medals is now in the possession of the New York Historical Society.

Page 57. The diagram is wrong as to the window in the north wall. It should be *west* of the fire-place, not east.

The building is now (1909) repaired and in good condition.

Page 84. The monument and its site are now owned by the American Scenic and Historic Preservation Society.

Page 107. Add after No. 194: "His Captors to André.

And after No. 196: 196 *a* Trifles in Verse, by a Young Soldier. (J. Marjoribanks.) Kelso, Scotland, 1784. Contains poem, "André to Washington."

196 *b* André's Ghost (*The Family Tablet*). Ed. by Rev. Dr. Abiel Holmes (father of O. W. Holmes) Boston, 1796.

Page 108. Add to No. 199: Horatio Hubbell, Phila., 1847.

Add after No. 201. "Boston, 1852."

Add to No. 201 *a:* André, by Rev. W. W. Lord. N. Y., Scribner, 1852.

FICTION ADDED

No. 202 *a* Secrets of Arnold's Treason; or Victors and Victims, by Charles P. Sumner, N. Y., Hilton & Co., n. d.

202 *b* A Great Treason, by Mary A. M. Hoppus, N. Y. Macmillan, 1883.

202 *c* The Eventful Nine Days. Tarrytown *Argus.* Dec. 19, 1885.

205 *a* Sad Tales and Glad Tales, by "Reginald Reverie" (Grenville Mellen). Boston, S. G. Goodrich, 1828. Contains "The Spy and the Traitor." 50 pp.

(Supplement to THE CRISIS OF THE REVOLUTION, December 1, 1915)

This is the only new letter on its subject which has turned up since the publication of our book. Dr. Hart's testimony to André's coolness perfectly agrees with that of others who have been quoted for more than a century, since the event. The introduction is chiefly from the History of the Massachusetts Society of the Cincinnati.—[ED.]

LETTER FROM AN EYEWITNESS OF THE EXECUTION OF ANDRÉ.

Communicated by HON. PRENTISS CUMMINGS, of Brookline, Mass., to the N. E. Hist. Gen. Register of July, 1915

John Hart, the writer of the letter which is here printed, was an Army surgeon in the Revolution, first in Colonel William Prescott's Massachusetts regiment, from May 1, 1775 until August, 1775, then in the Seventh Continental Infantry during the year 1776, and from January 1, 1777, in the Second Massachusetts regiment, serving directly under Washington. In November, 1783, he was retained in Jackson's regiment, in the Continental Army, and served until June 20, 1784. He died April 27, 1826.

He was appointed by Washington one of the medical inspectors to supervise the execution of André, and this letter is dated two days after the execution. It is written on the four pages of a sheet of paper about 12½ by 15¼ inches, the address being on the lower half of the fourth page, at right angles to the text of the letter.

Tappan, October 4th, 1780

Honourd Sir,

An Opportunity presents to write & As I am sensible you are fond of the news in Camp, will endeavour to give a perticculiar account of the greatest piece of villany that has come to my knowledge since the Commencement of the war—Major General Arnold has acted him self, that is the part of a Horse Jockey; he wrote to Genl. Clinton at New York that for a certain sum of money he would give up the Garrison W: Point into the Hands of the British, in Consequence of which proposal Genl. Clinton sent out Major Andrie Adjutant General to the British Army, to confer with Arnold in what way the matter should be carried into exicution, & this was agreed on between them, that Arnold would draw off as many of the men from the Point as he could, deprive the remainder of aminution & arms as much as possible without being suspected, Give a Draft of all the works & the best plans for Landing, & the number of men to Majr. Andrie; All which was Done, while this was carrieing (?) on there were three thousand British Troops at Fort

Washington with their Boats waiting for Majr. Andrie's return, after which they were to push up in the Night, take Arnold prisoner, and then take pession of the Point; which plan, Happy for us, miscarried—When the Affairs were detirmined between Andrie & Arnold,—Andrie procured A pass from Arnold to ("go" *blurred out*) pass our Guards to the White Plains & further if he pleased, Under a pretence of getting intelligence from the Enemy. Arnold likewise Desired one Joshua Smith (who was supposed to be a friend to our cause, but had a hand in this whol affair) to Escort Andrie through our Guards that he might not be suspected,—Smith went with Andrie Almost to Tarry-Town & left him; he (Andrie) went forward in expectation that he was out of Danger, but soon meeting three of our militia upon which he asked them if they were the lower Party; upon which they answered they were, he then said "I am very glad to see you, I am a British officer, have been up as a spy, hope you will not detain me long," upon which the men told him they would not, but desired him to get off of his Horse a minute upon which he did they serched him, & found in his Boots A plan of all our works at W: Point, the number of men at that Post, & every matter that was riquisit to carry their Infernal plan into exicution; they found Arnold was concerned in the matter, & would not carry Andrie to him, but to Genl. Washington who was then on his way from Hartford to camp: Arnold haveing notice of Andrie's being taken, & that Genl. Washington was very near, he was Imeadiately struck with Horror, and to save his Life took his boat & went to a British ship that Lay in the river under a pretence of being a flagg ("which" *crossed out*) in order to blind our people, who at that time knew nothing of the matter, otherwise he might of been secured, but Happy for him he got safe to the Enemy—Majr. Andrie was brought before a Bord of Genl. Officers, where he confessed every thing that he had been guilty of himself, but desired not to be asked any thing respecting any other carectors (?); which he was not, He was kept in close confinement & informe that he was to suffer death, which sentence he received with the greatest composure & said it was perfectly right for he came out as a spy, & his intinsion was to get what information he could, to our damage he was informed that he was to be exicuted at such an hour, upon which he caled his servant, ordered him to make tea, which he drank with out any perceivable Uneasiness of mind; he told his servant to dress & shave him, ordered his Cloathes to be brought, which were put on with as much composure as though he was going to a Ball, the time of Exicution Arrived, he appeared, & I think, the most, Agreable, pleaseing young fellow I ever see, the most agreable smile on his countenance that can be conceived of; when he came to the Gallos he said he was perfectly sensible of his fate but Did not like the mode of exicution, he put the rope round his neck himself, bound his eyes & said with an agreable smile "a few minutes will settle the matter," in doing this there was not the least tremor or appearance of fear: Such Fortitude I never ("saw" *crossed out*) was witness of, nor ever had I such disagreable fealings at an execution, to see a man go out of time without fear, but all the time smileing is a matter that I could not ("of" *blurred out*) conceived (*d crossed out*) of.

Mr. Smith was likewise taken, & is now on Tryal; it is supposed he will be hanged very soon, & no doubt he Justly deserves it, I think he does However——————————

This is all the news of impoitance that I have to communicate— Billy is well, & promoted to a serjant,—

Please to give my Duty to mamma & respects to all Friends

Your Dutiful son,

Jон Hart

(Addressed)
Capt. Abraham Gould
Stoneham

(Capt. Gould was his father-in-law.)

Plate 1

(Rector of St. Mary's Church, Burlington, N. J.)

Plate 2

FROM THE ORIGINAL BY TRUMBULL.

Plate 3

ANDRÉ'S LANDING-PLACE, FROM THE SOUTH. HAVERSTRAW IN THE DISTANCE.

Plate 4

ANDRÉ'S LANDING PLACE, FROM THE NORTH, TELLER'S POINT OPPOSITE.

Plate 5

"THE FIRS," JUST BELOW HAVERSTRAW.
Scene of the Arnold-André Midnight Conference.

Plate 6

JOSHUA HETT SMITH'S HOUSE, "TREASON HILL," HAVERSTRAW.

Major André's room is the second-story, left-hand.

Plate 7

JOSHUA HETT SMITH'S HOUSE, HAVERSTRAW.

The Rear and North End.

Plate 8

JOSHUA HETT SMITH'S HOUSE.

The André Window (whence he saw the firing on the *Vulture*).

Plate 9

JOSHUA HETT SMITH'S HOUSE, HAVERSTRAW.

The Dining Room.

Plate 10

John Lamb.

Plate 11

King's Ferry, Western End.

Plate 12

On the Kings Ferry Road, East of Verplanck's Point.

Plate 13

ON THE CROMPOND ROAD.
(West of the Miller House.)

Plate 14

RUINS OF ANDREAS MILLER'S HOUSE, YORKTOWN.

Plate 15

SITE OF STRANG'S TAVERN, CROMPOND CORNER.
(The site is just inside the bars.)

Plate 16

Plate 17

Plate 18

Sam.ᵈ B. Webb

Plate 19

The Underhill House, Yorktown.
The small rear window is opposite the "André door."

Plate 20

(The Dining Room Side.)

(The Outside.)

THE UNDERHILL HOUSE, YORKTOWN HEIGHTS.

The André Door.

Plate 21

Plate 22

THE THORNE HOUSE, NEAR CHAPPAQUA, N. Y.

(André came by the "Hog Hill" Road, which is not shown. That in front is the Chappaqua Road, and Kipp Street is seen ascending the hill.)

Plate 23

Sergeant Sylvanus Brundage's House, Pleasantville.

Plate 24

THE ROADSIDE SPRING, OPPOSITE THE SYLVANUS BRUNDAGE HOUSE, PLEASANTVILLE.

Plate 25

STAATS HAMMOND'S HOUSE, PLEASANTVILLE.

Plate 26

MEKEEL'S CORNERS, PLEASANTVILLE.
Here André mistook his way, taking the right-hand road.

Plate 27

THE CAPTURE OF MAJOR ANDRÉ.

(From the engraving by A. B. Durand.)

Plate 28

THE REED TAVERN, NOW LANDRINE HOUSE, EAST TARRYTOWN.

The André room is on right of entrance.

Plate 29

THE CAPTORS' MONUMENT, TARRYTOWN.

Plate 30

THE ROBBINS-WRIGHT HOUSE, KENSICO.

(Where the Captors expected to find Lieut. Col. Jameson.)

Plate 31

SANDS' MILLS, ARMONK, LIEUT.-COL. JAMESON'S HEADQUARTERS.

Sands' Mills (Barn) in town of Armonk (called Mile Square in 1780). André was confined in the left-hand windowed building (which was Lieutenant-Colonel Jameson's headquarters) just after his arrest.

Plate 32

John Jameson Col. Cont

plate 33

Solon Allen

Plate 34

Plate 35

THE GILBERT HOUSE, SOUTH SALEM.

(From the original sketch by Dr. Alexander Anderson, owned by Dr. Thomas Addis Emmet, N. Y.)

"There was a spacious yard before the door, which he desired he might be permitted to walk in."—*King*.

Plate 36

FROM ORIGINAL PAINTING BY STUART, OWNED BY MR. J. HOWARD KING, RIDGEFIELD, CONN.

Plate 37

Isaac Bronson M. D.

FROM THE ORIGINAL PAINTING BY TRUMBULL, IN THE POSSESSION OF MR. FREDERICK BRONSON, NEW YORK.

Plate 38

Plate 39

THE DINING ROOM, ROBINSON HOUSE.

(Made from the last photograph taken before its destruction, and never before published.)

Plate 40

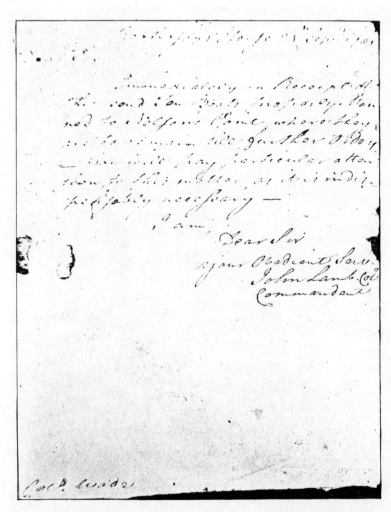

Letter from Colonel John Lamb, Commandant at West Point, to Colonel Nathaniel Wade, of a Massachusetts
regiment of militia there, relating to a (probable) design to board
the *Vulture* and capture Arnold.

(From the original in the possession of Francis H. Wade, Esq., Ipswich, Mass., grandson of Colonel Wade.)

Plate 41

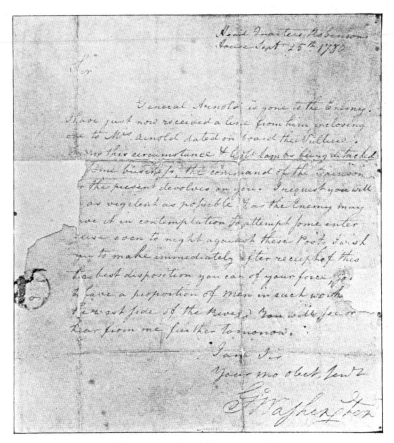

Letter from Washington to Colonel Nathaniel Wade, apprising him of Arnold's treason. Probably the first
letter written by Washington on this subject. The body of the letter is in the
handwriting of Alexander Hamilton.

(From the original in the possession of Francis H. Wade, Esq., Ipswich, Mass., grandson of Colonel Wade.)

Plate 42

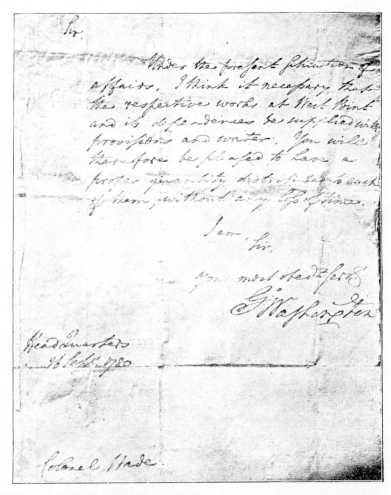

Letter from Washington to Colonel Nathaniel Wade as to provisioning the forts at West Point, then under Wade's command.

(From the original in the possession of Francis H. Wade, Esq., Ipswich, Mass.)

Plate 43

The Red Mills, Mahopac Falls.

(Destroyed by fire 1896.)

Plate 44

Plate 45

ST. PETER'S CHURCH, NORTH PEEKSKILL.
Built 1767.

Plate 46

The Hollman House, North Peekskill.

Plate 47

John Webb

Plate 48

THE ROBINSON HOUSE, ARNOLD'S HEADQUARTERS.

(Made from the last photograph taken before its destruction, and never before published.)

Plate 49

Ruins of Fort Putnam, West Point, Looking East, Over the Hudson.
(Major André was confined in a casemate on the north side.)

Plate 50

The Coe Tavern, Hempstead, Rockland County.

Plate 51

THE COE TAVERN, HEMPSTEAD, ROCKLAND COUNTY.
The Dining Room.

Plate 52

MAJOR ANDRÉ'S PRISON, TAPPAN. (THE MABIE TAVERN, OR '76 HOUSE.)
As it appeared for many years, before "restoration" in 1897. The right-hand room was his sitting-room, the left, Gen. Greene's headquarters.

Plate 53

THE MABIE TAVERN AT TAPPAN —

André's prison-room in the rear of the building. (It was originally two small
rooms, which were thrown into one in 1848.)

Plate 54

Colonel 1st New Hampshire Continentals.
Adjutant Gen'l Continental Army.

Plate 55

Jed Huntington

Plate 56

FROM THE ORIGINAL BY TRUMBULL.   BY PERMISSION OF THE NEW YORK HISTORICAL SOCIETY.
(SIGNATURE FROM THE EMMET COLLECTION.)

Plate 57

FROM MINIATURE LENT BY MRS. DAVID LYON GARDINER.

Plate 58

READING THE DEATH-WARRANT.

From Chappell's engraving, by permission of the Lenox Library.

"He evinced no surprise or evident emotion." — *Lossing*.

Plate 59

FROM AN UNPUBLISHED PORTRAIT BY TRUMBULL.
FROM THE FROSSARD COLLECTION, BY PERMISSION OF WILLIAM MACBETH N. Y.

Plate 60

ROAD UP ANDRÉ HILL, TAPPAN.

(The entrance to the field of execution is where the road bends to the left.)

Plate 61

Jo. Cilley. Col.

Plate 62

T. Hull M. D.

From an old painting.

Plate 63

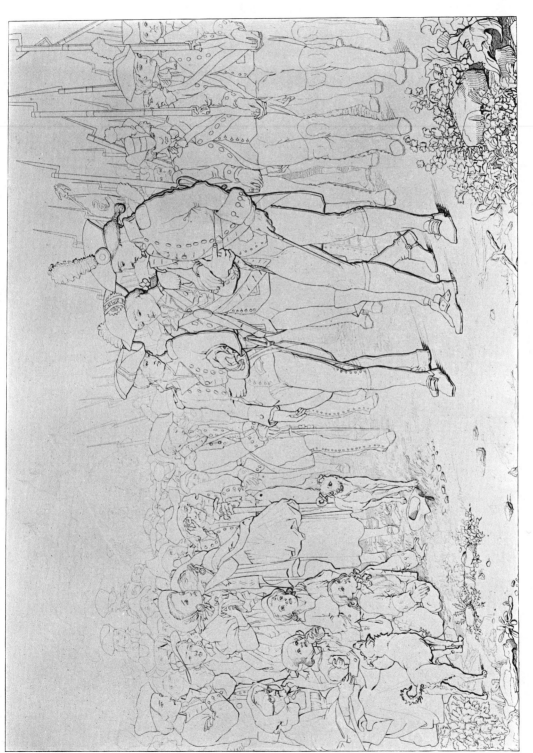

ON THE WAY TO DEATH.

After engraving by F. O. C. Darley.
"A vast multitude was assembled." — *Thacher.*

Plate 64

JOHN PAULDING'S MONUMENT.
St. Peter's Churchyard, North Peekskill.

Plate 65

THE MONUMENT, WESTMINSTER ABBEY.

In the South Aisle.

Plate 66

THE ANDRÉ CHAIR.

Inscribed on back — "*In this chair sat* MAJOR ANDRÉ, *Adjutant-General to the British army, when he wrote, at the quarters of Lieut. Joshua King, the letter to General Washington revealing the treason of Arnold.*" — (Owned by J. Howard King, Esq., Albany.)

Plate 67

THE ANDRÉ MONUMENT, TAPPAN.

By foreign hands thy humble grave adorn'd,
By strangers honor'd, and by strangers mourn'd.—*Pope*.

Plate 68

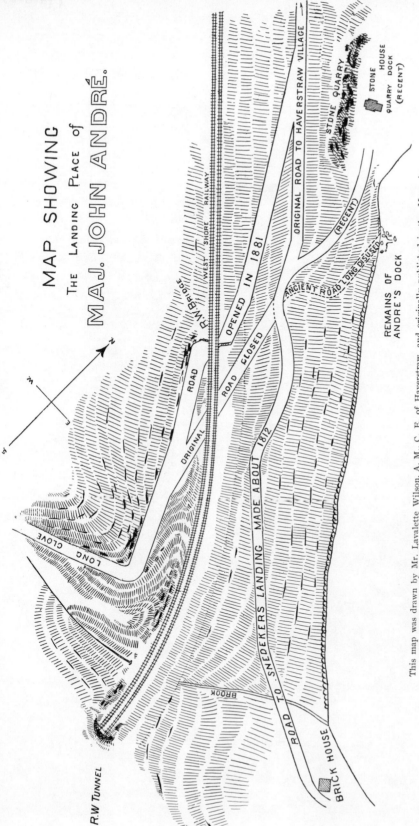

MAP SHOWING
THE LANDING PLACE OF
MAJ. JOHN ANDRÉ.

This map was drawn by Mr. Lavalette Wilson, A. M., C. E. of Haverstraw, and originally published in the *Magazine of American History*.

It has been enlarged to twice original size.

For its use I am indebted to Mr. S. Victor Constant of New York.

"The Firs," where Arnold and André met, is on a line a little North, or South, where the word "Ancient" ends.

Plate 69

MAP OF

HAVERSTRAW

IN THE TIME OF THE

REVOLUTION.o

By Lavalette Wilson A.M.C.E.

KINGS FERRY ROAD

KINGS FERRY

STONY POINT

Capt Jas Lamb

John Waldron

Jacob Waldron

FLORUS FALLS

FURTHER NECK

GRASSY POINT

John Crom

CROM ISLAND

Joshua Hett Smith

OLD LANE

Col. A. Hawkes Hay

HAYS LAND o

Wm Smith

Benjn Benson

NARROW PASSAGE

MAIN ROAD

Benjn Allison

MINESECONGO

CREEK 2/.

RAMAPO ROAD

PULLENS' POINT

HUDSON RIVER

Joseph Allison

Low Tor

MAIN ROAD

John DeNoyelles

W

E

High Tor

KAKIAT PATENT

SHORT CLOVE

Maj E.W.Kiers' Dock

ANDRÉ'S LANDING PLACE

LONG CLOVE

ONE MILE

CHEESECOCKS PATENT

Plate 70

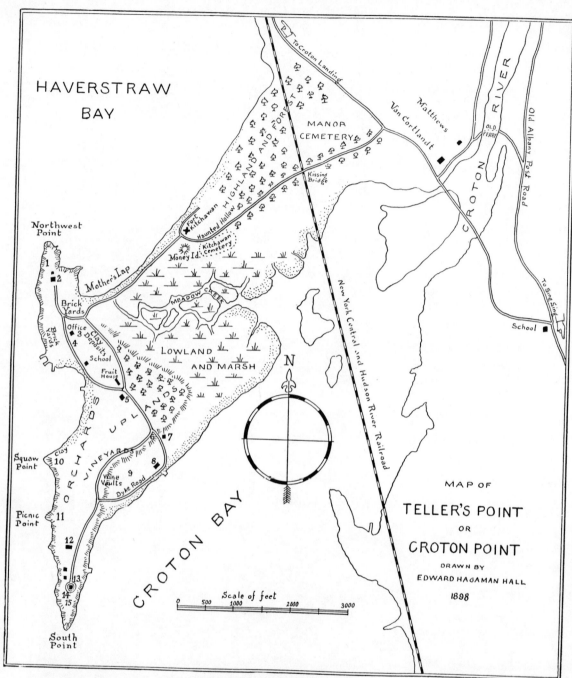

EXPLANATION OF MAP.

1. Place whence Peterson and Sherwood fired on the boat from the *Vulture*, September 20th, 1780. Descendants of Peterson have the musket. 2. Linden Cottage. 3. Cannon ball found by Eugene Anderson, who now has it. It weighs five pounds. 4 Old musket ram-rod found in clay. In possession of H. G Morehouse. 5. Underhill Homestead. 6. Old oak tree, a landmark. No one knows how old. 7. Vine Cottage. 8. Fish house. 9. Cannon ball weighing nearly six pounds, plowed up in meadow. 10. Squaw Point. Directly opposite, on the western bank, André landed from the *Vulture* and first met Arnold. 11. Picnic Point, where Enoch Crosby, Cooper's *Spy*, once enticed ashore and helped capture a boat-load of British soldiers. 12. Farm house 135 years old. 13. Italian villa built by Dr. Robert T. Underhill, deceased. 14. Cannon ball found lodged in a tree about eighty years ago, by Dr. Underhill. The ball is now in possession of S. W. Underhill and weighs about six pounds. The tree is not now standing, and the oldest inhabitant does not remember in which side of the tree the ball lodged. 15. Place where earthworks were thrown up by Americans* when they brought the cannon down to the point. Vouched for by S. W. Underhill, who lived there for sixty years. Dotted shore is low and sandy. Where the shore has declivity marks it is high and rocky.

E. H. Hall.

*Livingston's cannon may have been shifted from one place to another, as the *Vulture* got under way.

Plate 71

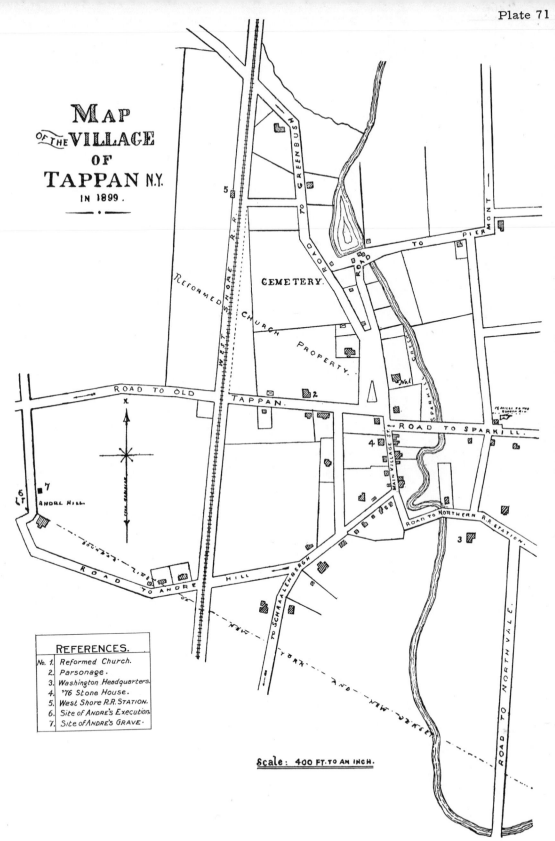

MAP OF THE VILLAGE OF TAPPAN N.Y. IN 1899.

REFERENCES.
No. 1. Reformed Church.
2. Parsonage.
3. Washington Headquarters.
4. '76 Stone House.
5. West Shore R.R. Station.
6. Site of ANDRE'S Execution.
7. Site of ANDRE'S Grave.

Scale: 400 FT. TO AN INCH.

André's route was from 4, North, to the road to Old Tappan, thence West, to the first road, which leads to the place of execution, marked 6.

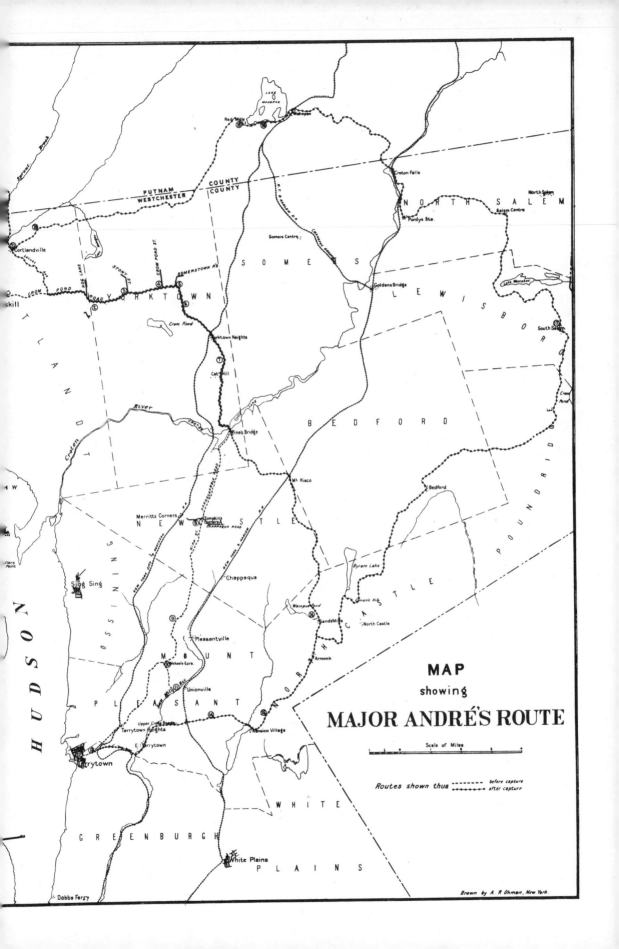

MAP

showing

MAJOR ANDRÉ'S ROUTE

Scale of Miles

Routes shown thus ----------- before capture
                    ·········· after capture

Drawn by A. R. Ohman, New York.